The
Literary
Lennon

ROCK & ROLL REFERENCE SERIES

pierian press
1983

The Literary Lennon

A Comedy of Letters

by
Dr. James Sauceda

*The First Study of
All the Major and Minor
Writings of John Lennon*

ISBN 0-87650-161-7
LC 83-62327

Copyright © 1983 by James Sauceda

All Rights Reserved

THE PIERIAN PRESS
Post Office Box 1808
Ann Arbor, MI 48106

DEDICATION

Let L = L

Contents

Foreword

By Friday, June 20, 1964, The Beatles had released their first two albums in the U.K. — **Please Please Me** and **With The Beatles** — and were less than a month away from the premiere of their first motion picture and debut of the accompanying album for "A Hard Day's Night." Two months before, John Lennon had accepted the coveted Foyle's Literary Prize at a luncheon honoring him for *In His Own Write*, published in March. On June 20, however, readers of *The Times* learned that John Lennon was actually "in a pathetic state of near illiteracy," and that his writing suggested that "here was a boy who ought to have been given an education that would have enabled him to benefit in terms of enjoyment from the talent he appeared to have."

Scathing barbs from *The Times'* literary critic? Abuse from the ranks of professional writers stung by the literary success of a mere mop-top pop idol? Neither. Simply part of a report on the previous day in Parliament, where a concerned Member had sought to illustrate the social consequences of excluding those with an "unsatisfactory education" from an increasingly automated labor market, where their inadequate skills would relegate them to a life without meaning or accomplishment. Case in point: Beatle John, whose book "seemed to show a great deal about the kind of education Lennon received in Liverpool."

"It appeared that he had picked up pieces of Tennyson, Browning, and Robert Louis Stevenson while listening with one ear to the football results on the wireless," continued Mr. Curran, MP from Uxbridge. His was a cry of alarm heralding "the danger of creating a great mass of alienated, embittered men and women" who felt rejected by a society which had ill-educated them for the rigors of the new industrial age. John Lennon's book was "singularly pathetic and touching" testimony to what lay ahead for Britain. The Right Honorable Mr. Curran, however, had made no allowances for art.

John Lennon became an accomplished, fulfilled, and well-rounded artist by anyone's standard. It is really not remarkable that creative individuals should excel and accomplish in more than one artistic area or medium; it is unusual that very many of them have the opportunity to do so, due to the constraints imposed on their lives by time and inadequate finances. A supportive patron or an early success which provides the time and money to develop one's talents, or the Spartan course pursued by those hardy souls who choose to starve and sacrifice everything for their art, seem to afford the only opportunities for full creative expression. (There are exceptions, of course: the occasional genius who pursues a life as a fisherman or registered nurse, survives a spouse and multitudes of offspring, and still seems to dabble successfully and effortlessly in many areas of the creative arena.)

Often it happens, too, that even those lucky artists who are blessed with an abundance of time and/or funds become noted for only one aspect of their multiple gifts, clouding their fame in one creative area or masking altogether their other endeavors. The American poet, e.e. cummings, for example, actually painted far more than he wrote, but few readers of his works would know this without consulting his biography.

And here we have, of all things, the first full-scale guide and analysis of the "writings" of John Lennon! Of the many who doubtless know that Lennon wrote two books, a small percentage have perhaps read them through (with still fewer understanding what they read), and only the most avid devotees are probably aware that there is more to read beyond *In His Own Write* and *A Spaniard In The Works*.

Works of literary criticism and appreciation often provide an enhancement of our enjoyment of original works, and this book is no exception. James Sauceda has here traced the development and illustrated the breadth of John's writing abilities, offering in the process an informed, intelligent and thoroughly engaging guided tour through the hitherto unexplored territory called the Literary Lennon. Lovers of Lennon the musician and recording artist are indebted to Professor Sauceda for broadening our understanding and appreciation of yet another dimension of this singular man and artist.

Tom Schultheiss

Acknowledgements

To Charles A. Marr (Elementary School teacher)
    Thanks for blowing my cover
To Mrs. Hack (High School English teacher)
    After e. e. cummings I was hooked
To "Bert" Potter (C.S.U.L.B. Dept. Secretary)
    Your sparkle started me
To Dr. "Lustre" Hauth (C.S.U.L.B. Faculty)
    Man, you really moved me
To Dr. Nancy Briggs (C.S.U.L.B. Faculty)
    Yep, you're a beautiful bridge
To Dr. Richard Porter (C.S.U.L.B. Dept. Chair)
    Damn it, you always encourage free flight
To John Dorsey (C.S.U.L.B. Acquisition Dept., Library)
    A quiet giant – your support always counts
To Shirley Touros and Sandy Lamprecht (C.S.U.L.B. Librarians)
    Ladies, we've shared laughter and scholarship
To Dr. Janet Bolton (U.S.C. Emeritus Professor)
    Elegant eloquence; so rare, so needed
To Dr. Jackson Cope (U.S.C. Faculty)
    Your Joyce lectures *enthrallllllllll* – I was stunned
To Teri Shannon and Chris P. (U.S.C., College Cont. Ed.)
    My Lennon seminar is thanks to your heart and vision
To Dr. Harrell Allen (Cal Poly, Pomona, Dept. Chair)
    "Send lawyers, guns and money!" *and* Lacey J –
To Dr. Bruce Loganbill – Dignity and daring –
    You offered no limits to interpretation – Thank you
To Tom Schultheiss (Author, editor extraordinaire)
    To begin with the best is a real privilege
To Harold Moskovitz (Literary agent, producer)
    My friend, you advance the culture with caring and style
To Patti McDermott (Psychologist, empath)
    No lies, no lectures, just feeling and focus
To Ruben and Bertha "Birdie" Sauceda (My Mom and Dad)
    Precious people, Real Friends, True loves

The author and publisher gratefully acknowledge permission to quote from the following sources:

Excerpt from the *Bag One* catalog reproduced with permission of the Lee Nordness Galleries, Inc., New York, New York. Copyright © 1970 by the Lee Nordness Galleries, Inc.

Selections from *Finnegan's Wake*, by James Joyce. Copyright ©1939 by James Joyce. Copyright renewed 1967 by George Joyce and Lucia Joyce. Reprinted by permission of Viking Penguin Inc.

Excerpt from *The Gay Liberation Book*, compiled by Len Richmond. Copyright © Ramparts Press, Palo Alto, California.

"The Goon Show Scripts," by John Lennon, from *The New York Times*, September 30, 1973. Copyright © 1973 by The New York Times Company. Reprinted by permission.

Lyrics from the song *A Hard Day's Night*, by John Lennon and Paul McCartney. Copyright © 1964 Northern Songs Limited. All rights for the U.S.A., Mexico and the Philippines controlled by Maclen Music, Inc. c/o ATV Music Corp. Used by permission. All rights reserved.

Selections from *In His Own Write*, by John Lennon. Copyright © 1964 by John Lennon. Reprinted by permission of Simon & Schuster, a division of Gulf & Western Corporation.

Selections from *Mersey Beat*, by John Lennon. Reproduced with the kind permission of Bill Harry.

Lyrics from the song *Mother*, by John Lennon. Copyright © 1971 Northern Songs Limited. All rights for the U.S.A., Mexico and the Philippines controlled by Maclen Music, Inc. c/o ATV Music Corp. Used by permission. All rights reserved.

Excerpt from *Oh! Calcutta*, by Kenneth Tynan. Copyright © 1969. Reproduced by permission of Grove Press, Inc., New York, New York.

Excerpt from *The People's Almanac*, by David Wallechinsky and Irving Wallace. Copyright © 1975 by David Wallechinsky and Irving Wallace. Reprinted by permission of Doubleday & Co., Inc.

Selections from *A Spaniard In The Works*, by John Lennon. Copyright © 1965 by John Lennon. Reprinted by permission of Simon & Schuster, a division of Gulf & Western Corporation.

Lyrics from the song *Strawberry Fields Forever*, by John Lennon and Paul McCartney. Copyright © 1967 Northern Songs Limited. All rights for the U.S.A., Mexico and the Philippines controlled by Maclen Music, Inc. c/o ATV Music Corp. Used by permission. All rights reserved.

Finally, our thanks to Yoko Ono Lennon for examining this book in manuscript form, and for allowing us to quote from John's work.

Introduction

I felt my life change as I stood in the Hollywood branch of Pickwick's bookstore. There I was, innocently browsing through paperbacks — you know, just glancing at covers or calmly previewing a paragraph or two before yawning. Then it happened. Right there in the "J" section, my unsuspecting eyes fell upon the following:

> "Come on, fool porterfull, hosiered women blown monk sewer? Scuse us, chorley guy! You tollerday donsk? N. You tolkatiff scowegian? Nn. You spigotty anglease? Nnn. You phonio saxo? Nnnn. Clear all so! 'Tis a jute. Let us swop hats and excheck a few strong verbs weak oach eather yapyazzard abast the blooty creeks."

My first response to this passage (and to all others I scanned in the hope of finding something written in coherent prose) echoed the reviews this book, *Finnegans Wake* by James Joyce, received in both its prepublished and first edition forms:

> "Judging from such selections as I have seen, it is likely to prove all but incomprehensible to anybody."

> "It is not English . . . it is not indeed language by any known tests."

> "Common honesty compels this reviewer [Richard Aldington] to state that he is unable to explain either the subject or the meaning (if any) of Mr. Joyce's book; and that, having spent several hours a day for more than a fortnight in wretched toil over these 628 pages, he has no intention of wasting one more minute of precious life over Mr. Joyce's futile inventions, tedious ingenuities, and verbal freaks."

Now the funny thing is — especially to someone who has never

xiii

heard of James Joyce — this author's reputation is so vast that many consider him to be the *most* influential writer of the twentieth century. The fact is, the day I wandered into Pickwick I had not only studied *all* of his previous works (short stories, novels, his play, poems, even his critical essays) but had written a Masters Thesis on the guy. So even though I was convinced he was "the best," my brief excursion into his last work made me wonder whether Joyce was on a bad acid trip when he wrote *Finnegans Wake!*

Appropriately, Joyce's strange dream book appeared in 1939, the same year as "The Wizard of Oz." Today *Finnegans Wake* is still thought to be the most experimental novel ever written. Also, after four decades of study, many critics, including William York Tindall, Clive Hart, Michael Begnal, Bernard Benstock, Jackson Cope and others, consider it to be among Joyce's greatest work. This is high praise indeed for the same author of *Ulysses* (1922), a novel which T.S. Eliot hailed as "the most considerable work of imagination in English in our time."

So in 1977, while John Lennon was already a couple of years into being a happy househusband, I went off to U.S.C. to happily write a Doctoral Dissertation on *Finnegans Wake*. Was it difficult? Well, as Anthony Burgess put it, "Oh yes difficult . . . but difficulty is the small price to pay for excitement, richness, and originality."

Scene two, 1980: I am back at Pickwick, post Ph.D. Yep, I had conquered *Finnegans Wake* (it took 200 of my pages, but I had successfully analyzed 12 pages of his!). I feel invincible as I move among the "L's" in the paperback section. Nothing can startle me now. Then, right in the middle of my egotism, my unsuspecting eyes fall upon this passage:

> " 'I night as welp hev a chocolush birskit as well, wile I do noddy.' So saying so he marshed offer to that teapod and tap it to that sing: bud to he grey suffice — what! — bat noo warty. 'Goob heralds! What's all of thiz goinge awn? Doe mein ice desleeve me? Am I knot loofing at me owen singunice, and there be know warty?' He was quait raight, lo! the warty didn noo apear, trey as he maybe."

Wait a minute! What is this? An undiscovered sequel to *Finnegans Wake*?! Impossible! Joyce died in 1941; this was written in 1965!

Of course, it wasn't "the master" James Joyce — it was "the Beatle" John Lennon. What a shock! Like millions of others, I had "studied" all of the Beatles stuff (and most of John's solo work). And also like millions of others, I knew he was simply "the best," meaning the best musical poet, the best rock artist, the best personality; I was stone-cold ignorant of the *literary* Lennon.

Oh, sure, I remembered John had written a couple of books way back (I hadn't bought them). And as I stood there, quite startled by what I had read, I seemed to recall his books were even bestsellers (an accomplishment that Joyce would never achieve). So even though I can be a pompous asshole sometimes (a bad trait), I can also admit when I need to be taught (a good trait). So off I went, just as I had done with Joyce, only now to read all there was about Lennon the writer.

For Joyce it had been easy finding sources. There were any number of books available — in-depth critical biographies, a two-volume set of his letters; there were concordances and lexicons, books on specific themes, books on the work as a whole (and, of course, lots and lots of dissertations!). Aside from such sources, there were also many journal articles available, a *James Joyce Quarterly* and an ongoing journal solely on *Finnegans Wake*! (There was even a recording of Joyce himself reading from the book.)

But when I hit the library to research Lennon's literary contributions, I was in for a second shock. NOTHING! I mean *zero, nada, the absence of, black hole in space, vacancy, nobody home!* Even though it had been *seventeen* years since John's first book appeared in March of 1964, not *one* book had been written on the subject. Why?

The answer came slowly, only after I had read all I could get my hands on regarding John Lennon and the Beatles. Only after I reflected on how I had reacted to John Lennon and the Beatles over the years.

The first thing I discovered from my research was that almost all of the books supposedly on John Lennon were *really* about the Beatles. The next thing I learned was that these books were seldom about the artistry or the musical contribution of either Lennon *or* the Beatles, but instead focused on the "phenomenon" of the Beatles. That means they simply chronicle the *publicity* the group or John generated, their "surface," while completely ignoring the art they created, their "substance."

The third fact of these Lennon/Beatle books was that they not only lacked any insight into John's or the Beatles' significance, but were often very poorly written and riddled with inaccurate data. Fortunately, some interstellar exceptions were found.

The Music of the Beatles by Wilfrid Mellers emerged in 1973. At the time of its appearance it was virtually the only book that was actually on the *art* of the Beatles. It not only provided the reader with fascinating observations on the musical mechanics of Beatle songs, but also offered a comprehensive perspective of the Beatles' career and its import.

For my money, *All Together Now* (the discography for 1961--

xv

1975) is still the single most scholarly and important book on the market. Harry Castleman and Walter Podrazik, in scrupulous detail, present a *complete* catalog of when, where, with whom, etc. the recorded art of the Beatles occurred. It also traces (with equal accuracy) the solo careers up to 1975. Their follow-up books, *The Beatles Again* and *The End Of The Beatles*, continue their invaluable work.

Among the spate of Beatles biographies, *Shout* (1981) is without question the finest. Philip Norman offers us the best documentation of the lives and careers of the Beatles (with an emphasis on John). But even here, out of the 400 pages that form the body of the book, only *two* paragraphs have to do with John's published writing (and those paragraphs are not even on the writing itself, but on a luncheon sponsored by Foyle's bookstore!). Why?

A simple answer would be that Lennon's books aren't worth the trouble, that they are just plain lousy as literature. That while Beatle music was authentic art, John's writings were pure hype, a verbal hoola hoop, churned out for mass consumption. (Maybe okay for a quick snack, but certain *not* a memorable meal.)

But not only is this position a simple answer, it is clearly a *wrong* answer. Now, while the publisher's initial motive may have been for profit only (hoping to get a share of the Beatle wig market), and the public's favorable response part of nondiscriminating Beatlemania, another fact remains: these writings are sophisticated, highly inventive and truly satiric, and they would be outstanding on their own terms as literature, even if Jack Schlurp wrote them!

But Foyle's literary luncheon, mentioned above, was to honor the serious author John Lennon, not Jack Schlurp. (If anything, the difficulty of John's prose has inhibited or scared off writers who otherwise would have tried to capitalize on the Beatle market.) But this doesn't answer the question either. So, why hasn't anyone written a book on the literary Lennon?

The answer is painfully complex; we *still* refuse to think of John (or Paul or George or Ringo) outside of their place within the orthodox mythology of the Beatles — a mythology that both the media and the Beatles themselves created. It was a myth so completely attractive that the Beatles, as well as the world at large, wanted desperately to believe in it. And so both parties, unconsciously, satisfied their hunger for Utopia, by accepting a delusion as truth.

Once the religion was established, the Beatle mythos was, and yet remains, quite heavenly: a secure sanctuary, beautiful, irresistible, outside the chaos of the real world.

But fortunately or unfortunately, John Lennon was a troublemaker in Eden. From the very beginning it was inevitable that he would be the first to escape from the prison of paradise and the box of Beatleism. In fact, the same dynamic power John wielded to help create the Beatle myth was later used by him to destroy it: "I don't believe in Beatles, I just believe in me."

Of course, no one really noticed how much John was changing on us, because we were all Beatle-Blinded. If John said or did something contrary to our image of perfect purity, the media just ignored it. (It was much more profitable to preserve the hype of "those fun-lovin' lads from Liverpool.") In *Lennon Remembers*, John reveals what few of us suspected: "There's photographs of me groveling about . . . on my knees, coming out of whorehouses." Yoko responded, "How did you manage to keep that clean image? It's amazing." John's reply is telling: "Because everybody wants the image to carry on . . . . Everybody wants to keep on the bandwagon . . . . We were the Caesars. Who was going to knock us when there's a million pounds to be made? All the hand-outs, the bribery, the police, all the fucking hype . . . . Everybody wanted in."

So, actually it was impossible for John to do *anything* wrong (that was a major doctrine of the religion). The same went for the other Beatles, but John was particularly infallible because he was the undisputed leader. Also he was allowed more freedom of behavior than anyone else (since he was the "intelligent" and "witty" one).

But John's expanding perception of reality made his rebellion necessary. "One has to completely humiliate oneself to be what the Beatles were, and that's what I resent. I mean I did it, I didn't know, I didn't foresee; it just happened bit by bit, gradually, until this complete craziness is surrounding you and you're doing exactly what you don't want to do, with people you can't stand, the people you hated when you were ten."

The legacy of Pope John really ended for the public when Yoko Ono made our closet satyr a card-carrying virgin. The naked truth (pun intended) was too much for everybody. Now it became popular to voice any doubts we had ever had about John — but not all at once. At first John was exempt from blame; "it was all Yoko's fault."

After all, Yoko Ono was literally and metaphysically a foreigner. We couldn't assimilate her. She was dark and strange, a threat, a woman fatal to John's future. She must be sowing discord among our four consecrated clergymen. And, for awhile, the John-will-come-to-his-senses-once-she's-gone mentality prevailed. Paul and George foolishly conceived of her as "the flavor of the month." Unfortunately, their flippancy and cruelty was matched by our own.

What we failed to understand was that Yoko was right when she said, "Actually the Beatles was like cutting him down to a smaller size than he is." That's because the Beatles were about perpetuating pleasure, while John Lennon was about discovering the pain of perception. The Beatles wrote songs with no rough edges and in the third person; John composed hard visions in the first person. The Beatles were "Penny Lane"; John was "Strawberry Fields Forever".

Furthermore, it was Yoko Ono who enabled John to realize: "I didn't become something when the Beatles made it or when you heard about me, I've been like this all me life." The dream was over. The Beatles were no longer a comfort station, but a cage. John realized "I could no longer artistically get anything out of the Beatles, and here was someone that could turn me on to a million things."

At first John naively didn't see the inevitable. "You see, I presumed that I would just be able to carry on and just bring Yoko in our [Beatle] life. But it seemed that I had to either be married to them or Yoko." So Lennon, as usual, took us to our breaking point; he actually married this arch enemy of idols. At the time, lost in self-righteous indignation, we condemned him. It was stupid and hateful; we wanted John Lennon to live inside our dream only.

Since John did not recant, it was clear he too must be a renegade. John and Yoko's bagism, bed-ins, and sundry events were not in the approved script. Those two were making their *own* music and movies without the others! And so, our worst fears were realized. John and Yoko became the first blasphemers of Rock religion; they were Anti-Beatle.

Yoko simply would not need scripture: "Thou shalt worship the image of the Beatles; or seek ye wisdom by removing thyself from our sight." Certainly all of the *other* Beatle wives accepted their blessed station as mute mates, so why didn't Yoko? The answer, of course, was that Yoko Ono was an artist *before* she had even heard of the Beatles; she fully intended to *remain* an artist after she married John Lennon; and (for those who don't know it) she remains an artist even without John.

On the one hand, John didn't care what we thought; on the other he cared too much. For above all, John was a humanist and truth-seeker, and even though we mocked him and the woman he loved, he couldn't just let us (or himself) passively live in lies. He had to keep growing and express the discoveries, the new mirrors that he'd found. He wasn't some God-above who sinned and failed us, but a man who succeeded in finding himself (and not with the help of heaven, but with another human on earth).

Now, to a certain extent, we *had* to accept John's "official" solo albums, simply because they came after the Beatles broke up. But we never had to accept them on their own merit — only in comparison to the Beatles (which shows how afraid *we* are to let go of Eden). In fact a recent example of this was seen in one of John's last interviews, the one published in *Playboy* in January, 1981. It's embarrassing how David Sheff repeatedly pursues John on the "Beatle reunion" idea, and how he cannot view John's work apart from the Beatles — who had disbanded eleven years before! Also, we certainly wouldn't take seriously anything John did with Yoko on his own while still a member of the High Priesthood — pun intended.

So, I believe a real answer can now be given to my initial question. There are no books on the writings of John Lennon because they are *not* part of the Beatle myth. His two books are expressions of an individual, not a group, and the themes and plots are painfully *real*: hypocrisy, betrayal, fragmented personalities that heap mindless cruelties upon each other, etc. In short, there is nothing happy-go-Beatle about them; they are the work of John Lennon, cynic and realist. In addition, John's literary art is difficult to understand, unpredictable, and generally defies easy labeling, so we've tried to forget they ever existed.

John confirmed that his books formed a distinct separation from the Beatles. "To express *myself* I would write *A Spaniard In The Works* or *In His Own Write*, the personal stories which were expressions of my personal emotions . . . I'd have a separate songwriting John Lennon."

The only person in the entire Beatle entourage who seems to have fully understood this fact is Brian Epstein. In Epstein's *A Cellarful of Noise* (1964), he states "John's lyrics . . . are only a fragment of his real aptitude for words . . . I was deeply gratified that a Beatle could detach himself *completely* from Beatleism and create such impact as an author."

So, in a manner of speaking, John Lennon first "broke up" the Beatles in 1964 when he published *In His Own Write* (a title that reeks of independence from his corporate identity). John "broke up" the Beatles again in 1965 when he wrote *A Spaniard In The Works*. He "broke up" the Beatles once more in 1966 when he flew to Spain to be featured in the film "How I Won the War." John was on location for six weeks, and he stated "It gave me time to think on my own, away from the others. *From then on*, I was looking for somewhere to go, but I didn't have the nerve to really step out on the boat by myself and push it off. I was always waiting for a reason to get out of the Beatles from the day I filmed 'How I Won the War.' I just didn't have the guts to do it."

Significantly, all of this restlessness and separation occurred *before* John Lennon had even met the "Ocean Child," Yoko Ono. John personally dates the irrevocable "break up" after August 27, 1967, the days that followed Brian Epstein's death (of course the actual dissolution of the group occurred when John told Paul, "I want a divorce . . . the group is over, I'm leaving" — in September, 1969).

In light of all this, it is really so wrongheaded, insensitive, and redundant for us to ask Paul, George, or Ringo about tributes or reunions. An excerpt from Merv Griffin's show, May 4, 1981, is typical of our arrested understanding of these individuals, in this case Ringo Starr:

> Merv: Are there regrets, Ringo, that you didn't once again reunite . . .
> Ringo: There's no regrets.
> Merv: . . . before John's passing?
> Ringo: No regrets.
> Merv: No?
> Ringo: No.
> Merv: We've never known how that happened, did you all sit down one day and say 'that's it'?
> Ringo: Everybody actually knows what happened . . . I'm really getting, you know . . .
> Merv: Tired of . . .
> Ringo: Tired of it.
> Merv: I know, but it's such a legendary story!
> Ringo: And the problem is, we've come to do this movie [Caveman], show you this great piece of film here, you know? Let's get into today . . . I've just done a week's tour of promotion and it's getting silly, because I'll do a two-hour interview and we talk about the movie and that, and the movie gets one line . . . but twenty years ago gets a page and a half . . . that's *not* why we're here!
> Merv: Testy little devil!

I think Ringo is right, "Let's get into today." All three gentlemen — Paul, George, and Ringo — have done a damn good job of being *significant individuals*, and they have been "solo" for over a decade. After all, the *entire* recording career of the Beatles was just seven years (October 1962 — August 1969). In fact, the complete catalog of the Beatles consists of just thirteen items: ten full length albums, one "abbreviated" LP (**Yellow Submarine** which only has Side One done by the Beatles), one double EP (the six songs of **Magical Mystery Tour**), and one double LP (the 30 songs on "The White Album"). In America, however, due to insatiable greed, and channeled through endless repackaging techniques, these same thirteen items have been turned into 25 albums! And, they're not through yet.

John Lennon's solo catalog (including works with Yoko) has eleven LPs — almost equaling the entire Beatle legacy! Within that catalog we find the literary Lennon, and this book attempts to put some long overdue perspective on that aspect of John Lennon's persona.

The goal of *The Literary Lennon* is to spur people to read Lennon's writings. It is designed, in fact, as a companion volume to the Signet/New American Library Edition entitled *John Lennon, 1940–1980, In His Own Write & A Spaniard In The Works*. All page numbers cited refer to this paperback edition. I will, however, also comment on other editions for clarification or the highlighting of certain stylistic aspects.

Because of the experimental nature of John's writing, the basic critical tool used will be the paraphrase. That is, I will rephrase difficult passages in "plain words," and then comment on why Lennon chose to write the way he did.

Returning to the two quotations which open this section, I will present a brief demonstration. First, the Joycean passage as it appears in *Finnegans Wake*:

> "Come on, fool porterfull, hosiered women blown monk sewer? Scuse us, chorley guy! You tollerday donsk? N. You talkatiff scowegian? Nn. You spigotty anglease? Nnn. You phonio saxo? Nnnn. Clear all so! 'Tis a jute. Let us swop hats and excheck a few strong verbs weak oach eather yapyazzard abast the blooty creeks."

Now in paraphrase:

> "Come on, how do you do, blond sir? Excuse us, Charlie! You speak Danish? No. You talkative Norwegian? No, no. You speak English? No, no, no. You pronounce Saxon? No, no, no, no. All so clear! 'Tis a Jute. Let us swap hats and exchange a few strong words with each other haphazardly about the bloody Greeks."

Easy, right?! Now I can't dwell on Joyce, but I will say the passage becomes even more clear when you realize, one, it's a dialogue between "Mutt" and "Jute" (all Jute says are the negative replies). And two, each line of Mutt's is delivered in a *different* accent. The first is bad French for "Comment vous portez-vous aujourd'hui, blond monsieur," the second is Danish, the third Norwegian, the fourth Italian, the fifth British, and the sixth Irish.

Now the original Lennon passage:

> " 'I night as welp hev a chocolush birskit as well, wile I do noddy.' So saying so he marshed offer to that teapod and tap it to that sing: bud to he grey suffice — what! — bat noo warty. 'Goob heralds! What's all of thiz goinge awn? Doe mein ice desleeve me? Am I knot loofing at me owen sing-

unice, and there be know warty?' He was quait raight, lo! the warty didn noo apear, trey as he maybe."

Now in paraphrase:

" 'I might as well have a chocolate biscuit as well, while I do nod [off to sleep].' So saying this he marched off to that tea-pot and takes it to the sink: But, to his great surprise — what! — but no water. "Good Harold! What's all of this going on? Do my eyes deceive me? Am I not laughing at me own sink with ice, and there be no water.' He was quite right, lo! the water did not appear, try as he might."

A snap, huh?! Well, once the underlying action is recognized, it becomes much easier to zero in on John's sophisticated use of puns. The key to comprehending Lennon literature is the realization that virtually all the important information of a story or poem is found *inside* the puns. That is, instead of writing the usual way (with sep-arate paragraphs describing the scene, or a character's appearance, movement, or personality), John imbeds everything within the multi-ple meanings produced by his well-chosen puns. We'll delve a bit into the levels of meaning found in this selection (which is excerpted from the short story "Silly Norman" in *A Spaniard In The Works*, page 150).

If John were just an ordinary writer, one lacking the genius to push the conventions of style to a more provocative and inventive place, he would have written just the way the paraphrase is: " 'I might as well have a chocolate biscuit as well, while I do nod.' " But what does that sentence offer us? Very little, other than a literal statement. But John is a brilliant writer, so he transformed that simple sentence into " 'I night as welp hev a chocolush birskit as well, wile I do noddy.' " But why?

In this way John achieves greater mileage of meaning. He tells us, through the puns, that Norman not only eats chocolate biscuits at "night," before he goes to sleep ("wile I do noddy"), but that Nor-man is a chocoholic! — a "choco*lush.*" We discover that this late-night snack is a routine, probably repeated every night — repeating "as well" suggests this — and it's like a performance of a "scene" from a play (a "bir*skit*").

We get a clear visual picture of Norman as an awkward, clumsy, overweight street fighter. The evidence is right there inside the puns ("I night as welp hev" may mean "I might as *well* have" or "might as *belt* have" — that is, "I might as well ignore this belly over the belt!"). "Welp" also lets us view Norman's welts (as well as antici-pate his yelps). And his slow movements just heave ("hev") along.

There's even a hint as to what Norman's secret night activity is, because he "wiles" away the night "while I do noddy," which can mean "while I do nod off to sleep" or, taken as a homonym, means "while I do naughty" — which, most likely, means masturbation.

Now all of that is in John's first sentence! And you don't have to accept *my* interpretation, because that's only provided as a springboard for your own. It's fun to experiment with possible meanings, but I do try to keep my versions text-based, and not based solely on my imagination. The point remains that Lennon literature is full of surprises and is highly evocative.

The next sentence reenforces Norman's regimented lifestyle, and also shows us his slushy movement as he marched (*"marshed"* over to his "tea*pod*" (the teapot *is* like a "pod," a pouch holding possible refreshment, a cylindrical case, etc.). It seems Norman usually tap dances and sings as he gets his nightcap of tea ("tap it to that sing"). But while Norman may have fits of joy, he is more susceptible to stronger fits of anger. For his violent temper "buds" (breaking open the "pod"), turning Norman "grey" with sufficient ("suffice") rage. So upset is he that he swings at, and hits, the faucet (bats the tap!) — thus starting a war with water (*"bat* noo *war*ty").

All of this behavior only confirms Norman's silliness, and he caps off his childish actions by yelling out like a giant baby: "*Goo*b." His personal expletive, "Harold," is an excuse just to "herald" his anguish. Unfortunately, Norman lets the entire event go over his head like an awning ("goinge *awn*"). His total frustration prompts his French Normandy roots to come out: "What's all of *thiz goinge awn*?" But, as Norman is basically a military mentality, his dialect switches to German as he analyzes the situation: "Doe mein ice desleeve me?" Not only can we discern the line "Do my eyes deceive me," but also we can see how Norman's singing ("Doe"-ra-me etc.) has moved from his throat to his sleeve ("desleeve").

Sadly, Norman's own words mock how tied-up-in-a-knot he is; standing there goofing off, looking, laughing ridiculously at his own sink, all with icy eyes ("Am I knot loofing at me owen sing-unice").

The narrating voice enters to inform us, with an ironic tone, that Norman looks quite quaint ("quait"). Also the narrator, with tongue still in cheek, tells us Norman was correct in his observation. The truth comes out, however, because "right" is spelled wrong: "raight"! Norman still tries to get the faucet to work three more times ("trey"), but the drops of water, which would have looked like a couple of small pears appearing, "didn noo apear." So we leave this excerpted scene with Norman's halfhearted attempt to get a cup of tea, "try as he might" becoming "trey as he maybe."

So there you have it, sports fans! A fairly close analysis of one part of one paragraph of one story of one John Lennon! Now before anyone freaks on me, or figures I must be on acid to spend so much time on one small segment of John's work, let me soothe some of your fears. First, "Silly Norman" is *the* most difficult of all Lennon's stories. I took time (and will take more time later), not because I'm into boring the reader, but because I want to help the reader find his way in the "apparent" jumble of words. Also, John's writing is tremendously varied; poems, stories, fake letters, play scenes, mock articles, and lots and lots of *very* interesting drawings are to be enjoyed. Many of the writings reveal early versions of John's lyrics, relate an experience of the Beatles, or even explore John's own complex personality. So hang in, folks, because as Anthony Burgess said of Joyce's "difficulty": "it is a small price to pay for the excitement, richness, and originality."

In a nutshell, here's how the rest of the book is organized:

Part I: The Major Works

> **Chapter One** — This lets you know what critics said when *In His Own Write* first appeared in 1964. It gives you a review of how right and wrong they were, and it also puts Lennon in a definite literary tradition.

> **Chapter Two** — If Chapter One is a pleasant appetizer, this is the main course. It is literally a page-by-page explanation of *In His Own Write*. So if you are the restless type, you can jump to *any* story or drawing in John's first book, and I'll have something to say about it.

> **Chapter Three** — This lets you in on what the critical reception was like in 1965 for *A Spaniard In The Works*. In addition, it lets you see if people learned anything from John's first book. It also establishes whether John improved as a writer.

> **Chapter Four** — Yep, just like Chapter Two, a page-by-page analysis of *A Spaniard In The Works*. This chapter, perhaps, is fuller than its predecessor, because I can cross-reference back and forth. In any event, you get a real sense of the integrity and progression of the author John Lennon.

Part II: The Minor Works

> **Chapter Five** — The Early Writings (1947–1962). This chapter chronicles John's literary work from his childhood up to the time he wrote *In His Own Write*. It includes the stories

and poems he published in *Mersey Beat* (the important Liverpool beat magazine begun in 1961 by Bill Harry).

Chapter Six — The Late Writings (1965–1979). This chapter collects together the works John wrote after *A Spaniard In The Works*. It includes short stories, poems, his scene in *Oh! Calcutta!* and John and Yoko's 1979 "Love Letter."

Part III: The Future Works

Chapter Seven — This final chapter does three things. First, it reviews the adaptation work of Adrienne Kennedy and Victor Spinetti in *The Lennon Play: In His Own Write*. Second, it summarizes John Lennon's significance as a writer. Third, it suggests areas for future research.

So, go out and get John's books, and let's get started on Mr. Lennon's literary voyages!

Part I
The Major Works

Chapter One

In His Own Write: Reviewing the Reviews

(Or, Why Do the Critics Say John Lennon Falls Into the Tradition of Edward Lear, Lewis Carroll, James Thurber, and James Joyce?)

What the Critics Said

John Lennon, in speaking about the critical reception to his first book, remarked: "You know, I was very pleased . . . . To my amazement the reviewers liked it." This gave John pleasure, of course, but what really made him feel "acknowledged" was the fact that critics "wouldn't have been biased by the fact I was a Beatle, even if the fans were." So here's how the critics reacted to *In His Own Write*.

The *London Times* Literary Supplement, Thursday, March 26, 1964, had only praise for John's short stories and poems:

> "They are remarkable; they are a world away from the . . . underdeveloped language of the . . . songs [hovering] in a linguistic never never land somewhere between Joyce, Lewis Carroll . . . with decorations . . . part Thurber. They are also very funny . . . the nonsense runs on, words and images prompting one another in a chain of pure fantasy.
>
> The book is beautifully designed . . . it is worth the attention of anyone who fears for the impoverishment of the English language and British imagination . . . humorists have done more to preserve and enrich these assets than most serious critics allow. Theirs is arguably our liveliest stream of 'experimental writing' and Mr. Lennon shows himself well equipped to take it farther. He must write a great deal more."

All in all, Lennon was found to be "a real and lively talent." John couldn't have dreamed that the London report would be so positive. After all, he was still a Northerner, just a Liverpool lad, and in John's own words, "that's where the despised people were. We were the ones that were looked down upon as animals by the Southerners, the Londoners. So we were hicksville."

3

A couple of years earlier, no one would have thought it possible that a Liverpool group could break open the closed shop of London — yet that's exactly what the Beatles did. Now John Lennon, on his own, not only entered the inner circles of London, but he had managed to walk through its most intellectual gate. He wasn't a "Beatle" to the *London Times* reviewer; he was an important new author. John must have been greatly gratified to be at the vanguard of Britain's experimental writers — as far from "hicksville" as one could go!

Peter Schickele's review in the *Nation*, June 8, 1964, aptly presents America's reaction:

> "Even people with a predisposition toward the Beatles . . . are almost sure to be pleasantly shocked when they open up *In His Own Write*. This little volume by John Lennon . . . not only has a style of its own, but at its best has a very sure and delightful style. A collection of . . . pure fancy and nonsense concocted by someone who loves jumbling words and images. In reviews of the book, all sorts of literary wheels have been mentioned as influences — Edward Lear, Lewis Carroll, James Thurber . . . even James Joyce has been mentioned . . . . But Lennon is Lennon, he has his own brand of jumble-word and his own satiric way of looking at things. Sometimes his satire is extremely cutting . . . . The pieces range from quietly clever to outrageous and occasionally there is a touching moment."

In short, Schickele's critical position is "my applause for John Lennon."

Time magazine, May 1, 1964, found the book "a startling collection of verse and prosery. Lennon has rolled Edward Lear, Lewis Carroll and James Thurber into one great post-Joycean spitball. Much of the book's charm is typographical . . . Lennon's unorthodox orthography . . . as if pages had been set by a drunken linotypist. Besides playlets, Lennon provides teasingly evocative dramatic fragments."

Newsweek, April 27, 1964, notes that John Lennon "has been hailed as an heir to the Anglo-American tradition of nonsense: Lewis Carroll, Edward Lear and James Thurber . . . . Several reviews, discussing Lennon's wordplay, recalled the elaborate puns of James Joyce's *Finnegans Wake*."

But *Newsweek*, in addition to restating these usual literary influences, took a definite stand on whether or not it was accurate to view Lennon's writing through these predecessors. *Newsweek* decided — at least as far as Carroll and Joyce were concerned — that the comparison was faulty. "In fact, there is in Lennon *very little* of the orderly Victorian pedantry with which Lewis Carroll crafted . . . nor is there really *any* of Joyce's erudite multilingual allusiveness." (I disagree, however, and will provide evidence in the next chapter.)

Still, the point made by *Newsweek* was a positive one; like the review in the *Nation*, it stresses John's uniqueness rather than focusing on his similarity to other authors. "Lennon comes on frothing with *original* spontaneity. The yeasty stream of word distortions would be perfect . . . even if one didn't keep remembering that the writer is a Beatle. As he is, there is an extra dimension of pleasure in a book that suggests that when John Lennon sings 'I Want To Hold Your Hand' he is wishing he could bite it."

The *Newsweek* review is also notable because it attempts to identify the major themes which unify *In His Own Write*. These themes were found to be no less than "littleness, isolation and unfair cruelty."

The Virginia Quarterly Review, Summer, 1964, opens this way:

> "At last those intellectuals who have become struck with Beatlemania have a serious literary excuse for their visceral pleasures, for John Lennon's first book is a true delight . . . the skill (one even toys with the word 'genius') which Lennon shows in this collection . . . places him [with] the best of the new seriously comic novelists in this country. Written in a sly, pseudo-Joycean language, the book is a mordantly humorous expression of . . . a disengagement from the political and social world, a rejection of realism, and a faith in the efficacy of the freed imagination."

And the review concludes that although other critics may not like it, "John Lennon is now very much a part of the modern literary scene."

The *Saturday Evening Post*, instead of reviewing *In His Own Write*, previewed it by featuring several examples of Lennon's writing under the heading "Beatalic Graphospasms." The only critical comment made was implicit; it described the selections are "wild fiction . . . by the brainiest Beatle of them all."

Certainly the most stylistically interesting review came from *Mersey Beat* (the Liverpool periodical in which John's work was first published). In fact, *Mersey Beat* was ahead of everyone else in heralding John Lennon's first book. Nearly two months before publication of *In His Own Write*, an article appeared in *Mersey Beat* entitled "Beatcomber in Book Form" — as an advance notice of the book. ("Beatcomber" was the occasional column John penned for *Mersey Beat*; the text of the "Beatcomber" column can be found in Chapter Five.)

The *Mersey Beat* review appeared on March 26, 1964. It reveals Bill Harry's ability to parody the rhythm and look of Lennon literature. I will present the opening of the review without comment, and then provide an interpretation:

> "Paul and Robert and Jonathan and Fleming and Humbug (Baylout Ump) Lester on paper said by Charles Dickens and crew Ump, bound up by Clay Pidge Upm of Bung Ho, Suffy have assembungled with John Lennings to pollute this book about Harold and Arnold and Eric Hearble and Nigel and Partly Dave . . . and all etc."

> "Paul [McCartney] and Robert [Freeman, the book's designer] and Jonathan [Cape, the publisher] and Fleming ["Lennon" punned from "Lennings" that follows] and Humbug [Dicken's character Scrooge; foreshadows Dickens, possibly "Hamburg," too] (Baylout Ump) [Bail out LTD] Better on paper said by Charles Dickens and crew, LTD, bound up by Clay Pidge [Richard Clay of The Chaucer Press; also Clay Pidgeon, clay picture] Upm of Bung Ho, Suffy [LTD, Bungay, Suffolk; the location of the printers of the book] have assembled with John Lennon to publish this book [the names that follow are all characters from *In His Own Write*]."

Remaining excerpts from the rest of the article will come with necessary clarifications:

> "[It] has lots of pidgers by John what drawed them all, he did already. Dear John Lennings, I say, congrastulations on bebeting your book what hast three stories from *Mersey Beat* with [On Safairy With] Whide Hunter [co-written by Paul, which is why Paul's name is mentioned earlier; first published September 6, 1962] and Kakky Hargreaves ['I Remember Arnold' first published August 17, 1971] and Liddypool [first published as 'Around and About,' September 14, 1961].

> Conceive some more books and let's have some more stuff

6

for the *Mersey Beat*."

[— They never received any more Lennon material.]

The review itself is actually a short essay of self-stroking (deservedly so) on *Mersey Beat*'s close affiliation with John Lennon; i.e., "Previously *only* readers of *Mersey Beat* had read John's works, and his contributions were well received." The only appraisal of the *book*'s content is a statement of Harry's, expressing fear that John's "first book is liable to create a great deal of controversy — and that many fans who buy the book purely because John has written it, will be puzzled by its way-out, off beat and sometimes sick humour."

The review concludes with a rather safe prediction: "Almost certainly [it] will be a best seller." [And as a matter of fact, the British First Edition sold out completely the *same* day it went on sale!]

Now you must be thinking, "Surely John got some bad reviews?" Well, of course you're quite right! The worst two I could find are included here, although undoubtedly there are worse ones lurking in the minds of slimy scholars:

Book Week, May 3, 1964, Tom Wolfe reviewing, had this to say:

> "This is nonsense writing, but one has only to review the literature of nonsense to see how well Lennon has brought it off. While some of his homonyms are gratuitous word play, many others have not only double meanings but a double edge . . . nonsense humor is a bit of an easy crutch, even for James Joyce. John Lennon's real test will come when he turns loose his wild inventiveness and bitter slant upon a heavier literary form."

Disappointed? Not bad enough? Well, Wolfe's criticism does seem half-hearted (he immediately counters his negative statements with positive ones). I mean, he's putting down Joyce as much as he is Lennon — which is itself an acknowledgement of John's talent. Ultimately Wolfe sounds angry that John didn't write a novel instead of short stories and poems — certainly not too damaging a charge.

So, the "Most-Negative-Review-on-*In His Own Write* Award" goes to Christopher Ricks for his *New Statesman*, May 1, 1964 review:

> "Hard to see how anyone unaware that John Lennon is a Beatle could get much pleasure out of *In His Own Write*. A

few expressive drawings, and one or two nice puns, but most of the time it is feeble. Nonsense-punning needs a nightmarish logic or else it becomes mere wool-gathering."

Interestingly enough, the positive reviews offer the more specific and valuable observations about "problem areas" in the book. Returning to the *London Times*, "Only the occasional forced bathos or neo-conventional sick joke . . . intrudes." "Forced bathos" means that John can sometimes be too predictable in a comic formula. The "sick joke" reference is in response to John's use of "spastics, sudden slaughter, amputations."

The *Nation* review included this statement: "Several stories are marred . . . by a sort of surface viciousness that comes out like the cute snicker of sick jokes." This parallels the *Time*'s momentary reticence about certain parts of *In His Own Write*, but in both cases the error is considered slight. "These places, however, are more than balanced by pages of inspired madness," says Schickele.

Newsweek's review was not without a negative comment: "Considered with psychiatric solemnity, the works of John Lennon might give an impression of superannuated adolescent self pity." But if that sounds like a heavyweight indictment, that weight is again lifted quickly: "However, this mood is transcended by the jabberwocky of his own writing."

So what have we here? We actually have a critical consensus which views John Lennon as a highly inventive, funny, and sophisticated writer. We also have seen a consensus as to his literary influences: Edward Lear, Lewis Carroll, James Thurber and James Joyce.

So what *don't* we have here? We don't have any explanation as to *why* Lennon is in the tradition of these writers. Therefore I'm going to briefly let you see how Lear, Carroll, Thurber and Joyce form the tradition that Lennon continues.

What the Critics Did Not Say

Edward Lear (1812–1888) was a nineteenth-century specialist in nonsense writing. A glimpse of his major collection, *The Complete Nonsense Book*, reveals startling similarities to John's work.

First of all, Lear not only wrote poems (what he called "Laughable Lyrics") with titles like "The Dong with the Luminous Nose," "The Courtship of the Yonghy-Bonghy-Bo," "The Pobble Who Has No Toes," and "The Quangle Wangle's Hat," but he personally illustrated these verses with original line drawings.

Second, Lear (like Lennon) indulged in special topics such as "school courses" (a science series investigating "Washtubbia Circularis," "Shoebootia Utilus," etc.), "playlets," "recipes" (how to make "Crumbobblious Cutlets," or "Gosky Patties"), and crazy "Alpabets."

What follows next are a few examples of Edward Lear's work . . . a poem entitled "Mr. and Mrs. Discobbolos," several limericks (with Lear's original illustrations), and an excerpt from a playlet called "Eclogue." From reading these selections, you'll be able to clearly see why Lennon shares some stylistic aspects with Lear. Note, however, that Lear is almost exclusively a writer of verse, whereas Lennon's focus is prose.

One last similarity is Lear's own attitude towards his work, a lighthearted Lennonlike view of his writing: "No assistance ever having been given me in any way but that of uproarious delight and welcome at the appearance of every new absurdity."

MR. AND MRS. DISCOBBOLOS

I

Mr. and Mrs. Discobbolos
Climbed to the top of a wall.
And they sate to watch the sunset sky,
And to hear the Nupiter Piffkin cry,
And the Biscuit Buffalo call.
They took up a roll and some Camomile tea,
And both were as happy as happy could be,
Till Mrs. Discobbolos said, —
"Oh! W! X! Y! Z!
It has just come into my head,
Suppose we should happen to fall!!!!!
Darling Mr. Discobbolos!

II

"Suppose we should fall down flumpetty,
Just like pieces of stone,
On to the thorns, or into the moat,
What would become of your new green coat?
And might you not break a bone?
It never occurred to me before,
That perhaps we shall never go down any more!"
And Mrs. Discobbolos said,
"Oh! W! X! Y! Z!
What put it into your head
To climb up this wall, my own
Darling Mr. Discobbolos?"

9

III

Mr. Discobbolos answered, —
"At first it gave me pain, —
And I felt my ears turn perfectly pink
When your exclamation made me think
We might never get down again!
But now I believe it is wiser far
To remain for ever just where we are." —
And Mr. Discobbolos said,
"Oh! W! X! Y! Z!
It has just come into my head —
— We shall never go down again —
Dearest Mrs. Discobbolos!

IV

So Mr. and Mrs. Discobbolos
Stood up, and began to sing,
"Far away from hurry and strife
Here we will pass the rest of life,
Ding a dong, ding dong, ding!
We want no knives nor forks nor chairs,
No tables nor carpets nor household cares,
From worry of life we've fled —
Oh! W! X! Y! Z!
There is no more trouble ahead,
Sorrow or any such thing —
For Mrs. and Mrs. Discobbolos!"

There was an Old Man with a nose,
Who said, "If you choose to suppose
That my nose is too long, you are certainly wrong!"
That remarkable Man with a nose.

There was a Young Person of Smyrna,
Whose Grandmother threatened to burn her;
But she seized on the Cat, and said, "Granny, burn that!
You incongruous Old Woman of Smyrna!"

There was an old Person of Dutton,
Whose head was as small as a button;
So to make it look big he purchased a wig,
And rapidly rushed about Dutton.

There was an Old Man of Coblenz,
The length of whose legs was immense;
He went with one prance from Turkey to France,
That surprising Old Man of Coblenz.

There was a Young Lady of Hull,
Who was chased by a virulent Bull;
But she seized on a spade, and called out, "Who's afraid?"
Which distracted that virulent Bull.

ECLOGUE

Composed at Cannes, December 9th, 1867

(Interlocutors — Mr. Lear and Mr. and Mrs. Symonds.)

Edwardus. — What makes you look so black, so glum, so cross?
Is it neuralgia, headache, or remorse?

Johannes. — What makes you look as cross, or even more so?
Less like a man than is a broken Torso?

E. — What if my life is odious, should I grin?
If you are savage, need I care a pin?

J. — And if I suffer, am I then an owl?
May I not frown and grind my teeth and growl?

E. — Of course you may; but may not I growl too?
May I not frown and grind my teeth like you?

J. — See Catherine comes! To her, to her,
Let each his several miseries refer;
She shall decide whose woes are least or worst,
And which, as growler, shall rank last or first.

Catherine. — Proceed to growl, in silent I'll attend,
And hear your foolish growlings to the end;

Lewis Carroll (1832--1898), though a contemporary of Edward Lear, seems to never have met him. Also, between Lear and Carroll it appears certain that Carroll provided John the most direct influence. Although in one of the initial reviews of John's first book (in *Time* magazine) it was reported that of all the writers suggested as Lennon's models, John "admits only to a small debt to Lewis Carroll," John also had characterized his work in *In His Own Write* this way: "There were very *Alice in Wonderland*."

It makes sense that John as a schoolboy (both bored and angry) would find to his liking the poems and stories of Carroll's *Through the Looking Glass* and *Alice's Adventures in Wonderland*. Carroll, like Lennon, loved playing with words; there was also fantasy to free the imagination, and an offbeat texture that John must have enjoyed. In the last *Playboy* interview with John, he remembered his isolation:

> "I always was so psychic or intuitive or poetic . . . that I was always seeing things in a hallucinatory way. It was scary as a child, because there was nobody to relate to.
>
> Playboy: Were you able to find others to share your visions with?
>
> Lennon: Only dead people in books. Lewis Carroll, certain paintings."

In particular, John's attention seems to have settled on "Jabberwocky." This also is quite understandable, since "Jabberwocky" is considered to be the greatest of all nonsense poems in English.

It is a curious coincidence that Carroll first penned the famous opening stanza of "Jabberwocky" in 1855, when he was twenty-three years old; John was the same age when he completed *In His Own Write*. John's style is Carrollian because Lennon's puns share a logic and goal (while Lear's puns have no logic). In fact, Carroll's idea was to combine more than one emotion or reaction into a single word. This multiplication of meaning in language is explained to Alice by Humpty Dumpty, who calls such puns portmanteau words (because they open up like a suitcase, with two separate compartments). Let's look at the text of "Jabberwocky," and then listen to some of Humpty Dumpty's interpretation.

JABBERWOCKY

'Twas brillig, and the slithy toves
Did gyre and gimble in the wabe:
All mimsy were the borogoves,
And the mome raths outgrabe.

"Beware the Jabberwock, my son!
The jaws that bite, the claws that catch!
Beware the Jubjub bird, and shun
The frumious Bandersnatch!"

He took his vorpal sword in hand:
Long time the manxome foe he sought —
So rested he by the Tumtum tree,
And stood awhile in thought.

And, as in uffish thought he stood,
The Jabberwock, with eyes of flame,
Came whiffling through the tulgey wood,
And burbled as it came!

One, two! One, two! And through and through
The vorpal blade went snicker-snack!
He left it dead, and with its head
He went galumphing back.

"And hast thou slain the Jabberwock?
Come to my arms, my beamish boy!
O frabjous day! Callooh! Callay!"
He chortled in his joy.

'Twas brillig, and the slithy toves
Did gyre and gimble in the wabe:
All mimsy were the borogoves,
And the mome raths outgrabe.

According to Humpty Dumpty, " 'slithy' means 'little and slimy.' You see it's like a portmanteau — there are two meanings packed up into one word. 'Mimsy' is flimsy and miserable (there's another portmateau for you.)"

In addition to portmanteau words, Carroll has Humpty Dumpty identify another form of linguistic invention:

> "When I use a word . . . it means just what I choose it to mean — ."

> "The question is," said Alice, "whether you can make words mean so many different things."

> "The question is," said Humpty Dumpty, "which is to be the master — that's all."

Carroll is referring to the fact that words can have a private or purely nonsensical meaning. "Well, 'toves' are something like badgers — they're something like lizards — and they're something like corkscrews . . . also they make their nests under sun-dials — also they live on cheese."

As Martin Gardner has convincingly shown in his delightful and insightful book, *The Annotated Alice*, "The fact is that Carroll's nonsense is not nearly as random and pointless as it seems . . . . In the case of Alice we are dealing with a very curious, complicated kind of nonsense . . . and we need to know a great many things that are not part of the text if we wish to capture its full wit and flavor." Gardner's evaluation of Carroll applies to Lennon as well. We need to know the details of Liverpool geography, history and Merseyside lifestyle (sometimes we need to know the private history of John's life or the Beatles' career) to understand "its full wit and flavor." So in the same way that Martin Gardner researched Carroll, I have tried to research Lennon; and Gardner presents this reasonable approach: "There is much to be said for [the] plea not to take Alice too seriously. But no joke is funny unless you see the point of it, and sometimes a point has to be explained . . . . Some of Carroll's jokes could be understood only by residents of Oxford, and other jokes, still more private, could be understood only by the lovely daughters of Dean Liddell."

George Harrison, quoted in *Mersey Beat* (February 13, 1964) said of *In His Own Write*, "The 'with-it' people will get the gags and there are some great ones." When one realizes that George is not only speaking to the general readership of *Mersey Beat* (already a small Liverpool audience of insiders) but also, and in particular, to the hip members *within* that group, one can see that the private meanings of some of Lennon's jokes rival Carroll's.

16

So now, on to James Thurber. Again, here we have a predecessor setting the trend that John would unconsciously follow. Thurber (1894--1961) illustrated his work, just as Lear did, with simple line drawings; but *unlike* Lear or Carroll, Thurber specialized in the mini-short story — the precise length used by Lennon throughout *In His Own Write*.

Probably the best way to witness the Thurber style (as it relates to Lennon) is in his *Fables of Our Time*, 1939. Incidentally, this is the same year Joyce's *Finnegans Wake* was published. What Thurber has — something that Lear and Carroll do *not* have — is a sense of satire bordering on menace. It is quite akin to Lennon's black humor.

Let's look at "The Fairly Intelligent Fly," for example: in this fifteen line fable, Thurber presents to us a fly whose "intellect" allows it to avoid being trapped by a spider's web — only to be caught by fly paper! The fly's problem, and often our own, is that it pompously relied on a faulty assumption, in this case the idea that in numbers we are safe. Therefore, the veritable mob of flies found on the paper signaled "sanctuary" to our hero, not a death-trap.

There is a wonderfully offbeat tone to Thurber's work, and a very real cynicism lurking in his fables. Lear and Carroll lack this bite, or hard edge; Lennon has it in profusion. Two more stories will confirm Thurber's sense of irony: "The Bear Who Let It Alone" and "The Green Isle In the Sea." The latter story is accompanied by Thurber's own illustration, and both express the same themes found in *In His Own Write* — "littleness, isolation, and unfair cruelty."

It is important to note, however, that in these stories Thurber does not employ puns; he simply allows the vocabulary of each "children's story" to create all the adult humor. (This reminds us that Lennon said he wrote his own first book in the language "of Winnie-The-Pooh.")

In "The Bear Who Let It Alone," a two paragraph fable, we find another example of Thurber's insight into the complexity and irony of human behavior. An alcoholic bear is pictured returning home, and we watch as he habitually destroys his furniture, hurts himself, and generally creates havoc until he passes out.

The twist in the tale is that our bear "reforms," becoming a health enthusiast whose physical workouts at home cause him to habitually destroy his furniture, hurt himself, and generally create havoc until he passes out! Thus, Thurber illustrates well how we may swap one compulsion for another, deluding ourselves into believing that we have changed.

Finally, in Thurber's "The Green Isle In The Sea," we discover a structure that Lennon excelled in, that of the progressive destruction of a character. We are introduced to a kindly, elderly gentleman as he awakens to a beautiful sunfilled day. Upon opening the windows of his bedroom, he is attacked by a poisonous spider. At breakfast, he falls to the floor (the victim of his grandson's prank), and during his stroll toward a favorite park he is hit by a hoop rolled at him by a little girl. Finally, he is accosted by a thief and robbed. When, at last, he arrives at his "Isle" of calm and beauty — the park — he is horrified to find it blighted and barren of leaves, and instead of the anticipated solace, the park provides the overflying bombers with a clear view of its solitary target: the little old gentleman.

The fourth and final author most often cited as influential to John's writing is, of course, James Joyce (1882–1941). It is interesting to learn that in a 1965 interview, John denied "any knowledge" of James Joyce — saying of his own unique style, "It just comes out. I sit down and write and this is what happens." Yet John also said that both of his books "were written in a sort of Joycean gobbledygook," which implies that Lennon must have had some knowledge of the author. Perhaps it was knowledge gained solely from literary reviews, but I doubt it.

I believe it is James Joyce who forms the predominant tradition which Lennon is heir to — because Joyce combines all the stylistic devices of Lear, Carroll and Thurber with his own personal vision — and John did the same thing.

Carroll used the word "portmanteau" for his puns, but Joyce went further; he called his words "polyhedrons." Now a polyhedron is a mathematical concept, but here it means that instead of only two meanings being packed into a word, many more may be accommodated. Indeed, one of Joyce's critics claims that a single polyhedronic word in *Finnegans Wake* has, on the average, 12 different meanings!

It is more than misleading to say that Carroll, Joyce and Lennon are "nonsense" writers; they would be more aptly termed "newsense" writers — with the intentional homonym on "nuisance," revealing the difficulty of the language they employed. Do not fear, however — it's my job to take the nuisance out of their newsense!

In the "Foreword" I compared an excerpt from Joyce's *Finnegans Wake* with a cutting from Lennon's *A Spaniard In The Works*. The result of that comparison was the discovery of distinct similarities in style between the two authors.

In Chapter Two I will establish, in a page-by-page analysis of *In His Own Write*, further commonalities of style shared by Lennon and Joyce. But before I do that, let's recap the discoveries made in Chapter One.

So In a Few Words, What Does This All Mean?

It means that John does indeed fall into an established tradition of literature. The main members of this group — another four-man combo — are: Edward Lear (on nonsense), Lewis Carroll (on portmanteau), James Thurber (on black humor), and James "Jumble Jim" Joyce (on polyhedronic prose). And that means something else again — that we can safely and correctly think of John as a major talent, one whose work is impressive on its own ground even as it continues a literary style dating back to the previous century.

Chapter Two

Annotation of
In His Own Write

This chapter is organized in such a way as to enable the reader to zero in on specific areas of interest:

The Overview. This first section offers the reader a concise plot summary. In addition to establishing the literal sequence of action, the overview offers observations made on the structure of the selection as a whole.

The Key Themes. In this section, direct statements about central themes are provided for easy reference.

The Interpretation. Only in this section are the metaphoric aspects of each selection discussed. Furthermore, detailed analyses of Lennon's language, point of view, and style will be explored together under this heading.

Before we systematically progress through *In His Own Write*, the work at large will be considered.

The Overview

John Lennon's first book consists of fifty-seven items: fifteen mini-stories (ranging in length from two paragraphs to about two and a quarter pages); eight poems (running from eight lines to ten stanzas); five special forms (one letter, one lesson, one report, one travelogue and one editorial); three play scenes (from one page to just over two pages in length); and twenty-six drawings (including four self-portraits and two Beatle portraits).

The Key Themes

John tells us of *In His Own Write*, "It was my version of what was happening then. I suppose they were all manifestations of hidden cruelties. I was very hung up then." This may account for the excessive violence and emphasis on deformity in the book. In fact, there are eight selections depicting people or animals being killed, as well as eight items that deal with or portray deformity and the physically handicapped. It would not be fair, however, to say that John was morbidly obsessed with these topics. There are also eight items on the Beatles: two drawings, one letter, one report, one poem, three stories. However, it *is* fair to say that John does have a penchant for the shocking and the provocative.

John's fascination with and mockery of the "crippled" date back to his childhood. By the time he reached college, John had developed a notoriously "sick" sense of humor. As a matter of fact, John's particular brand of comic writing was coming to the attention of others by the end of the fifties. It was in early 1959 that Bill Harry met John at Ye Cracke (a student pub) and read Lennon's poetry for the first time. Harry observed that John's writing had "freshness and originality in its sheer lunacy . . . . [but] His individual sense of humour was almost surreal and I began to notice the strangeness and wit in his personality, actions, and activities . . . his humour seemed absurdly cruel with its obsession with cripples, spastics and torture."

A more contemporary reason for John's featuring of cripples throughout *In His Own Write* lies in the Beatle experience itself. Few of us realize that the Beatles were actually bombarded by people with physical handicaps. In fact, these people seemed to believe that the Beatles could heal them merely by their presence or their touch. In *Lennon Remembers*, John says, "We were just surrounded by cripples and blind people all the time and when we would go through corridors they would be all touching us. It got like that, it was horrifying." Jann Wenner of *Rolling Stone* responded, "You must have been still fairly young and naive at that point." John replied, "Yeah, well as naive as *In His Own Write*." And so John was incorporating such strange and horrifying Beatle experiences into his stories, using the stuff of life for his art.

Other key themes of *In His Own Write* involve the foibles of politics and the narrowmindedness of Christianity. "I've been satirizing the system since my childhood," reports John. So in his first book, his two main targets were "the . . . church and state . . . I was pretty heavy on the church . . . there's many knocks at religion and there is a play [scene] about a worker and a capitalist."

One can safely say, however, that close behind that humor there is pain — or perhaps because of the pain, there is humor. John said he tried "to express what I felt about myself" in *In His Own Write*, but "I always had to write in that gobbledegook . . . my usual way, because I was never honest enough." Overall, I personally feel that *Newsweek* best capsulizes the themes of the book as "Littleness, isolation, unfair cruelty."

Because there is no way to effectively interpret a book of such diversity in only a few paragraphs, I will simply present some general background on *In His Own Write*: how it was compiled, how it got to publication. In order to do this, I will contrive a question and have John answer in his own words (all questions are based on the original interviews):

Q. Did you ever expect that *In His Own Write* would be published?

A. "When I wrote the original stuff, over a period of four or five years (but most of it last year [1963]) it was *not* meant for a book. Basically these things were just for me . . . I wrote it to read among my friends."

Q. Do you plan to write more?

A. "Yes. Tomorrow. I wouldn't mind just writing books . . . I plan the more the merrier, if people like it as much as I do."

Q. What was your usual procedure for writing?

A. "I write when I feel like it. When the Beatles started going on tour, I used to take out my typewriter after the show and just tap away as the fancy took me."

Q. How do you organize your manuscripts?

A. "I put things down on sheets of paper and stuff them in my pocket. When I have enough I have a book."

Q. Are you still composing poetry?

A. "The poetry bit? I still churn out odd verses whenever something strikes me as being particularly ludicrous . . . . When I collect all the cigarette packets together [they] go into a book."

Q. What about *In His Own Write*'s unique language?

A. "I just made it up. Mostly it's really just puns on words."

Q. How did *In His Own Write* reach a publisher?

A. "A friend of mine took some of the material to Cape, the publishers, and the man there said: 'This is brilliant. I'd like to do this.' And that was before he even knew who I was."

Q. What did you think of the positive critical reception to the book?

A. "I really didn't think the book would even get reviewed by the book reviewers — maybe in the record columns as a new 'single' by one of the Beatles. I didn't think people would accept the book like they did. To tell you the truth they took the book more seriously than I did myself. It just began as a laugh for me."

Notes on the Front Cover. The Signet Edition, published by the New American Library (hereinafter referred to as "our version") features a photograph of John that never appeared on the original covers of either *In His Own Write* or *A Spaniard In The Works*. The photograph used for the original cover of *In His Own Write* was taken by Robert Freeman (our version is by World Wide). Freeman is the same top London fashion photographer who shot the outstanding album covers used on **Meet The Beatles** (on Capitol Records in America; called **With The Beatles** on Parlophone in Britain) and **Rubber Soul**.

Freeman's cover photo of John for *In His Own Write* is in black and white and shows a smiling and relaxed Lennon wearing a pea coat and a cap. This original photograph is still available in the Penguin paperback edition (hereinafter referred to as Pp.).

A final note on the cover concerns the Simon and Schuster First Edition (hereinafter called SS.). For this cover adds "The Writing Beatle!" next to John's name — an addition which appeared only in America.

Notes on the Back Cover. Our version simply prints scanty excerpts from reviews on both of Lennon's books. Unfortunately, the reader has no way of knowing which *one* of John's books is the referent for a particular critical comment.

More importantly, our version totally omits John's hilarious "biography" (which appears on the SS. and Pp. editions). To rectify this significant omission, I have reprinted John's original biography below:

About The Awful

I was bored on the 9th of Octover 1940 when, I believe, the Nasties were still booming us led by Madalf Heatlump (who only had one). Anyway they didn't get me. I attended to varicose schools in Liddypool. And still didn't pass — much to my Aunties supplies. As a member of the most publified Beatles my and (P, G, and R's) records might seem funnier to some of you than this book, but as far as I'm conceived this correction of short writty is the most wonderfoul larf I've ever ready.

God help and breed you all.

The Interpretation

The information is correct. John Winston Lennon was born on

the 9th of October, 1940, when the Nazis were still bombing Liverpool (led, of course, by Adolf Hitler, who did only have one testicle). He did indeed attend various ("to varicose") schools: Dovedale Primary and Quarry Bank High School For Boys. It is also true that John "still didn't pass" (most of his exams in school, especially the National Tests required in the British school system). So Aunt Mimi (who really raised Lennon and who supported him with all the "supplies" he needed) was much surprised ("much . . . supplies") at John's failure in school — she knew he could succeed if he tried.

Because the Beatles ran their lives like a never-ending pub party, they were literally "publified," as well as publicized and even vilified. John's closing statement ("this collection of short writing is the most wonderful laugh I've ever read") is made all the funnier by the incisiveness of his puns.

A few examples: John jokes about his unorthodox spelling by implying his "collection" needs "correction." He uses "writty" because it combines "witty" and "writing" into one word — a typical portmanteau for John. Certainly the book is filled with wonderfully "foul" laughs (by using "larf" for laugh he incorporates the "arfing" of a dog to suggest the gutteral sound of laughter). And even in the short space of this biography, some *Joycean* similarities are evident. Joyce used "bored" as "born" (*FW* 136.08 — hereinafter all *Finnegans Wake* citations refer to the Viking Press paperback edition. I will supply both page and line numbers in all *FW* references). But while John used "awful" for "author," Joyce preferred to emphasize the godlike strength of the writer: "arthor" (*FW* 52.17), meaning "art-Thor" (probably King Arthur's power is there also).

The tag "God help and breed you all" is double-edged: it can be taken either as a benign benediction or as an indictment of Christianity — "God help and *bleed* you all."

I hope our version restores this biography in future printings — it's too rare to miss.

"Title Page" (p. 9)

Hunter Davies (and no one else, I might add) asserts that "Paul came up with the title." Whether or not he did is irrelevant; the title itself establishes Lennon's independence from the Beatles.

Drawing One (p. 10)

This is the first of four self-portraits found in *In His Own Write*. Here John depicts himself as naked because he *feels* himself to be so: "Up to now we've done everything together, and this is all my own work. I keep thinking I'm breaking my contract."

Lennon's lenses are off, his hair is pulled back; and unlike "old flattop" of *Come Together* there are no "feet down below his knees." The missing feet express John's fear he has nothing to stand on — except his potential to fly. Thus there are eleven birds in the drawing.

John's initial feelings of vulnerability and fear of failure disappear by the time we reach his third self-portrait. For now, however, as we begin the book, John tells us with Drawing One that he has nothing to hide.

It is interesting to note that in the SS. and Pp. editions, Drawing One *precedes* the title page; I believe that Drawing One is better placed in these editions, for the reader's focus rests entirely on John's image before the book begins. Furthermore, the Pp. edition has more detailing and highlighting than our version. For example, the birds on John's hands have black-tipped beaks (while other birds have strong shadows on their beaks). I admit this is a minor point — but such details do make the portrait more satisfying.

Drawing Two (p. 11)

This is John's first portrait of the Beatles. This interpretation becomes the more plausible when we remember what Paul said at the time: "The thing is, we're all really the same person. We're just four parts of the one." So what we have, then, is a representation of the corporate identity of the Beatles: one head and four extensions. Though John's drawing is abstract it remains, nonetheless, accurate even to the smallest detail. For three of the hands appear right handed, and one, Paul's, looks left handed. Years later, in *Lennon Remembers*, Jann Wenner brings this concept to John's attention: "Always the Beatles were talked about and the Beatles talked about themselves as being four parts of the same person." John's reply is quite telling: "You see we believed the Beatles myth, too."

Our version of this Beatle portrait is preferable to that of SS. and Pp., because ours is free of the printed credits: SS. proclaims the portrait "designed by Robert Freeman," and in Pp. we find (above the head of the Beatles) this announcement: "drawings by John Lennon and design by Robert Freeman."

"Introduction," by Paul McCartney (p. 13)

As I stated in my Introduction, inaccuracies of date and place abound in regard to John Lennon and the Beatles. This generally confusing situation becomes particularly ironic when even Paul (presumably one who should know the facts) supplies the reader with misleading and incorrect information. I will now briefly highlight the introduction in order to separate fact from fiction.

1. "At the Woolton village fete I met him." This statement is true, but requires some clarification. Woolton is a suburb of Liverpool and is, in fact, a city and not a "village" (I think that whenever

Americans think of "villages" in England, they conjure up visions of Doctor Doolittle's house). The "fete" (an outdoor festival with entertainment) was not organized by Woolton per se, but by St. Peter's Parish Church in Woolton. These things aside, Paul did first meet John at the fete, having been invited by a mutual friend (Ivan Vaughan).

2. "I realized he was drunk." This is, as you might imagine, true; John was indeed drunk.

3. "We were both twelve then." This, however, is competely *untrue*. Yet while it is easy to verify that Paul's statement is false (John would have been fourteen to Paul's twelve), it is difficult to establish how old each of them actually was. It sounds ridiculous, but as of 1981 the date of this event remains in dispute. In 1964 the *Original Beatles Book* reports *John's* recollection of his first meeting with Paul: "We can both remember it quite well. We've even got the date down. It was June 15, 1955." If this date is correct, then John *was* fourteen and Paul was twelve (Paul, however, would turn thirteen in just three days). But in 1981, Philip Norman's *Shout!* records that this same event occurred on July 6, 1957 (making John sixteen and Paul a newly-turned fifteen). So either John's memory is faulty or Norman's research is erroneous. Personally, I accept Norman's date for the following reasons:

A. John would easily forget the years in which his major works appeared, just as he would forget words to his songs. As a matter of fact, John would blank out over how to play them. This would seem to indicate at least the possibility of a hazy recollection of the "fete."

B. *Strawberry Fields Forever: John Lennon* (1980) claims that Lennon was in his "fifth form" at Quarry Bank High School when he formed the Quarry Men. A British book on English educational terms informs us that a student is *sixteen* years of age during his fifth form.

C. Norman provides more details of this event than does any other author — and Norman's Beatle research is generally the best documented.

D. Norman provides further evidence by printing the "*earliest* known picture of the Quarry Men." It is dated "summer 1957."

(The real point, at the moment, is that regardless of which date you choose, John and Paul were *not* "both twelve then.")

4. "He had written a poem for the school magazine about a hermit who said: 'As breathing is my life, to stop I dare not dare.' " There are two errors in this statement. First, the poem that John wrote, "The Tales of Hermit Fred," *never* appeared in — nor was it written for — a school magazine. This is simple to verify, for we

know from *Shout!* that John's original copy of the poem, first given to his pal Pete Shotton, then "enjoyed wide under-the-desk circulation." Furthermore, the poem was entered in one of John's "exercise" books. So where did Paul get the school magazine idea? Possibly by misinterpreting a line of John's that was similar to the following: "I used to write *magazines* in school and hand them around." Maybe Paul assumed that John's "private" magazine was the school magazine? At any rate, "The Tales of Hermit Fred" was first published on February 27, 1964 in *Mersey Beat*. And from that issue we learn that Paul apparently misquoted the poem — his second error in this regard. The hermit *actually* said, "As breathing is my very life, To stop I do not dare." (The entire poem is reprinted in Chapter Six.)

5. "None of it has to make sense and if it seems funny then that's enough." Just a point of clarification: I agree that John's writing doesn't have to "make sense" to be enjoyable; however, I assert most emphatically that it *does* make sense. Also, I believe the humor in the book may be intensified, and not by searching for so-called "hidden meanings," but simply by unmasking what's already there.

Drawing Three (p. 14)

This is an illustration of "Little Bobby," complete with his birthday hook. (The actual story, "A Surprise for Little Bobby," appears towards the end of the book, p. 72.) The only additional detail added to this drawing by the story is the fact that Bobby is thirty-nine years old.

Unfortunately, the size of our version is greatly reduced from that found in SS. and Pp. As a result, the reader will have a difficult time realizing that Bobby is dressed as a priest: he wears a clergyman's collar and a crucifix around his neck. Furthermore, if you place your index finger on Bobby's mouth and then angle the drawing to the right, the head of a lamb is suggested: the lamb's nose is to the left of your finger, the eye is at the center of your finger, and a floppy ear appears at the right. Thus John has effectively presented one of God's flock, in this case a priest, as literally resembling "The Lamb of God."

Interestingly enough, there is a discrepancy in the illustration: the hook should be on the other hand! Yet John (in several instances) doesn't seem to mind having his illustrations deviate from the text of a story.

"Partly Dave" (p. 17)

The Overview

Dave, a salesman, gets up in the morning, has breakfast with his wife Betty, and then leaves for work on the bus. Basuboo, a black conductor, gives Dave some advice before throwing him off the bus for having no bus fare.

The Key Themes

The pointlessness of the working class/survival/rat race routine. Also man's political naivety.

The Interpretation

A tale of fragmented personality: socially myopic automatons who lack any real purpose in life. The title "Partly Dave," I think, is a humorous way of expressing the woeful lack of self-awareness on the part of the main character.

Dave starts out each morning with a groan and a moan which grow in intensity ("groam"). James Joyce used a similar word which also captures a double meaning in the phrase "his corns were *grown-ing*" (*FW* 223.32). The line "he had a mission in life" is, of course, highly ironic: Dave has absolutely nothing in his life. He is, like the others in the story, a person whose only "mission" is To Exist. He doesn't realize that he both ignores his wife and unnerves his girl-friend, Mary; all they get from him is "I'm partly Dave" (literally). Dave also fails to realize that there is a "colored problem"; later on he doesn't even realize the conductor is black.

Now the black conductor is, in certain ways, no better off than Dave — Basuboo does not understand "the colored problem himself really." Yet the only truthful statement in the tale is spoken by Basuboo: "Your in a rut Dave." And "your" is very deliberately used in place of "you are," thus grammatically fragmenting Dave. How-ever, Basuboo is in a double rut himself: the literal rut of the bus route, as well as the rut of his subservience to the White Power Structure. Indeed, the name itself (Basuboo) evokes the feeling of nineteenth-century British colonialism on the Dark Continent.

There is a certain poignancy in the line "Dave used to think"; it refers both to his being used to (or accustomed to) thinking in cliches at the present, while it also suggests that somewhere in his past, "Dave used to *think.*" Unfortunately all we are left with is "a raving salesman" wildly jumping off a bus "like a burning spastic."

Stylistically, John has skillfully reenforced the redundancy of Dave's life by using parallel sentence construction: "which always unnerved Betty" and "which always unnerved Mary." By exploiting the same phrasing (and merely changing names), Lennon effectively reduces these people to interchangeable nonentities.

All in all, "Partly Dave" is a very successful sketch about empty lives — surreal in tone, ludicrous in detail, and aptly embodying a serious theme. It's to John's credit that so many images and ideas emerge from only eighteen lines of prose portraiture.

Drawing Four (p. 18)

This is an illustration of Frank's wife, Marian. She is four-foot-three and is pictured lying on the kitchen floor, virtually covered by flies; she has been dead now for two or three weeks. The humor of the drawing is intensified by the title of the story: "No Flies on Frank." At first the reader laughs at the apparent contradiction between the "No Flies" titles and the abundance of flies on the body — but a careful second look at the drawing reveals a woman's shoe. And so we read the story and discover it is Marian, and not Frank, who is blessed with all the flies.

"No Flies On Frank" (pp. 19–21)

The Overview

This is the story of Frank — who awakens on the morning of his wife Marian's thirty-second birthday only to find that his penis has grown twelve inches longer. Frank is shocked; at first he mentally compares his penis size with that of his brothers and ancestors, and then he dejectedly goes downstairs to his wife in the kitchen. Although poor Marian yells that she is not to blame, Frank nevertheless clubs her to death with the head of his penis.

After two or three weeks Marian's body is still lying on the kitchen floor; the flies are such a bother to Frank that he can't even eat his food. So Frank puts Marian into a sack and takes her over to Mrs. Sutherskill, Marian's mother. But Mrs. Sutherskill doesn't want the flies in her home either, so she slams the door in Frank's face. The tale closes with Frank carrying away the sack, presumably back to his own house.

The Key Themes

How sexual frustration, coupled with a bad marriage, can lead to murder! Also the numbness and loss of feeling (typical of our age) regarding the value of life.

The Interpretation

This story stands as a universally amusing male fantasy, but Frank's desperate attempt to escape a dead marriage finds its foundation in John's own experience. John admitted that his song "If I Fell" was a personal fantasy of leaving his wife Cynthia (the song was written early in 1964). It seems reasonable that John channeled at least some of his own maritial frustration into Frank's situation.

It is interesting to note that in *The Lennon Play: In His Own Write*, 1968 (a one-act play adapted from John's writings) this story is "staged" as a "B.B.C. Third Programme; A Play for Radio." A fine choice, for here the bizarre physical action of the tale is relegated directly to the mind' eye of the audience.

Also of note: the premise of John's story echoes that of Franz Kafka's "The Metamorphosis." In Kafka's classic short story, the main character wakes up one morning to discover that his entire body has turned into that of a giant insect. In Lennon's tale, only one part of Frank's body is changed.

I'm aware that the reader may initially suspect my sanity, as I have asserted it is in fact Frank's penis which grows twelve inches. Therefore, to quell any doubts and dissension, I will present the textual evidence for my interpretation.

Frank's discovery is made as he stands on the bathroom ("barthroom") scale. As he looks down to see what he weighs, the next line confirms exactly which part of his anatomy has changed: "his blood raised to his head" (meaning he'd gotten a giant erection). Frank then wonders what "hath taken me thus into such a fatty hardbuckle." This line refers to his now fat and hard prick, stationed beneath the area of his belt buckle. Also, the line alludes to the silent film star Fatty Arbuckle, whose sex-scandal exploits were well publicized in his day.

"Again Frank *looked down* at the awful vision . . . . 'Twelve inches more heavy, *Lo*!' " Both of these phrases further reenforce the location of his malady. Frank then compares his penis size to that of his brothers, in an attempt to rationalize its present enormity: "Am I not *more fatty* than my brother . . . ?"

We learn from the text that Frank's testicles, or balls, now resemble large rocks, and so they are called "his boulders." Also we discover that Marian can no longer arouse Frank sexually: Frank may be looking at Marian's face, but the sight will no longer "raise . . . poor Frank's head." And Marian's response to Frank's condition further corroborates my interpretation: "*Lo*! Frank – Am I to blame for this vast *burton*?" Lennon is now using the sexual exploits of another movie star, Richard Burton, as he had done with Fatty Arbuckle.

Finally we witness the culmination of Frank's problem, as he "took his head in his hands and clubbed her . . . dead." Now I hope the evidence I've presented convinces the reader that is was John Lennon who came up with the prick idea, and *not* yours truly! But this little story has much more to offer the reader than Frank's big surprise – the tale is not only very complex linguistically, but is also rich in syntactical invention and built upon a relentlessly funny running gag.

To begin with, there are the portmanteaus: "barthroom" and "Grate qualmsy." In "barthroom" we easily detect "bathroom" and "barfroom." But perhaps there is a further reference – one made to an author named "Barth" (which would also make the bathroom the reading room). "Grate qualmsy" seems to mean "a gratingly great, qualmy and queasy feeling" — an apt description of Frank's horror and shock at finding his bloated organ.

John also uses deceptive and teasing syntax, i.e., "I carn't not believe," which actually means "I *do* believe" — for Frank "cannot not believe"! There are the puns on surnames and place names. For example, Mrs. Sutherskill's name resembles "Mrs. Daughters-kill" and "Smother-Mother-Skill" (which make perfect sense in context). And certainly "Kenneth-through-Leslies" is a lurid geography, a take-off on the names of a typical English village as well as a specific indictment of Kenneth's sexual intercourse with Leslie — Kenneth and Leslie being Franks' grandparents.

The "wonderfoul" running gag "No Flies On Frank" is used five times within the story. Lennon calculates each appearance quite skillfully, for just when we've forgotten about the line, it resurfaces, i.e. "Frank — who as you know had no flies on him," etc.

But even more important than John's use of humorous devices is his ability to portray the emptiness of his characters' lives. Lennon's insistent use of irony allows us to feel some of the pain in the puns. "It was a typical Frank morning . . . . He journeyed downstairs crestfalled and defective" — carrying "a great wait."

Here we see Frank's real dilemma: A lonely, broken man without any self-esteem, Frank waits endlessly for his life to change. For years he has played out a pointless charade of marriage, and he views his wife only in a grotesque way: "a former beauty queer." In fact, Frank's wife isn't even given a name in the story until *after* she is dead! Even more invisible than Marian is their child, who is mentioned once at the opening of the tale and then is never heard from again. The child, however, is given no name at all.

Sadly for Frank, there is no consolation — Christian scripture, meant to provide hope and comfort, turns into a pungent parody. Instead of "Yea, though I walk through the valley of the shadow of death, I will fear no evil," we have "Yea, though I wart through the valet of thy shadowy hut I will feed no norman." The Christian myth melts into a Pagan one (echoing Odysseus telling the Cyclops that his name is "No Man" in order to escape being eaten.).

Also, John's parody of scripture is highly reminiscent of Joyce's brilliant blasphemy. For example, the Lord's Prayer opens with: "Our Father who art in Heaven hallowed be thy name, thy kingdom come, they will be done, on earth as it is in Heaven." In *Finnegans Wake*, it becomes "Our Farfar that arred in Himmal, haloed be her eve, her singtime sung, her rill be run, unhemmed as it is uneven." (*FW* 52.16, 599.05, 104.2–3).

The general irony in "No Flies On Frank" is heightened by Lennon's use of King James English. Here the language of the Royal

Court only highlights the lowliness of Frank's life: "Am I not the most miserable of men. Suffer ye not to spake to me or I might thrust you a mortal injury; I must traddle [travel/straddle] this trail alone." Frank's grandiose language announces that he is at his breaking point, untouchable, and murderous if his wife should dare attempt to communicate with him. Marian's reply (her last words, in fact) can be taken quite seriously: "Thou hast smote me harshly with such grave talk" (The pun on "grave" is classically Elizabethan).

Even though Frank "frees" himself of Marian, nothing really changes in his life. Her presence, unfortunately, lingers on — and now Frank is more alone than ever. He's done all he can, yet is unable to get rid of his initial "problem" — his wife. This strange and funny story concludes with Frank being rejected by Mrs. Sutherskill (another human being with no ties and no compassion). So Frank departs, cast off by Mrs. Sutherskill, a woman Frank could "never call . . . Mum."

"Good Dog Nigel" (pp. 22–23)
The Overview

A dog named Nigel happily pees on a lamppost, barks playfully and wags his tail as he goes on his merry way. Until it is abruptly announced that Nigel will be killed at three o'clock.

The Key Themes

The unpredictable dangers of existence, and the intense irony of life: just when we feel we've attained some small measure of tranquility, tragedy strikes. A theme made horrifyingly real by John's death.

The Interpretation

Lennon aligned himself with Nigel linguistically, for John's "larfing" is Nigel's "arfing." Also, John will use another dog as a symbol of the Beatles (pp. 28–29).

The humor of this eight-line poem derives from its puerile nursery-rhyme opening and its completely maniacal reversal of tone. In lines one through five, everything is "merry," "bright," and "nice." But in line six, potential danger is introduced: "Waggie tail and *beg*." (the begging could be taken either as a fun trick or as a demand to "beg for your life"). Line seven sets up the final irony, "jump for joy," i.e., "celebrate your own execution!" And then line eight breaks from the verse form entirely, announcing in unfeeling prose: "Because we're putting you to sleep at three of the clock, Nigel."

Drawing Five (p. 23)

This is an illustration of Nigel (apprently he's the most isolated dog in the picture) and his "little hairy friends." A quick note on dogs is appropriate at this point — there are eleven of them throughout *In His Own Write* (pp. 23, 29, 30, 32, and 61). Why so many dogs? Perhaps because John enjoyed watching them — especially at the circus! At any rate, more than a few diminutive canines wag their way into John's drawings.

"At The Denis" (pp. 24--25)

The Overview

This is the first of three dramatic scenes in the book. "At The Denis" concerns an elderly woman who goes to see Denis the Dentist. She tells him of her toothache, and he has her sit in his examination chair. The resulting diagnosis is that she must not only have the one tooth extracted, but all her remaining teeth as well. Denis also tells her she will look much, much younger with a set of false teeth. The woman is flattered and agrees to have *all* her teeth removed.

The Key Themes

The incompetence of medical services in general and of the dental profession in particular. Also, the gullibility of most people in accepting, without question, "Doctor's Orders."

The Interpretation

The first line of the scene reads like an excerpt from "No Flies On Frank": "I have a hallowed tooth that suffer me grately." The similarity is due to the mock-heroic style of the language and to the fact that "grate" was used in "No Flies." But then the similarity ends; "At The Denis" creates its own crazy world.

We get a clear picture of this woman known only as "Madam." First we surmise she is old because she has only eight teeth left in her mouth. We also see her as strange, sporting as she does a small, rodent-like smile. To convey that image, Lennon uses "mouse" for "mouth." In addition, Madam is quaint; she displays an antique manner which comes out in her language. She says "Alad!" (meaning not only the exclamation "Egad!" but also calling to mind some obscure expression of courtesy. As *Time* pointed out, "it is logical to assume that if a Sir says "alas," a Madam might say "alad." Joyce used "alick and alack!" (*FW* 166.3).

Madam's appearance and manner, to Denis at least, is that of a man gone insane (Denis reveals these feelings by accidentally calling her "Madman."). This interpretation is enhanced if you read the first two words of these scene as "Mad am I."

However, Denis is not really any finer specimen of humanity than Madam is: his chief talent is the ability to con his clients. We learn of Denis' slippery ways when he tells Madam to "sly down" (a portmanteau made of "slide" and "lie"). Further evidence of the dentist's duplicity is found in the false (but funny) information that he gives Madam just after she admits she has only "eight teeth left." Denis replies, "Then you have lost eighty three." (This is absurd, of course; it means Madam once had a total of ninety-one teeth.) Denis then compounds his prevaricating with the following: "Everydobby knows there are foor decisives, two canyons and ten grundies which make thirsty-two in all."

To begin with, "everydobby" sounds like an insult: i.e., "every dopey." It also has the ring of a patronizing version of "everybody." As for the rest of Denis' data, it is both true *and* false; there are eight incisors, not "foor decisives." But we do have two canines ("canyons"), even though we lack "grundies" (perhaps "grundies" refer to the grinding molars, which number twelve, not ten. Joyce might call such a molar "the grinder of the grunder," *FW* 353.23). Denis' addition is incorrect, but his conclusion is right: there are thirty-two teeth in all in the normal mouth.

A Joycean line which follows the above summarizes the likelihood of either Madam or Denis ever becoming any brighter: "Perhumps! but to no avague." It is interesting to note that Joyce actually used "perhumps" for "perhaps," (*FW* 602.24).

At first Madam agrees only that Denis may *look* at the infected tooth, but Denis extracts it before she can protest. Denis then rationalizes his action by saying, "It was all black and moody, and the others are too." Madam's fear of losing all her teeth is then assuaged when Denis tells her she will look "thirty years jungle" ("younger," perhaps, but still like an overgrowth of foliage!). Finally, Madam capitulates, giving Denis permission to pull out all the stops ("pull out all my stumps"). And Denis replies to our Granny, "O.K. Gummy," as the hilarious scene closes.

A final note: John's great dislike of dentists (extending beyond the physical pain that is associated with them) seems to have a broader base, dating back to his early education. Lennon has been quoted as saying, "A couple of teachers would . . . encourage me . . . to draw — express myself. But most of the time they were trying to beat me into being a fuckin' dentist."

"The Growth On Eric Hearble" (p. 26)
The Overview

One morning Eric Hearble wakes up to find a growth on his head. The growth calls out to him, but Eric just ignores it. That night the growth introduces itself as "Scab," and instantly Eric and Scab become fast friends. The story ends abruptly when Eric's boss fires him for becoming a "cripple."

The Key Themes

The concept that any definition of "cripple" is relative. Also, the implicit observation that most people are hypocritical and myopic when they encounter others who are physically "different."

The Interpretation

Structurally, the story is a variation of "No Flies On Frank" (pp.

19–21). For example, instead of it being a "Frank" morning, it is a "fat morning"; and of course both Frank and Eric awaken to find "growths" on their "heads" — Eric's head being on his shoulders, Frank's head being in a more delicate location. Instead of repeating Frank's story of being alienated, however, Eric's tale has the hero happily finding a friend.

It makes sense that Scab is described as "an abnorman growth," for not only is his presence "abnormal" — he is literally an "abnormal *man*." And so it also makes sense now that Eric must carry "on as Norman."

It is both humorous and sad how Eric "became very attached to his fat growth friend," for the implication is clearly that Eric had never had a friend until Scab showed up. To give Scab his due, however, he does seem kind, and while "bumpy," he yet has "aplomb" ("a bombly").

The punch line of the tale reminds us of the conclusion of "Partly Dave" (p. 17) because of the word "spastic." Here, however, it doesn't refer to the behavior of the main character, but to that of Eric's students. We're told that Eric's job is "teaching spastics to dance" (an old, bad joke, admittedly, and a cheap shot, if it were not used to make a point).

In partial vindication of the spastic joke, we see that it is used to show two things. First, that Eric's new friendship with Scab makes him a "cripple" in his boss's eyes. Second, that while it's fine to have a physically "normal" person teach the physically handicapped, society feels it is not okay to have a handicapped person assume the role of teacher.

The real joke is that Eric's boss is an emotional cripple himself and, ironically, is also a *"Head*master"! For although he is technically the master of Eric's head, he is not master of his own; he doesn't even see what stands in front of his eyes.

Drawing Six (p. 27)

This is, of course, a head shot of Eric Hearble and Scab. The fact that Eric and Scab are practically identical suggests that Scab is the symbolic extension of Eric's personality. It is worth noting that both the SS. and Pp. editions reproduce Drawing Six as *much* larger than does our version. Not only does the increase in size make for a funnier picture; it correctly emphasizes the "fatness" mentioned in the text.

"The Wrestling Dog" (pp. 28--29)
The Overview

Every year at harvest time, Perry (the Lord Mayor of a small island) provides a feast and entertainment for his people. This year

36

Perry has outdone himself: he's secured a wrestling dog to perform for his guests. The tale ends abruptly with a question and an answer: "Who would fight this wondrous beast? I wouldn't for a kick off."

The Key Themes

The anxiety and humiliation experienced by entertainers when they are treated like performing animals.

The Interpretation

This selection is the first of the Beatle stories. The tale expresses the emotional claustrophobia shared by the Beatles as Fame made them the biggest attraction in the world.

The first paragraph establishes the location of the tale as Liverpool — "hicksville" as John describes it — or, as the text would have it, "miles away from anyway over the hills." It follows that the "little island on a distant land" is England; after all, the entire country of Great Britain is, unbeknownst to most Americans, smaller than the state of California. (It's small.)

In addition, there's possibly a more subtle bit of evidence for the Liverpool interpretation. The story opens, "Once upon a *tom*," and this may well refer to another Liverpool lad that the Beatles' manager (Brian Epstein) handled. Tom, or Tommy Quickly, was the first solo artist ever managed by Epstein, and Tom's premiere engagement was on a Beatles bill.

Lennon adds a Joycean touch by calling the boisterous Lord Mayor the "Loud" Mayor (Joyce, in addition to using "Loud" for "Lord," *FW* 258.13, generally enjoyed punning on the title Lord Mayor, i.e., "lewd mayers," "londmear," "lorkmakor," and "lode mere": *FW* 550.28, 372.02, 342.28, and 248.07 respectively). Previously, the Lord Mayor had only presented sideshows or circus acts (billing performing dwarfs, for example, as "new and exciting; thrill and spectacular"). But today the Lord Mayor "had surpassed himselve by getting a Wrestling Dog!"

In my view, this story is based on John's accurate anticipation of a Beatle event which actually took place during July of '64 in Liverpool. The occasion was the second premiere of the Beatles' first movie, "A Hard Days Night." The film's title, in fact, was picked out of a Lennon story, "Sad Michael" (p. 37) by its director, Richard Lester (though originally the line was a "Ringoism" which John nicked for his story).

By early 1964 the Beatles were definitely paying an emotional price for their unprecedented popularity. Significantly, John's lyrics to "A Hard Days Night" reveal, for the first time in any Beatle song, real fatigue:

> "It's been a hard day's night
> And I've been working *like a dog*
> It's been a hard day's night
> I should be sleeping like a log"

And so, just like in John's story, the *real* Lord Mayor of Liverpool was able to show off the biggest act in the world! There was even a huge parade which culminated with the Beatles standing on the balcony of Liverpool's Town Hall with the Lord Mayor and his Aldermen. Needless to say, the Beatles were received in this case like a returning god — dog spelled backwards.

Predictably, the Lord Mayor had not just outdone "himself," but had surpassed all the various "selves" he represents — so John used "himselve." Joyce, it can be noted, often punned on "himself": "himpself," "himsalves," "himselfs," and "himshelp" (*FW* 313.33, 352.36, 234.10, 157.13 respectively).

The ending of the story is tongue-in-cheek, for John admits that no one can wrestle down their present fame: "Who would fight this wondrous beast?" John closes by saying, in essence, "the Beatles are so big *I* wouldn't challenge them myself!"

Drawing Seven (pp. 28--29)

This is the second "Beatle" portrait, only now the Beatles are depicted as a single performing dog. The SS. and Pp. editions are superior to our version, as their picture is greatly enlarged; therefore the dog properly dominates both pages. As the story states, there are thirty-nine people staring at the dog. The thirty-nine people represent the entire "island," or the entire *world* watching the Beatle phenomenon.

The dog, understandably, looks bewildered as it stands alone in the wrestling ring — quite a different portrait than the fans are used to. In short, we see the alienating side of Fame.

Drawing Eight (pp. 30--31)

This is a drawing of Randolf's "good pals." First, it's worth noting that some of Lennon's bizarre representations of these people will reappear in the brilliant animation of "The Yellow Submarine." Second, as is John's custom, this illustration doesn't strictly adhere to the text of the story.

The tale that follows names sixteen pals; however, if you count both the people and all of the "balloon heads" (an apt metaphor for the empty-headedness of these pals), you wind up with seventeen people. In addition, there's a very, very small dog present (maybe this is our "Nigel," p. 23, for one of the "pals" is named Nigel). Another good guess is that "Beddy" in the story is really "Little Bobby" (p. 72), for the drawing shows one person with a "hook" hand.

Once again, our version suffers from reduction. In both the SS. and Pp. editions the facial features of the smallest balloon head (located on the creased edge of p. 30) are clearly visible; in ours, the face doesn't exist.

"Randolf's Party" (p. 31)

The Overview

It is Christmas Day and Randolf, with only his father's Christmas card for company, sits alone. Sadly he arises to decorate the tree (all the while longing for his friends to visit him), when (right on cue) a knock on the door brings Randolf's buddies inside — shouting "Happy Gringle, Randolf."

Then, without warning, they all jump on Randolf, beating him to death as they yell "We never liked you," etc. The tale ends with the narrator bidding Randolf's *corpse* a "Merry Christmas"!

The Key Themes

Betrayal, and the treachery of those who are friends in name only. Also, the hidden evil and unpredictable violence of people. A minor theme is Anti-Christianity, which serves as a backdrop to the main story.

The Interpretation

The Lennon Play theatrically mounted the story as a televised Christmas party — wherein a joyous family gathering turns into horror. The fact is, this is (structurally) a prose variation of "Good Dog Nigel" (p. 22). The story teases us into believing Randolf will have a wonderful Christmas, but just as in "Nigel," we forfeit a happy ending; instead we suffer through the murder of the main character.

"Randolf's Party" is much more complex than "Nigel": It first develops our empathy with Randolf's isolation and loneliness. After all, who would *not* feel sorry for someone left all by himself on Christmas? Further, direct questions by the narrator create in us a sympathy for Randolf: "Where were all his good pals . . . . Where were they on this day?" And now add to this Randolf's poignant longing, his moody looks, and his sadly sagging spirit as he "*looged saggly* at his only Chrispbut card," and you've got quite a setup.

To top off the pathos, Lennon has Randolf speak as a vulnerable and hurt human being: "I can't understan this being so aloneley on the one day of the year when one would surely spect a pal or two?" John's language is very well-crafted, as usual: "understan" means not only "understand," but also refers directly to his friend "Stan," whom he misses. "Aloneley" emphasizes the youthful and tender emotions of Randolf (Joyce also used "alonely" and "alonety" for similar effect, *FW* 92.25 and 598.18, respectively).

This scene shifts dramatically midway through the second paragraph, apparently ending Randolf's loneliness: "All of a surgeon there was a merry timble on the door." Yet this sentence foreshadows Randolf's death, for "all of a sudden," when rendered "all of a surgeon," implies that the visitors will cut Randolf up surgically!

The techique of foreshadowing is again used in paragraph three, for even though Randolf is physically affectionate with his friends (he "welcombed" them, stroking their hair, etc.), he also has a "griff" on his face (a "grin" broken by a "riff").

The entrance of Randolf's old mates is written with a Joycean flair: "In they came jorking and labbing shoubing 'Haddy Grimmble Randoob." The jerking, joking ("jorking"), slapping, blabbing, laughing ("labbing"), shoving, shouldering, and shouting ("shoubing") of this group establishes them as a boorish mob indeed! Their greeting, "Haddy Grimmble," has a sinister side, too; in addition to meaning "Happy Chris Kringle day," it also suggests "Had thee grim rumble?" The group's disrespect for Randolf is revealed by their calling him "Randoob," which sounds like "Ran*boob*."

The murder scene is grizzly, for Randolf must listen to his "friends" revile and utterly reject him as they proceed to beat him to death! – "We *never* liked you *all the years* we've known you"; then Randolf's worst fear (of being "aloneley") is confirmed with the chorus "You were *never* raelly one of us" ("raelly" is "really" and "rally" combined). The relentlessness of Lennon's irony comes forth, for although Randolf lived alone, "At least he didn't die alone did he?"!

The Anti-Christian motif is present throughout the tale by John's deliberate trivializing of Christ's name. Lennon uses many distortions of "Christmas" (originally meaning "Christ's Mass"): "Chrisbus," "Chrispbut," and "Chrustchove," in parody of the day itself – the last, I think, being the most damning. "Chrustchove" takes the head of the church, Christ, and merrily substitutes the then-head of the Soviet Union, Khrushchev – an atheist-Communist. John further puts down Christmas and the church by referring to Christmas decorations as "desicrations"! James Joyce also had fun with Christmas: "chrissormiss," "Christienmas," "Chrysalmas," and "crossmess" (*FW* 6.15, 130.7, 416.26, and 619.05 respectively).

A final observation: John's use of "muzzle" toe for "mistletoe" is apt, for instead of being kissed by friends, Randolf's mouth is muzzled by their violence. Joyce would undoubtedly have called this Christmas of Randolf's "kissmiss" (*FW* 624.06) as well as "a muddy crushmess!" (*FW* 534.01).

Drawing Nine (p. 32)
This is one of my favorites, and certainly an offbeat choice: we see eight men moving "by the light of their faithful dog Cragesmure"! Once again, John's illustration does not adhere closely to the text, for at no time in the story are there eight people together.

"The Famous Five Through Woenow Abbey" (pp. 34–35)
The Overview
"The Famous Five" and entourage of friends, relatives and dog

take a holiday train ride to Woenow Abbey. Upon arrival, an old man warns them, "Don't you dare go on the mysterious Woenow Abbey Hill." Naturally, that very night they all go to the Abbey, only to encounter the very same stranger. The stranger is then overpowered by the group and is asked, "What is the secret of the Abbey?" The old man's answer, however, is defiant: "You can beat me, but you'll never learn the secret." And so the story closes with the old man being told, "Anything you say may be used in evidence against you," as the narrator concludes, "And it was."

The Key Themes

The search for truth in general, and the secret of success in particular.

The Interpretation

This is the second Beatle story, and virtually impossible to comprehend fully unless one is privy to detailed knowledge both of Liverpool and of the Beatles' early careers.

The title of the tale, "The Famous Five Through Woenow Abbey," is possibly the most complex of all the titles found in *In His Own Write*. To begin with the obvious, "The Famous Five" are, of course, "The Fab Four" plus Brian. As a matter of fact, Beatles manager Brian Epstein was even known as the "fifth Beatle."

Not so obvious is the fact that a certain district in the Beatles' hometown has been nicknamed "The Famous Liverpool 8." This area was once peopled by rich merchants, but in the Beatles' "college days" it was largely inhabited by artists, poets, and students. Hence the "Liverpool 8" residents metaphorically strengthen the theme, for artists, poets, and students share (theoretically, at least) a common bond: the search for truth.

The "Woenow Abbey" reference is highly evocative. Initially it triggers a recollection of the famous Woburn Abbey; but that's just a beginning. Before the Beatles became famous, they spent one nervous night at yet another Woburn — that being Woburn Place in London. It was during New Year's Eve, December 31, 1962, and the Lads were anxiously awaiting their first official audition for a record label (Decca). But although the Beatles may have pondered on this night the secret of success and hoped for sudden fame, Instant Karma eluded them — Decca turned them down, making Woburn Place a "Woe now place." And later on in the story, it becomes a "Woebeat" (they were, after all, a "beat" group).

There is also more meaning to "Abbey" than meets the eye. Brian Epstein, in *A Cellarful Of Noise*, stated that after October of 1963 "The Beatles had ceased to be purely a pop group and were becoming a cult." And this "cult" had its spiritual headquarters within the walls of a musical monastery: Abbey Road Studios.

The first line of the tale establishes the success of "The Famous

Five," for a travel agent ("Enig Blyter") is responsible for booking their annual holiday. By using "holliday," John evokes the image of musical legend B*illi*e Holiday — which in turn suggests that the Famous Five could also sing (the blues).

The text establishes that "For the past 17 years the fabled fibe had been forming into adventures." It is interesting that this time span approximates the rise of the Beatles' success (if you substitute months for years). For it was roughly seventeen months from the time *Love Me Do* was recorded in September of 1962 to the publication of John's book in March of '64. That the Beatles, like the Famous Five, travelled with an entourage is also well documented.

In the second paragraph, John uses a nursery-rhyme kind of onomatopoeia:

> 'Gruddly Pod, Gruddly Pod,' the train
> seemed to say, 'Gruddly Pod, we're
> on our hollidays.'

There is a humorous anecdote regarding John and his use of onomatopoeia. It seems that Lennon was always unwilling (or possibly unable) to discuss his writing on technical terms. So when John was asked, "Do you make conscious use of onomatopoeia?" he responded, "Automatic pier? I don't know what you're on about, son!"

At any rate, after the train comes to a stop, the group notices a stranger standing nearby; they find him suspicious: "a mysterious stranger who bode no ill?" In actuality, however, this man is not too mysterious at all, for the text tells us many things about him. We know he is a Cockney ("Oi, what's this 'ere"); that he is old and probably crippled ("an olde cypped"); that he lives on Abbey Hill in "a green hut;" and that he wears a large frayed and grey hat ("frae a great hat").

The crux of the story revolves around the group's question to the stranger: "Wart is the secrete of Woebeat, Doddy?" We may now view this query as an artful composite of the kinds of inquiries that the Beatles were typically bombarded with: the typical interview question, like "What's the secret of your musical sound?" Or "What does your name mean — four beat?" Or "What's the secret of your success?" etc.

The stranger's reply is correct, for we will never know the secret of Beatle music unless we get near to it (by pure experience) and let ourselves yell and secrete perspiration to its bouncing beat! ("ne'er ye'll learn the secrete").

The closing line renders "evidence" as "Everton" because knowledge is ultimately preserved in books and may be used to refute opposing ideas (Everton Library is in Liverpool).

In summation, the story is a funny montage of the Beatles' career and their advice regarding the best way to understand their music.

Drawing Ten (p. 36)

I take this picture to depict "Sad Michael," a Cockney member of the Jehovah's Witnesses cult ("Michael was a Cocky Watchtower"). He is seen squatting on a soapbox (what else?) and offering a Policeman a copy of *The Watchtower* (the official publication of this fundamentalist group).

Michael is certainly portrayed as being physically unattractive ("the little wretch" . . . "the scab"). Also, Michael appears to be very confused about his sexual identity (he wears women's shoes, fingernail polish, and a skirt!).

One stylistic feature of the illustration to take note of is John's technique of having one eyeball of a character (in this case, of the policeman) drawn *outside* the face. The effect is interesting: the face appears to be both in profile *and* looking face-forward to the reader.

"Sad Michael" (p. 37)

The Overview

Michael awakens in the morning quite sad. His wife gives him his usual lunch, and off he goes to his soapbox (to proselytize the world). At four in the afternoon a policeman comes around, just to pass the time. The policeman bids Michael "Good evening," but we're told Michael can't respond because he's deaf and dumb.

When the policeman, however, casually asks about Michael's wife, Michael retorts, "Shuttup about that!" And so, Michael has a crisis. Now that he's able to speak, he wonders what he's going to do with all his deaf and dumb books. The tale concludes with the narrator intoning: "here was a problem to be reckoned with."

The Key Themes

The lifelessness of the soapboxed street evangelist.

The Interpretation

Michael, the Jehovah's Witness, is a grotesque figure. He is not only arrogant in his belief, but emasculated in his identity ("a *Cocky* Watchtower"). Furthermore, "Michael" itself is ironic, for this "scab" has the same name as "St. Michael" the Archangel! However, not only is this Michael despised by others, he is also unhappy with his own life. And small wonder, for Michael's blurred sexuality is equalled only by his wife's — she's given a man's name: Bernie.

Michael's dogmatic and authoritarian religious beliefs definitely extend into his home: his wife Bernie is "well-controlled" by being beaten ("a wife to boot"). In fact, Michael is afraid the policeman is referring to his wife-beating when he asks, "How's the wive, Michael."

Michael is literally and metaphorically deaf and dumb (he doesn't hear the people putting him down, and he lets the church speak for him with its pamphlets). Structurally the story is quite novel, for it is a Miracle Tale *in reverse*. That is because the secular power (the policeman) triggers the miracle (Michael regaining his faculties), and Michael becomes a born-again-human! He realizes for the first time that his pile of religious material comprises nothing more than "deaf and dumb books."

The conclusion of the story is healthy: the secular conversion of our crooked Christian brings with it problems, and not paradisical dreams: "Michael realizing *straight* away that here was a *problem* to be reckoned with."

Stylistically there are many resonances to Joyce's work in this story. In fact, Lennon's line "he was debb and duff and could not speeg," particularly in association with his "Practice daily but not if you are Mutt and Jeff" (p. 47), seems *very* influenced by the following famous passage in *Finnegans Wake* (16.12-16):

Jute	—	Are you jeff?
Mutt	—	Somehards
Jute	—	But are you jeffmute?
Mutt	—	No ho. Only a utterer
Jute	—	Whoa? Whoat is the mutter with you?

A quick surface translation reads:

Jeff	—	Are you deaf?
Mutt	—	Some (times) hard (of hearing)
Jeff	—	But are you deaf mute?
Mutt	—	No no, only a stutterer
Jeff	—	What? What is the matter with you?

It's close similarities like the above (plus John's exact use of other Joyce puns like "parse" for "pass," *FW* 204.1) that make me wonder how extensively Lennon may have browsed among the "langwedge" (*FW* 73.01) of Joyce.

However, John's linguistic genius and his innate ability to spontaneously create sophisticated and funny puns may also account for the uncanny similarity between the two writers. In either case, Lennon's writing remains most impressive.

"I Wandered" (p. 38)
The Overview

This is the first (and one of the few) selections from *In His Own Write* in which there is no discernible plot line, no real characters, and no coherent action. It is a fifteen-line poem in three stanzas.

The Key Themes

It seems — possibly — to be about the loneliness of wandering by oneself in a chaotic world. Or about one's search for adventure, relaxation, and entertainment.

The Interpretation

John, in the lyrics of several songs, reveals an ability for soundsense writing: that is, using words for minimal meaning and for maximum rhythm or sound play. In particular, *What's The News Mary Jane, Candle Burns: Peace Of Mind* (both songs unreleased), *I Am The Walrus, Come Together*, and *I Dig A Pony* have significant amounts of soundsense in them. This poem predates *all* of the above; it may be a linguistic exercise in pure sound which paved the way for those later compositions.

The poem is, however, not without some traceable meaning — it simply never coheres into a specific point or goal. To begin with, the title instantly brings to mind Wordsworth's "I Wandered Lonely As A Cloud" (and indeed the penultimate line of each stanza has a variation on Wordsworth's title). But no clear satire or parody is made on Wordsworth's poem.

The first line of the first stanza is straightforward enough. It begins as an adventure-nursery rhyme — of "seas and schooners." But the remaining four lines are, to this reader at least, soundsensical.

The second stanza seems to focus on an infant's night of sleeping. We might imagine the baby, nestled past the rattling window ("ratters"), and staring at the "sheep" placed in the crib. The baby looks like a monkey ("resus"), "stooped" and curled next to a stuffed "hairy . . . dog." All the while, the baby is trying to get a good (a "goo") night's sleep. Admittedly this interpretation is stretched, and perhaps ill-founded. The third stanza almost begins with another nursery rhyme adventure ("Down lovely lanes and stoney caves"), but once again the remaining lines don't hold any ideas together.

In sum, the verse can be reduced to the following skeletal structure:

> "I wandered happy . . . to meet good . . .
> I wandered hairy . . . to get good . . .
> I wandered humbly . . . to meet bad . . . . "

If the short selection has any logic at all, it would be an intentionally blurry tale of the search for meaning. For my money, however, I think this is a string of non sequiturs — spun out for the hell of it!

Drawing Eleven (p. 39)

This is a portrait of a twenty-two year old British prostitute named Christine Keeler. She also serves to represent the German fan-prostitutes enjoyed by the Beatles when they played in Hamburg. There is a sharp seductiveness expressed in the picture, and the "letter" that follows confirms this edge.

"A Letter" (p. 39)
The Overview

A female fan asks why more photographs and articles have not been published about her favorite group. She says she likes the group because they are very theatrical on stage, and that she would like a publicity shot of them performing live. She closes her letter as "An admirrer . . . Afan."

The Key Themes

Because this selection is a composite of documentary information, there is no theme per se.

The Interpretation

This is truly a "private" letter, for *intimate* details of the Beatles' early career must be known in order to decipher it. There is no single time frame in this epistle, for it is a montage of events that span three years.

1. In 1960, when the Beatles first performed in Hamburg, their manager (Allan Williams) and their German employer (Bruno Koschmider) demanded that the group "Make Show" on stage. That is, that they create as much of a spectacle of themselves as possible (in order to entertain their rough and rowdy clientele). Needless to say, the Beatles (John, Paul, George, Pete Best, and Stu Sutcliffe) quickly learned the art of how to "Make Show." They would do everything and anything on stage: dance, eat, get drunk, curse, clown, jump wildly, etc., all much to the fans' delight.

One ancillary benefit of their extravagant performances was the free and easy "love" of the Hamburg prostitute; the girls came to the Beatles as readily as the V.D. they brought with them. Another permanent fixture of the Kaiserkeller Club was Bruno's brutal bouncers, called "Hoddel's gang."

2. In August of 1960 two of the Beatles (Paul and Pete) were deported for allegedly trying to burn down one of Koschmider's enterprises, a sleazy cinema. The Beatles' lodging was behind the screen of this theatre, and Philip Norman tells us that "In their haste to desert the Kaiserkeller, Paul and Pete Best left most of their things."

3. In 1961 the Beatles (now a quartet, minus Stu Sutcliffe) sent Allan Williams a letter from Hamburg, informing him that the group had decided not to pay his commission. To a man who had worked very hard on the Beatles' behalf, this was a stab in the back. Williams had, in fact, most recently helped the Beatles by sending a letter to the German authorities — persuading them to allow the group reentry into Germany for a Hamburg engagement.

4. During the summer of 1963, a major sex scandal dominated the British media. The breaking story involved Christine Keeler, a young prostitute who had had lucrative liasons with several high-ranking members of government.

It takes all of the data provided above to enable the reader to understand the seven-line paragraph of "A Letter"! From this we can surmise that John Lennon, like Lewis Carroll or James Joyce, at times felt no obligation whatsoever towards his reading audience — no compunction to help us perceive the "real" story lurking behind the syllables. In this case John simply wrote how and what he wanted, and he left the treasure hunt to others.

Fortified with the historical context provided in One through Four above, the "Letter" makes perfect sense. The name of the group — "Berneese und zee Rippers" — is a jab at "Bruno (Koschmider) and the Rippers (his gang of bouncers)." There is also a pun on "Berneese"; it means "Burn ease" — referring to the alleged cinema fire.

The line "Alec jumb about and shoes" (meaning "I like" ("Alec") performers who jump about and dance") refers, of course, to the Beatles "Making Show." The letter sent by the Beatles to Allan Williams is alluded to in "Pleese send a *stabbed* undressed envelope," and "Bern and Ern" means "burn and earn" (combining the Koschmider "fire" with "burning" Williams for the respect and money owed him).

The Beatles themselves are here "a most deserting group" (deserting Williams, deserting the Kaiserkeller); and the closing line combines the cinema fire, the Kaiserkeller, and the sexual fire of Christine Keeler: "hope this fires you as you keeler."

Drawing Twelve (p. 40)

This would more properly be called a "decoration," rather than an illustration. The drawing depicts an old and ornate curtain, raised to reveal "Scene three Act one." At the top of the curtain appears a regal emblem (which makes the reader a member of the audience at a Royal West End theatre in London). The most interesting feature of the "decoration" is a small head which peeks out from the curtain, to stage left of and below the regal emblem. Who this person is, or what business he has high in the curtain, remains a teasing mystery.

"Scene three Act one" (pp. 40–42)

The Overview

The scene is set in the study of a wealthy capitalist named Fatty. The action is as follows: Fatty is speaking with Scruddy Taddpill, a working-class union representative, in order to avert a strike. Fatty wants to negotiate, but Scruddy prefers to hurl insults at Fatty rather than discuss issues. Their discussion is then stalemated as Mammy enters, carrying "a great bundle" and plopping it on Fatty's desk. Fatty tells Mammy to remove the bundle, but instead she eats it, informing Fatty that the bundle contained his daughter (by his second wife). Fatty insists, however, that he has never even been married — which causes Mammy to run "round the room crossing herself."

Scruddy then grabs his cap and leaves, but not before insulting Fatty one more time.

The scene closes with "Fatty, Mammy and fourteen little Jewish children all singing together a kind of hymn."

The Key Themes

The lack of communication between management and labor. Also the intrigue inherent in the lifestyle of the Bourgeoisie.

The Interpretation

This scene is best viewed as a parody of social melodrama — rather than as a scene with any serious political point to make. What I find most striking about it is a stylistic affinity with the modern form of drama called Theatre of the Absurd. In particular, Lennon's stage indications resemble those of playwright Eugene Ionesco in *The Bald Soprano*. For example, John opens his scene thusly:

> (Scene) A broadshouldered room . . . There are three or four or five chairs faceing the desk. One are occupied by a scruddy working clog, cap in hook what is gesticulated greatly but humble toward a big fat catipalyst boss. A white man carefully puts coal on the fire and steps back toward a giant door which seems to lead somewhere else. A cat . . . leaps up and smiles all on the carpet. A photy of Fieldimarcher Loud Montgomery . . . looks down on the two men, each of them looking up at it trying to place him.
>
> A dog is quietly gnawing at a pigmy under the giant desk . . .

Ionesco's *The Bald Soprano* opens as follows:

> Scene: A middle-class English interior, with English armchairs. An English evening. Mr. Smith, an Englishman, seated in his English armchair and wearing English slippers, is smoking his English pipe and reading an English newspaper, near an English fire. He is wearing English spectacles and a small gray English mustache . . . A long moment of English silence. The English clock strikes 17 English strokes.

Both of the above inaugurate a ludicrous tone and create a calculated form of confusion. Despite the Absurd elements in John's opening stage indications, however, his puns present the reader with some concrete information. We learn that Scruddy lives his life like a cog in a clogged-up machine ("working clog"). Interestingly, Scruddy, like Little Bobby (p. 72) has a hook for a hand ("cap in hook"). Later we discover that Scruddy, like many of Lennon's characters, is Cockney ("shut yer gob yer big fat get . . . going to France for yer 'olidays").

There is indeed a photograph of the phony ("photy") Field Marshal Lord Montgomery which stares judgmentally down upon them. Montgomery, undoubtedly, is considered to be a fraud by

John, because the real Lord ("Loud" mouth) Montgomery once denounced the Beatles' hairstyle! In fact, he publicly proclaimed that the British Army would solve the problem as soon as the Beatles were conscripted!

The real antagonist of the tale is, of course, the big fat capitalist boss. For it is clear that Fatty's one goal in life is to financially catapult himself upward, like a leaping cat ("catipalyst").

The dialogue and action of the scene are wonderfully melodramatic and intentionally loaded with plot formulas and cliches: the imminent strike, the family problems of the union representative, the sexual intrigue of the boss, the boss's black maid, the maid's pent-up hatred of the boss, etc.

Scruddy, like "Partly Dave," literally repeats himself, which reveals the redundancy of his personality and the fact that Scruddy has the I.Q. of a clod ("clog"). The physical appearance of Scruddy's boss is likened to that of a fat budgie ("fat Bourgies"); the description also makes him a corpulent member of the Bourgeoisie. I should mention that "The Fat Budgie" is also 1) a poem, and 2) the title of a drawing that appears in *A Spaniard In The Works* (pp. 99--101; this selection is discussed in Chapter Four).

Fatty resembles "Partly Dave" in that he too does not realize "the colored problem." When Mammy enters singing about the Black plight ("Old Man River": "Tote that barge, lift that bale"), Fatty instantly dismisses her. "What is it Mammy, can't you see I'm haveing a prodlem with Taddpill and you come in here all black and singing?" Mammy's response is in the subservient language of British colonialism: "O.K. Kimu sahib bwana massa."

Mammy's attempt to injure her boss by eating his child is a failure, and Scruddy exits with an overly dramatic flourish. Here John makes it clear that he is totally aware of his use of melodrama: "he half turns like in the films and shakes his fist." Scruddy, we find, is as racist (and as blind to Mammy's oppression) as Fatty is, but Scruddy is also *sexist*: "Get this black woman out of this factory . . . or yer'll 'ave a strike."

The completely illogical ending of the scene fits the genre perfectly, for no matter what horrible things have happened here, a "happy family" is produced to conclude the drama in an upbeat fashion!

Drawing Thirteen (p. 43)

This drawing is a variation on the theme of the wealthy capitalist exercising his power over the impoverished worker. The man holding the sword is dressed in opulent regalia and is smiling as his weapon finds its mark on his opponent's neck. The other man wears only a hat, and is frowning at his plight − being at the mercy of his enemy.

The period costumes preview the story to follow (though there is nothing in "Treasure Ivan" that is specifically illustrated by the drawing).

"Treasure Ivan" (pp. 44–46)
The Overview

Large John Saliver enters a small seashore pub to make merry before he sails off to an island far across the ocean. Inside the pub, Large makes small talk with Blind Jew; and he is pleasantly surprised by the entrance of Jack Hawkins.

Large John and crew (Captain Smellit, Squire Trelorgy, Disreali Hands, Jack Hawkins, etc.) set sail the next morning. While sailing, Jack overhears Large John and others plotting a mutiny; Jack's discovery, however, goes unnoticed, for a cry of "Land Ho" is heard.

Once they are ashore, a bearded old man (Sten Gunn) jumps out at them, complaining of cruel Captain Flint. But before anything else can happen, the tale comes to an abrupt end: we're told that Jack Hawkins was really a thirty-two years old midget; that Sten Gunn is a young politician; and that the entire crew was arrested "for development."

The Interpretation

The obvious source of much of the tale's teasing is Robert Louis Stevenson's classic adventure novel, *Treasure Island*. However, superimposed over some of Stevenson's plot and (names of) characters are several of Lennon's own private jokes.

For instance: "Large John Saliver" not only implies self-mockery on John's part (regarding his weight), but it also alludes to the Beatles' past. The phrase "Long John and the Silver Beatles" was, early in 1960, suggested to John as a good name for the group. John took the suggestion – made by Cass of "Cass and the Casanovas" – and shortened it to "The Silver Beatles." In fact, the name change was made to accommodate Larry Parnes, an important rock impresario who was responsible for booking the Beatles' first professional gig.

The character name "Jack Hawkins" also has a Beatle referent: one "Jim Hawke" was at the helm of the Seamen's Mission in Hamburg, where in 1961 (and during subsequent engagements) the Beatles often took their meals.

But beyond such subtle resonances in the tale, we find Lennon's more explicit sexual aspects. The Squire's name, Trelorgy, sounds like "we'll orgy;" and the shipmates do, after all, go off to sea in search of great treasure-trash ("serge of grate treashy"). And where better to have an orgy than on "whore island" ("horivan") – lying under misty palm trees that are laden with "cockynuts"! In fact, Lennon's conclusion to the story more or less confirms this lascivious interpretation: all were "arrested for development," a charge that resembles development of prostitutes, or pimping.

There is the usual-unusual Lennon language. It makes sense that the parrot who tells stories, perched from on top of Large John's shoulder, is called a "Parable." And Jim, hiding in a wine barrel stolen from a monastery, is "in a *bar*ret of abbeys" — having, no doubt, as much fun as a barrel of monkeys!? Also, it stands to reason that if you are a sailor studying a plan of mutiny, you are really "planting to botany"!

All in all, "Treasure Ivan" is a funny burlesque of *Treasure Island*, peppered with Beatle allusions and a pinch of sexual innuendo.

Drawing Fourteen (p. 45)

This is, most certainly, an illustration of "Large John Saliver" — complete with his faithful "Parable" on his shoulder. In addition, and following through with the Hamburg association in the text, the drawing can be viewed as a caricature of Bruno Koschmider. As Philip Norman describes him in *Shout*, he had a "dwarfish stature," a "large head," and "an artificial leg." And the photo of Koschmider that Norman provides makes such an interpretation even more plausible.

A final point of interest in this drawing is the quirky "foot" crutch that Large John is leaning on. It provides the exact kind of visual novelty that the animators of the Beatles' "Yellow Submarine" brilliantly elaborated upon years later.

"All Abord Speeching" (p. 47)
The Overview

This is a "school lesson" in three parts; hence there is no plot.
The Key Themes

The boring condition of educational instruction, and the incompetence of teachers.
The Interpretation

In *The Lennon Play*, this lesson is theatricalized by using a schoolteacher lecturing from a blackboard. It's worth noting that Lennon's attack on pointless education closely resembles Eugene Ionesco's scathing satire, *The Lesson* (a one-act play).

The title of this selection is one of the most polyhedronic in the book: "All Abord Speeching" may be read as "All About Speaking/ Teaching," "All Are Bored Speaking/Teaching," "All Abort Speaking/Teaching" or " 'All Aboard' [for] Speaking/Teaching." The lesson itself will be interpreted using its own three-part division.

1. The speech rule presented here completely contradicts itself.

51

To speak "clear" is *not* to speak "nasal." Also, by using "for distance" to mean "for instance," John is able to make another joke on voice training, i.e., vocal projection.

However, the real rule offered in this section is the parental rule of "mind your mother and forgive her ("forgiver") for her cruelty." John effectively presents the hidden rage of children against "motherly oppression" by saying "Many people express great *hate* ("height") with the word *Mom* ("Mam").

2. This section opens with another mock rule of voice projection. The instruction, however, specifically relates to radio work (in fact the lecture veers off into a radio weather report!): "Deep breathing and inhaling is very important for broadcasting and outlying areas . . . visibility nil in Rockall" etc. John's puns in this section cleverly subvert the value of the instruction: "important" is rendered "impotent," and the entire piece is called a "discharge"!

3. The calculated assault on scholarship and pedantry in this section is also reminiscent of Joyce. The opening instruction translates into "the word, physically written, must be changed grammatically with both vowels pronounced strainingly, e.g., 'While talking to you my irons are getting cold . . . we must strike the iron while it is hot.'"

The closing portion satirizes the "Oxbridge" (Oxford and Cambridge) pronunciations of "Iron" ("Ivan"); "The bowel thus strethed pronuned-piglo" is translated "The vowel thus stretched and strengthened pronounced below."

"All Abord Speeching" remains a concise and highly comedic indictment of educational systems everywhere.

Drawing Fifteen (pp. 48--49)

This composite illustration is made up of seven small television screens. Together these TV's represent the usual range of programming. On page 49 we definitely see a religious show and a soap opera (the other sets on this page seem to represent documentaries and movies). On page 50 we see an interview talk show, a comedy, and an educational program. The only commonality among these various TV shows is the grotesque and distorted type of individual that appears on them.

A footnote to this selection is that our version has fully-drawn TV sets of various shapes and sizes, whereas the Pp. has only screen and dials. I do not know which variation is closer to John's original work.

"The Fingletoad Resort of Teddiviscious" (pp. 50--51)
The Overview

This selection is written as three separate television surveys or reports; therefore there is no plot to establish.

The Key Themes

The stupidity of both the questions that are asked and the responses that appear on television polls.

The Interpretation

The title of the piece carries an indictment against television violence and TV coverage of the Teddy Boy phenomenon in England. This becomes clear when the title is translated either as "The Fingletoad Report of Teddy [Boy] Viciousness" or "The Fingletoad Resort [Playground of] Telly-Viciousness."

(The "Teddy Boys" emerged around 1956. They were English teenagers who wore "Drainpipe" pants, velvet trimmed drape jackets, and particularly frilly shirts. The name "Teddy Boys" was derived from their use of Edwardian fashions. These youths, with their greasy duck-tail hairstyle and wild clothes, were considered to be street punks, gang members, and generally disrespectful hooligans.)

The first report requires considerable knowledge of Beatle history in order to decipher its content. For "Peckle and Braces (Granarthur)" identifies the *first* television show on which the Beatles ever appeared: "People and Places" (Granada TV), which aired November 7, 1962.

"The Doddipottiddy Poll" ("Doddi" — old and doddering; "Potti" — crazy or irrational) seems to ask its older viewers the following question: "Do you like the new Beat groups (i.e., "Big Grunty," which may be a joke on "Kingsize Taylor" — one of the first Beat group leaders), or do you prefer your own silverhaired bands?" ("Grey Burk"). At first the respondents seem stumped by the question ("questiump"), but then they offer an honest reply: "Who are we to judge?"

The second report appears on the BBC show "Panorama" ("Panorasthma"), and it asks a question regarding the preferred pronunciation of Ringo's name! Ringo, of all the Beatles, had the most markedly working class upbringing, and so it stand to reason "more kind worjing folk" are surveyed. Richard Starkey ("Richie" to his friends, "Ringo" to the public) was raised in the Dingle section of Liverpool. Thus the question, "Do you prepare Rinkled Dinglebone or Tichie Bimplebean?" may be translated: "Do you prefer Ringo Dingle-born or Richie Dingle-Bean?" (As Ringo was the short Beatle, he was "the bean.") The answer we get is an honest one: "Who the hell is . . . he?"!

The third and final report supposedly refutes yet another journalistic piece, "The Piltdown Report." This title is amusing: "Piltdown" refers to a famous anthropological dig-site in East Sussex, England. On this site was perpetrated an elaborate hoax, "The Piltdown Man," which fooled a worldwide public into believing "The

Missing Link" had been found on English soil.

Anyway, the conclusion of the Piltdown report is that:

A. More people are watching the radio rather than TV!

B. There are too many commercials on Britain's ITV. (*I*depen-dent *Tele*vision). Also, ITV pulls some of the audience from BBC's documentary programs.

C. Only 9½ people watch ITV! Also, those not watching ITV or BBC shows are reading newspapers: *The Daily Express* ("Deadly Excess") or the *Daily Mail* ("Davey Grail").

Possibly, John called *The Daily Express* the "Deadly Excess" be-cause of a photograph he sent to *Mersey Beat* that captured his own excesses (potentially deadly) while he was in Hamburg. The snapshot shows John casually standing on the street named Grosse Freiheit (part of the rough cabaret district in Hambrug). What makes this photo startling is that John is standing only in his underwear, reading *The Daily Express*!

"Alec Speaking" (p. 52)
The Overview

The action of this poem is in three parts: a short narrative open-ing (lines 1–3), where Alec's casual attitude and hostile classroom manner are established; Alec's Latin lecture (lines 4--8), which has no coherent thread at all; and finally, one student's response (lines 7--13), which completely dismisses both Alec and his lecture.

The Key Themes

The schoolteacher as egomaniacal dictator. Also, the unfortunate fact that one must strive to make one's life (even) *after* graduation: "school's (never) out!"

The Interpretation

This is a young schoolboy's recollection (whereas "All Abord Speeching" is a parody on college instruction). There is textual evi-dence to suggest that John Lennon himself is the schoolboy in ques-tion. Lennon recalls that most instructors were "trying to beat me into being a fuckin' . . . teacher."

The opening of the poem may be paraphrased as follows: "Alec is putting it lightly, blithely when he says: 'Squabble and grumble in the class. You students stray and strap down the Saturdays.' "

The lecture that follows is a parody of Latin (the scholar's langu-age). Watch how John's daydreaming mixes into the lesson, produc-ing some humorous results: "Amonk amink a minibus" – here the dry drone of Alec (teaching like a monk) gives way to John's fan-tasies of wealth ("a mink") until John's mind pauses on his favorite type of car ("a minibus"). Lennon's fanciful imagination lets loose and envisions "Amarmylaidie Moon" (an image predating the "mar-malade skies" of *Lucy In The Sky With Diamonds*). Within the word "amarmylaidie" we can hear another lyrical line, "my ladie moon."

The next line confirms that John is the student in the poem, for Lennon's personal nickname for his Menlove Street home, "mendip," mixes into Alec's lecture. Furthermore, the only major exam John ever passed (called "The Eleven Plus") is referred to as "muliplus."

It is schoolboy John who closes the poem, "caring not a care" for study, but encouraging himself to succeed:

> Onward, Onward, Onward.
> Onward, my friends to victory and
> glory for the thirtyninth.

These closing lines break the sing-song nursery rhyme of the poem, signifying John's break from school into the pursuit of his musical career. The "glory for the thirtyninth" may mean glory for England, as the Island of England is said to be home to 39 inhabitants in "The Wrestling Dog," p. 28.

Drawing Sixteen (p. 53)

This is John Lennon's second self-portrait. Here he stands as a young grammar-school lad (fully arrayed in his school uniform). He looks stiff and glazed as he listens to Alec, his teacher.

Alec is portrayed as a literally wild-eyed pedagogue. The message we get — from John's distortions of Alec's physical appearance — is that Alec is totally inhumane, and lost within his own world.

Drawing Seventeen (pp. 54--55)

This is John's third self-portrait from *In His Own Write*. It is a beautifully positive rendering, for the absence of landscape, clouds, or background (found in John's first self-portrait, p. 10) has given way to hills, trees, and big, billowing clouds. John is no longer naked *or* anchored to the ground. Instead, Lennon is fully-clothed and soaring (his long hair is freely flowing; his arms, like outstretched wings, are allowing him to fly on the power of his imagination).

From this portrait we learn that John has found his stride as an individual artist, *outside* of the Beatles. It makes sense that John used twice as much space in this self-portrait as he did with his first or second. For Lennon has truly expanded and has found freedom in flying.

Drawing Eighteen (p. 56)

This is a depiction of other Merseyside Beat groups. John's idea of using one head and four legs to represent a quartet (p. 11) is continued here — and quintets are also represented. Further evidence for my interpretation is found in the unedited, original version of "Liddypool" (in which eight Beat clubs are identified and satirized).

In essence this drawing represents the first picture of "The British Rock Invasion," for at least *20* groups are in the picture.

"Liddypool" (p. 56)

The Overview

As this is written as a travelogue article on Liverpool, there is no plot present.

The Key Themes

This selection has no theme per se, save for its comedically derogatory tone regarding John's hometown.

The Interpretation

Unfortunately, this piece appears in a significantly shortened version. In fact, it's impossible to fully appreciate "Liddypool" in its present form: nearly one-half of the selection has been cut. Entirely missing is the amusing Beat club section, as well as John's parody of Personals in newspapers. To rectify this problem, the restored, original version appears in Chapter Five, complete with commentary. However, for now I will interpret "Liddypool" just as it appears in our version.

This travelogue opens with the announcement that a renewed burst of social activity, as well as a return to former traditions, is now being enjoyed by Liverpudlians. Now, one has to remember that "Liddypool" was written specifically for *Mersey Beat* (under the title "Around And About"): John assumed the reader to be intimately aware of Liverpool's history and geography. As a matter of fact, most of the article consists of spotlighting locations in Liverpool:

1. "The Peer Hat is very popular for sun eating." I take "The Peer Hat" to be a pub; "The Pier Head" is a traditional name for a waterfront pub. Perhaps this pub is located near The Port *Sun*light of Merseyside.

2. "Boots for Nude Brighter is handys when sailing." Boots is a large drugstore chain in England, and I think it is saying that "Boots provides good suntan lotion (for 'nude brighter') and is handy to have when sailing." ("Nude Brighter" refers to the seaside resort of New Brighton.)

3. "We are not happy with her Queen Victorious Monologue." The Queen Victoria Monument caused quite a stir in Liverpool because, from one angle, it is said to be "obscene"!

4. "Walky Through Gallery is goodly when the rain." The illustrious Walker Art Gallery once had on display the works of then-Beatle Stu Sutcliffe (in 1959). And, of course, there's nothing quite like a fine gallery in which to pass a rainy day.

5. "Georgie House is black and white . . . . " St. George Hall is Liverpool's chief public building, and as such it serves both the black and white communities.

6. "Hellsy College": probably just a derogatory remark about

higher education.

7. "Talk Hall" is both the Liverpool Town Hall and Speke (Speak) Hall.

8. "Shout Airborne" is Speke Airport.

9. "L.C.C.C." The N.S.P.C.C.? The National Society for the Prevention of Cruelty to Children? — which originated in Liverpool. Certainly *L*iverpool *C*ounty *C*ouncil applies.

10. "The Mersey Boat" is, of course, the publication for which the article was written: *Mersey Beat.*

"You Might Well Arsk" (p. 57)

The Overview

As this selection consists of one-line editorial questions, there is no plot.

The Key Themes

The hopeless chaos caused by people in politics. Also, the incompetent coverage of world events by the media.

The Interpretation

It appears that John took various world figures and newspaper headlines and had some fun pasting them together. This specialty item carries no serious editorial comments (in fact, the punchline after each question is "You might well ask").

Several examples will show the tone of the editorial: "Why were [French] President De Gaulle and Conrad Adenauer [Chancellor of Germany] getting so friendly? Why did [Prime Minister] Harold Macmillan ["*Harass*ed" into resignation for his involvement in the Christine Keeler sex scandal] go golfing with Bob Hope? Why is Frank Cummings [head of a powerful trade union in Britain] . . . against the Common Market? Why did Princess Margaret ["Priceless Margarine" because she's an expensive imitation of royalty: she lacks class] and Bonny Armstrong [her husband] gives Jamaka away?"

And so, the article asks, "Why?" "You might well arsk"!

"Nicely Nicely Clive" (p. 58)

The Overview

Roger anxiously prepares for his wedding day. He thinks back to the bachelor parties he's had; he rehearses his wedding vows; he imagines his bride, Anne, in her wedding gown and wheelchair.

Roger dresses and primps in the mirror, as Anne polishes the footrest of her wheelchair. Meanwhile, Anne's mother comments about the imminent ceremony.

The story comes to an abrupt end when Anne's father returns and gets rid of Roger.

The Key Themes

One of Lennon's favorites: marriage viewed as a crippling and absurd institution.

57

The Interpretation

Structurally John does something very interesting with this story. It seems that in order to deflate the subject, he forces our attention onto Clive — a character not at all central to the story. Nevertheless, it's Clive's name, and not Roger's or Anne's, which appears in the title; and it's Clive's life that opens the tale. In fact, Clive Barrow is the only character here who is graced by the author with a full name! Why? Because all of the attention Clive gets only undercuts the "importance" of Roger and Anne.

The wedding day has been firmly established, through Clive, as "ordinary . . . nothing unusual or strange about it." So when Roger announces this to be a "red letter day," it seems ironic. And a close reading of Roger's excitement about the impending marriage only serves to reveal the pointlessness of it all: Roger is simply going through the motions. He is "happy" because Mother told him he should be, and because he gets to wear "his best suit and all that." The facade breaks down, however, because Roger's grinning face is really a *"grim*ming" one.

The clincher to this ill-fated "love affair" comes in the form of the marital vows: "To have and to harm . . . till death duty part"! For even the vow was rented for the occasion, foreshadowing that the wedding was off: "he knew it all off by hertz."

Between Clive's indifference and Roger's unconsciousness, a very cynical view of marriage emerges. The bride-to-be is more interested in the spokes of her wheelchair than she is in her own appearance. In addition, she wears a perpetually imbecilic smile: "Anne smiled the smile of someone who'd seen a few laughs."

Finally, even the narrative voice takes sides against the wedding: "Then *luckily* Anne's father came home from sea and cancelled the husband." "Cancelled" *could* mean that Roger is murdered by his almost-father-in-law; it certainly establishes that the marriage is definitely off!

Drawing Nineteen (p. 59)

This, of course, is Anne. She sits in her wheelchair, displaying her vaguely simian fact, unstyled hair, and crippled body. The one fashionable touch? Her Dusty Springfield eyelashes.

Drawing Twenty (pp. 60--61)

This two-page illustration is, I feel, the best one in the book. It very effectively captures the off-kilter, drugged perceptions of the patrons of the Neville Club.

The sketch is also noteworthy because of John's further use of a novel technique (first seen in Drawing Ten, p. 36): the placement of an eye *outside* the face in order to create the illusion of double exposure — in this case, of the person seen just below the wild woman dancer. This man's body is facing right; yet his head is turned 180 degrees facing left, and his face is simultaneously in profile and facing out to the reader! Quite a complex depiction, I'd say, of being totally stoned! The man on the floor (p. 61) is more dog than human, while the hunched man, standing like a gorilla (p. 61), is partly created (right shoulder and arm) by the giraffe-neck of another man.

All in all, this is a highly inventive illustration. I also find the excerpt accompanying the drawing to be the most evocative in the book.

"Neville Club" (p. 62)
The Overview
An unidentified person narrates his experience in the seamy dive called "Neville Club." He describes a wild scene: people smoking hashish, watching films, and dancing naked, all oblivious to the world. He is particularly shocked by one girl who's exhibiting herself to the crowd (for rounds of applause and money).

Our visitor heads for the exit and is temporarily halted by the doorman. A brief power-play ensues; the doorman finally asks if the patron is "friend or foe." Our hero says "foe" — and the scene is over.

The Key Themes
The entertainment excesses of modern man. Specifically, the pathetic attempt by some people to have "fun" by using strong drugs, sexual anonymity, and the hypnotic effect of chaotic crowds.

The Interpretation
This is the next to last Beatle item in *In His Own Write*. In "Neville Club" John has combined the Beatle experience of the Cavern Club with both the London disco scene, circa 1963-64, and the Beatle tour orgies. The result is a single montage.

In *Lennon Remembers*, John speaks frankly of this aspect of the Beatles: "The Beatles tours were like Felini's *Satyricon* . . . wherever we went there was always a whole scene going . . . orgies and shit . . . If we couldn't get any groupies we would have whores."

The Beatles' disco days are recalled in an interview with Lennon for WNEW-FM, in September of 1974. "When we [the Beatles and the Rolling Stones] were riding high [1963–64] there was a disco-teque scene in London and the main club was the Ad Lib. We used to go there and dance, talk music and generally get drunk, stoned and high . . . looking super stoned."

Philip Norman quotes Paddy Delaney, the doorman of the Cavern Club, in order to establish the atmosphere: "You could feel it [the unbearable heat and sweat] as you went down those eighteen steps climbing up your trouser legs. The lads used to faint as well as the girls." Norman adds a descriptive detail by telling us that the dance floor was so crowded, you had to move "in the glue of bodies."

Moving directly to the text, in the opening paragraph we spot John in his teenage brown sweater. He tells the reader he "easily micked with crown at Neville Club . . . " — which could mean that he easily mixed with the Irish crowd (micks) — or that he and Mick Jagger had mixed drinks, "crown" referring to the royal emblem on the liquor. There is nothing royal about the club, however; it's described as "a seemy hole" (steamy and seedy, like the Cavern Club; also, a place for exhibitionists, as in "see-me").

All of a sudden, the location becomes London: "all of a *Southern.*" Lennon looks around more carefully; he sees the boys (bloated and discolored — like "boils"). The girls ("girks") fair no better, for their very name intimates that they're jerks, who probably dance that way too. Everyone is smoking "Hernia" or Irish hash (Hibernia hashish) and taking opium ("Odeon"). The word used here not only emphasizes the odor, but also suggests the people are watching movies: Odeon cinemas are all over England.

Much of the language of this tale is akin to *Finnegans Wake,* but none more so than the following: "Puffing and globbering they drugged theyselves rampling or dancing with wild abdomen, stubbing in wild postumes amongst themselves." Paraphrased this sentence reads: "Puffing on hash pipes were globs of people clobbering and slobbering ["globbering"] as they dragged and drugged themselves . . . . " ["They self"] signifies they are one nameless group.] The people sample each other sexually or dance in wild abandon (abdomens exposed), their cigarette stubs snubbing and rubbing ["stubbing"] the wild old costumes. The people look dead in their party outfits ("postumes" = posthumous) as they mingle amongst themselves."

In short, the members of this evil club (Club N*evil*le) were like Dicken's orphan Oliver: "They seemed Oliver to the world." As the narrator of the story, John is shocked and lost within this maze; finally he heads for the door.

Then it seems we're back in Liverpool, for the doorman is Irish (like Paddy Delaney of the Cavern). John is caught in a surrealistic swirl of people and sound. He boldly tells the doorman he's not a friend to this foreign lifestyle, but instead a "foe" to it. The narrative ends with John in jeopardy for having refused to join this orgiastic nightmare.

"The Moldy Moldy Man" (p. 63)
The Overview
This eight-line poem breaks down into three mini-sections. In the

opening, lines 1–3, the persona declares that we just would not believe he is "a moldy man." Lines 5–7 reiterate the man's encrusted state and his shyness. Line 8 closes the poem with the announcement that he is also humble.

The Key Themes

The surprise of others and their disbelief at our heartfelt expressions of pain.

The Intepretation

To be "moldy" is to be covered with fungus or to be crumbling. In this poem I believe we can sense John's inner feelings of pain and his withdrawal. John is covered with, actually engulfed by, his fame (the fungus), and in the poem we see him crumbling "thru and thru." John also knows that most of his fans "would not think it true."

Lines 5 and 6 resemble early experiments with lyrics which eventually led us to *Come Together*. The final line is ironic (a typical Lennon technique, employed particularly when he fears he's sounding too serious).

Drawing Twenty-One (pp. 64–65)

The original story illustrated by this drawing was first published in *Mersey Beat* on September 6, 1962; however, *no drawing* accompanied the story at that time. The drawing reproduced in our version, as well as in the Pp. and SS. versions, is not reproduced in its entirety. Our version cuts off Whide Hunter from the knees down and eliminates the face of a native (extreme edge of p. 65). But what is more important, our version utterly destroys an illusion that John must have worked very hard to create: that of the text being the cargo carried by the natives. Ideally, their hands should disappear into the cargo of words, and the printed text should rest on their shoulders.

As it is, our drawing shows the natives carrying a flat-line board. The ornamental canopies of the two carriages are so reduced in our version that neither can cover the words. The small decorative circles on the canopy (better seen in the Pp. or SS. versions) suggest skulls. Perhaps these skulls are the fruit of Whide Hunter's gun?

It is significant that the great white hunter is depicted as the smallest of the nine people in the drawing. For his power comes solely from his weapon, and not from any heroic stature of personality. Hence, Whide Hunter is the least powerful of all.

"On Safairy With Whide Hunter" (pp. 64–65)
The Overview

Whide Hunter sleeps as his personal servant, Otumba, sings to him. Otumba, we're told, is in charge of feeding fellow natives (as snacks) to the poisonous snakes.

The next day Otumba awakens his master, and they head off towards the jungle. Whide tries to identify another hunter in the bush, but quickly gives up. Soon Whide and Otumba set up camp in a clearing. (It should be mentioned that Whide's name tells us not only that he is fat, but also summarizes his whole attitude about the safari: Why hide from animals when you can hunt them?! Of course, "Whide" can also emphasize the exploits of "Whitey" in Africa.)

Jumble Jim moves towards their camp — unaware that Whide is watching him. Then Whide tells Otumba to "get a bus," but Otumba replies, "Maybe next week." Jumble Jim spots Whide and a Doctor shooting rhinos, hippos, *and* Otumba. "Stop shooting those animals," Jim calls out, but it fails to stop them. The story concludes with Whide and the Doctor continuing to shoot alligators, wild boars, giraffes, leopards, and people.

The Key Themes

The mindless slaughter humans perpetrate upon all species of the planet, including their own.

The Interpretation

This story is the only collaborative effort in the book, having been "written in conjugal with Paul." Unfortunately, there is no way to verify the extent of Paul's contribution; it seems minimal, for the piece reads as pure Lennon. In fact, the original version — which aside from a few minor spelling changes is *identical* to our own — does *not* cite Paul as collaborator at all!

Anyway, in *The Lennon Play* this story was conceived as an adventure comic book, an understandable choice — but hardly the most telling interpretation. For this tale is a black comedy that carries a serious indictment against "white hunters" everywhere. In particular, the story characterizes British colonial policy as totally self-serving — and ruthlessly insensitive to the indigenous population.

The opening lines are really lyrics to a hit from the early sixties that was based on an African folk song. The incorporation of these lines beautifully typifies the commercial crassness brought by white hunters into the African culture.

Otumba is yet another fruit of conquest: the Uncle Tom, the sellout. Otumba literally feeds his own people to Whide's pet snakes. As for Whide himself, he's inept, physically deteriorating: he wears dentures, always has a runny nose ("Wipe Hudnose"), and is a closet homosexual ("Whide" = Why Hide?! And *Why*-take-it-out on the *Hide*s of animals?). Indeed, Whide is on "Sa*fairy*" as he watches Jim undress. Whide's final act is to shoot his most devoted servant (Otumba), after which he embarks on a killing spree which neither differentiates man from animal or endangered species from legal bounty.

John's puns are as sophisticated as ever in this selection. For example, John tells us that a hippo is killed simply by saying "hippo-posthumous," or that a rhino goes down with flared nostrils: "rhinostrils." A Joycean footnote is that "hwide" is used in *Finnegan's Wake* for "white" (*FW* 13.34).

The appearance of the story's end on the printed page in our version is far less effective than in the original *Mersey Beat* version, where we retain the visual redundancy of Whide's murders:

> Uncle Tom Cobra and all . . . Old
> Buncle Ron Gabble and all . . . Bold
> Rumple Bom Doddy and all . . . Bad
> Runcorn Sad Toddy and all.

Here the death list seems to conform to nothing more than some grotesque word game. It should be mentioned that "On Safairy With Whide Hunter" can be viewed, in part, as an early version of John's *The Continuing Story Of Bungalow Bill*. Not only is "Jungle Jim" the equivalent of "Bungalow Bill," but we even have the name "Elephant Bill" ("Elepoon Pill") in our version. If you investigate the lyrics, you will find several other correspondences to this story.

"I Sat Belonely" (p. 66)

The Overview

A fat man sits all alone by a tree. He hears a woman singing, and though he looks around for the source of the song, he sees no one. He calls out for the stranger to show herself, but nobody appears; and so he simply falls asleep, lulled by the soft singing.

All of a sudden, on a nearby twig, what should the fat man see but a tiny pig — singing! "I thought you were a lady," says the man . . . when to his surprise, "the lady, got up — and flew away."

The Key Themes

The elusiveness of truth — and of love. Also, the idea that behind every cloud lurks a not-so-silver lining.

The Interpretation

This is a poem about John's search for something to believe in: ultimate love. From *In His Own Write* forward, Lennon has characterized religious thought as being female. For instance, John admits of *Girl*: "I was trying to say something about Christianity, which I was opposed to." The search for Christianity is replaced, in Lennon's world, by the search for The Girl, The Truth, etc., "the one that alot of us were looking for." John would later have another woman, *Sexy Sadie*, represent the Eastern philosophy of the Maharishi.

In retrospect, then, "I Sat Belonely" reveals John's vulnerability, and his longing for some miraculous truth. John was primed for meeting Maharishi Mahesh Yogi when, three years later, "The Great

Saint" appeared — looking quite authentic at the time.

The juvenile language of the poem is apt, for it is at once an expression of innocence and gullibility. In the first stanza, the persona admits to spiritual blindness: "I couldn't see at all." The second stanza expresses his irresistible need ("I . . . have no choice") to find her. It is poignant to learn that — on some level at least — John thought "The Truth" might be put in so many words. Phillip Norman recounts how John once said of the Maharishi: "Maybe if I go up with him in the helicopter her may slip me the answer."

By the fourth stanza the fat man drifts off to sleep, courtesy of the singing. This suggests that the truth he will find will not awaken him, but instead will keep him unconscious. During the fifth and final stanza, the man verifies for himself that the song was produced by a pig — and not by the wise and winsome woman he'd wanted to find.

The poem concludes with John laughingly rejecting what only a moment before he had been seeking; this cycle was repeated, almost exactly, with the Maharishi. Finally, the last line suggests that the pig will fly off — in hopes of finding someone else, who would make a better convert.

Drawing Twenty-Two (p. 67)

I take this to be the fourth, and final, self-portrait in the book. John sits, bloated with success, but empty of any happiness ("humbled fat and small"). We see (for the first and last time) his Beatle "mop top" haircut and a large tear on his face (the hidden part of his public personality). John sits, like Buddah, under a tree, awaiting enlightenment. It is a sad and soft scene to behold.

"Henry And Harry" (p. 66–67)

The Overview

Henry is told by his father, Harry, that he must take over the family business. Henry is not interested in the business, and so he successfully gets his father off on a tangent.

Henry then confronts Harry by telling him, "I want to be a golfer, Dad," but his father flatly rejects his son's vocational choice. As a result Henry runs away from home. Soon Henry discovers he "could not get a golfing job anywhere," so he decides not only to return to the fold, but also to follow in dad's footsteps.

Upon Henry's return he sees his mother digging a hole. His mother at first ignores him, but then remarks, "Can't you see I'm burying . . . your father." The story abruptly ends with Henry "assuming responsibility."

The Key Themes

The destructive and symbiotic relationships of fathers and sons.

Specifically, parents as unfeeling dictators of their children's lives.

The Interpretation

This is a funny-sad tale of a son unable to escape his father's control. The opening line is revealing: "Henry was his father's son," so much so that their names are nearly identical. Harry wants his son to continue the tradition of "Brummer Striving." If you will recall, Paul McCartney asked the reader in his introduction, "What's a Brummer?" Well, below are some workable ideas (and like all my interpretations, they don't have to be "right" to be helpful):

1. A "Brummer" is one who produces "Brummagems"! Yes, the dictionary states a "Brummagem" is something "cheap or inferior," which could account for the business being described as a "farce and fast ["Farst"] dying trade."

2. Joyce used "brumming" as a musical term (*FW* 44.19), but I don't think it has any association here.

3. Personally, I go for "Brummer" as meaning "one who sweeps rumors about like a broom." John's strong dislike of gossip is thoroughly evident in "Victor Triumphs Again And Mrs. Weatherby Learns A Lesson" (p. 79), and I sense there are similar sentiments behind the scenes in "Henry And Harry." Perhaps it was even a "tawdry rumor" that was responsible for Harry's "prize stumps"!

What's most intriguing about this story is the way John makes father and son completely interchangeable. On the bottom of page 68 we read, ' "There's something in what you say, I dare say,' said *Henry* eyeing his *son* proudly" (well, Henry *is* the son). John uses this technique again on page 69: " 'It seems I'm a born Brummer like dad Harry says I am,' said *Harry*." Obviously, the "mistakes" are deliberate, and accurately represent both Henry's low self-esteem and his inability to separate himself from his father's domination.

The actual death of father Harry is ambiguous. Did mother, the "right old hag who was living with them," do it? If so, we achieve a balance of sorts, for "No Flies On Frank" (pp. 19–21) has a husband kill a wife; and here we'd have a wife kiling her husband.

But of greater importance is the fact that regardless *how* Harry died, it is *Henry* who "assumes responsibility." Henry's statement can be taken in several ways:

1. Henry assumes that he personally caused his father's death. This would have been achieved by his refusal to join the family business and by his running away from home. The result of his belief would be that Henry assumes all the guilt of his father's death.

2. Henry only assumes the responsibility of being the "head" of the household (i.e., breadwinner and provider).

3. Henry assumes the responsibility of being truly separated from his father (thus pursuing his own personhood for the first time).

Personally, I suspect that Henry's behavior consistently points to number one; in that case, Henry will unfortunately accept and live out a guilt trip, rather than be liberated, or free from his father.

"Deaf Ted, Danoota, (and me)" (p. 70)

The Overview

This is a six-stanza poem narrated by an unnamed "me." It begins by describing the countryside: hills, groves, daisies, trees, etc. Then it establishes that Deaf Ted, Danoota, and the narrator "clobber" bad guys.

The second stanza expresses the trio's unity, swiftness, and fighting prowess. Stanza three introduces the group's "faithful frog," and restates their power.

The fourth stanza reveals that the group is a *mercenary* force that fights "baddies" for "colour, race and cree[d]." Stanza five basically reiterates the first stanza; and the final stanza simply tells the reader to keep a lookout for our heroes.

John can't resist a funny footnote to the poem: "(sometimes we bring our friend, Malcolm.)"

The Key Themes

The false romance of the American West in general, and the harsh reality of vigilante justice in particular.

The Interpretation

The *London Times* Literary Supplement, March 26, 1964, referred to this selection as "The Ballad of 'Deaf Ted, Danoota, (and me)," whereas *The Lennon Play* approached this poem as a movie western. Both approaches are in tune with the piece, for it is a wonderful satire on the American Wild West and its folk ballads of rustic justice.

To my thinking, the unidentified narrator is none other than the horse! This startling conclusion is reached by the following process of elimination:

1. The person called the "frisky dyke" must be "Danoota." Being an hermaphrodite, her name has both male ("Dan") and female ("Anita," "Uta") parts.

2. The person called "The battle scab" must be Deaf Ted.

3. The faithful frog's presence is established by the narrator. So either the horse is speaking, or there is a hidden narrator — because we've run out of dramatis personae! (The "and me" concept reminds us of how John wanted to stay "hidden" for Yoko Ono's exhibit, "Half-Wind Show," and so he designated his role as producer in the phrase "Yoko Plus Me.")

Returning to the text, the ballad opens in a Jabberwocky-like manner: "Thorg hilly grove and burly ive." Paraphrased, this reads: Like the god Thor, we moved through thorns, hilly groves, trees with burls, and ivy. The phrase "burly ive" almost assuredly conjures up "Burl Ives" — that quintessential American folk balladeer. (It may surprise you to know that Ives' "Little Bitty Tear" was number nine in *Mersey Beat*'s Top Twenty in February of 1962!)

The unity and loyalty of the trio is revealed in "Never shall we partly stray" of stanza two. However, in stanza four we disover this "Big mighty club" really consists of small-time hired guns who indiscriminately fight for anything and anyone. They will champion some guy named "Bernie" as readily as they'll protect a sacred "creed," etc.

The poem is a droll portrayal of the American way of worship (of the anti-hero). Of course the poem never becomes too serious, and so it playfully leaves us watching the trio "ever gallup," so if we:

> hear a wondrous sight,
> Am blutter or at sea,
> Remember whom the mighty say
> Deaf Ted, Danoota, and me —

Drawing Twenty-Three (p. 71)

This is an illustration of Deaf Ted (man in plumed hat and frilly shirt), Danoota (naked woman behind him), faithful frog (wearing a hat similar to Ted's!), and the horse. It is somewhat curious that although the poem is in the style of the American Western, Ted's costume is closer in style to the clothes worn by a European nobleman. But then again, John has never strictly adhered to the rules of "realism."

"A Surprise For Little Bobby" (p. 72)

The Overview

On Bobby's thirty-ninth birthday he receives his lifelong dream: a hook for his amputated right hand. Unfortunately, the hook fits the left hand, so Bobby chops it off to find the hook "fitted like a glove." The narrator ends the tale in hopes that next year Bobby will get a hook for his *right* stump.

The Key Themes

The self-destructiveness of people.

The Interpretation

In *The Lennon Play*, this piece is presented by a storyteller on a children's television show. This is a clever approach, for it amplifies the story's black humor by first establishing a safe, "fairy-tale" ambience.

In the text itself, Bobby is immediately set up for a tragic future. His birthday is called a "birthmark" (Bobby being marked for pain from birth). The first surprise for Bobby was "The War," which took his right hand in combat. Today's surprise is a birthday hook, a gift received after thirty-nine years of prayer. (By the way, Lennon uses "p*way*er" to emphasize that Bobby is looking for "the way." Joyce's focus is different: he uses "preyers" (*FW* 351.25) to show Christians as spiritual scavengers — or "brayers," (*FW* 342.11) to portray prayer as inarticulate noisemaking.

John spells "everybody" as "ebry doddy" (we've already seen "everydobby" in "At The Denis," page 24).

The entire story views life as a cruel joke; even Bobby's "answered prayer" brings further mutilation. Lennon leaves us with a boxing metaphor: "Maybe next year he will get a right hook." That is, another slug in the jaw!

"Halbut Returb" (p. 73)

The Overview

For fourteen years Rosebeen has waited for her husband, Halbut, to return from war. At last he returns — and with a slave for Rosebeen — though she had only asked for butter. Halbut then refuses to show Rosebeen her slave, and the story concludes with Rosebeen asking "Am I not your very own?"

The Key Themes

The absurdity of both war and marriage.

The Interpretation

The title "Halbut Returb" establishes a flippant tone for this scene: it suggests "Hell, I'll but return," or "Halbut Returns to Disturb." Or: "He'll But Disturb."

Rosebeen's name makes her a has-been or faded rose; and even though Halbut has returned "to make an honest womb of her," his gift to Rosebeen of a dead slave is hardly a romantic gesture. At any rate, whatever commitment these two have made to each other is threatened when Halbut refuses to show his gift. Rosebeen wonders what gruesome truth ("grurth") Halbut hides: doesn't he care? Of course, neither Halbut nor Rosebeen have much love to spare after fourteen years of separation, at least judging from their reunion.

"Unhappy Frank" (p. 74)

The Overview

Frank is unhappy about every aspect of his life: his house, his work, his mother, etc. In fact, Frank feels that all he ever does is take care of his aging mother and clean house. So Frank gets rid of both his house *and* his mother — in order to move to another country.

The conclusion of the tale is that — in spite of all he's done — Frank remains unhappy.

The Key Themes

Unhappiness.

The Interpretation

This story has the most Joycean "langwedge" (*FW* 73.01) found within the pages of *In His Own Write*. I believe that this is because the tangle of Frank's pain is best expressed through a jumble of words.

I will first excerpt the most difficult passage, lines eight through nineteen, in its original form, and then offer a paraphrase of it:

'Just look at that garbet all filby
and durby. How am I supposed to
look affaffter all this garby rud-
dish. Wart am I but a slave tow
look upon with deesekfrebit all the
peegle larfing and buzing me in
front of all the worled. How can I
but garry on? How? Hab I no live
of my own to do but wart I must ever
jub gleening and looking aretor
theese damn owld house of my own?'
Frank went over to his dubb old
mother, whomn was stikl liffing
with him. 'What are you larfing at
you dubb owld boot?'
'Havn' I nuff treble without you
kakking in the korber?'

Now the paraphrase:

'Just look at that carpet all filthy
and dirty. How am I supposed to look
after all this garbage rubbish? What
am I but a slave to look upon with
the-sick-free-bit, all the people
laughing and bugging me in front of
all the world. How can I carry on?
How? Have I no life of my own? To
do but what I must? Ever job cleaning and looking after this damn old
house of my own?' Frank went over to
his dumb old mother, who was still
living with him. 'What are you
laughing at you dumb old boot?'
'Haven't I enough trouble without you
kicking in the cupboard?'

This surface narrative reveals Frank's years of frustration — and his utter hatred for his mother. Lennon, however, has used polyhedronic prose (those multiple-meaning puns) to significantly deepen the texture of the story.

To begin with, you can just *bet* on seeing *gar*bage on Frank's *car*pet — hence, "garbet." You will also find (on the floor) the hat Frank wears at the derby horse races (a dirty derby: "durby").

However, Frank's anger clearly stems from the fact he takes care of his mother — that is to say, the-sick-free-bit ("deesekfrebit"). I would translate this further as: "Because I'm your mother and sick, you must take care of me." Frank's feelings of hopelessness are found in his stuttering laughter over a simple word like "after": ("affaffter"). The truth is, Frank considers his mother to be either a yelping dog, or a dumb old boot: " 'What are you *larfing* at you dubb owld boot?' " If you remember, Paul McCartney in his Introduction quoted "dubb owld boot" as a phrase he thought would cause people to "search for hidden meanings." The meaning, however, is hardly hidden; in fact, it's quite evident by John's consistent usage and by the clear context in which he places the phrase.

Returning to the story, we learn in the following line that Frank will kill his mother: " 'I'm going to sell this daft shed and you to aswell, also Mummy.' " Here it is confirmed that Frank does not consider his mother to be human, but rather a "thing" that can be bought and sold. Also, Frank will personally entomb her like an Egyptian *mummy*! (stuffing her in the cuboard/coffin).

The ending of the tale is as cynical as its beginning. Frank's unhappiness will never abate, no matter what he does; a judgment that *just* ("judd") goes "to show what happens" in real life.

Drawing Twenty Four (p. 75)

This picture of Frank is the second and last head shot among the illustrations (Eric Hearble, page 27, is the first). I prefer the much-enlarged versions found in the SS. and Pp. editions, in which Frank's face completely covers the page. His pinpoint eyeballs and complacent half-smile suggest terrible doings lurking inside his mind.

"On This Churly Morn" (pp. 76--77)

The Overview

This soundsensical poem is made up of ten four-line stanzas, which makes it the longest poem in the book. There is no plot, but a rather curious montage of ideas and incidents.

The Key Themes

Chaos!

The Interpretation

This is the most baffling piece in the book. ("I Wandered," page 38, comes in a close second.) There are three possibilities with this selection:

    1. "On This Churly Morn" has *no* coherent meaning at all.

    2. There was an abundance of *private* meanings for John.

3. There is some subtle structure behind the apparent chaos.

Just for fun, and because there's at least some evidence for it, I'll proceed as if we've got a combination of two and three. To begin with, it can be fairly well documented that John alludes to at least six selections from *In His Own Write* in this poem:

1. "Scene three Act one" (pp. 40–42). The line "I crivy like a black," in the first stanza, vaguely harkens to "you come in all black and singing." Also, both "Scene three Act one" and "On this Churly Morn" use a middle English font type for their closing words — "The End" and "God Speed," respectively.

2. "The Fingletoad Resort of Teddiviscious" (pp. 50–51). In the second stanza, "The Piltdown Retord" is called "blink down booltoad."

3. "I Remember Arnold" (p. 80). In the second stanza this title is rendered, "I'll december barrold." Also, "Kakky Hargreaves" becomes "haughty bygraves" in stanza five.

4. "Deaf Ted, Danoota, (and me)" (p. 70). "Thorty skive" and "bad Ive" in the second stanza allude to "Thorg hilly grove and burly ive."

5. "At the Denis" (pp. 24–25). In the seventh and eighth stanzas, "Graddie," "Groppy," "gribble" and "grapple" resemble "grately," "gorble," "grundies" and "gummy."

6. "The Fat Growth on Eric Hearble" (p. 26). This is referred to in stanza nine, as "My tall but little Eric."

So why did John cite other passages from *In His Own Write* in this poem? I think for the same reason James Joyce alluded to himself: the sheer pleasure of self-indulgence. After all, Joyce cited (in punned form) the titles of *all* his short stories in only three paragraphs of *Finnegans Wake* (186.13–187, 1–13)!

Lennon's songs also contain lyrics which reflect back on earlier songs: check out *If I Fell, Glass Onion,* and *How Do You Sleep?* So it was a penchant of John's (not only in his poems and short stories, but in his music as well) to make references to his other work.

Regarding an overall structure for this poem, I submit the following:

The date of "this Churly Morn" is Saturday, May 2, 1964. Now, I realize John's book was published in March, but Brian Epstein tells us the "plans" were made months in advance.

It is the morning of the Beatles' most elaborate attempt yet to escape world notice and to have an unmolested holiday. So complete was the secrecy surrounding this vacation that the Beatles' regular travel agent was bypassed in favor of a small unknown agency. The group, and their companions, were all issued code names and disguises.

With this in mind, look at stanza one. The persona is thinking, "I should be farlorn" — that is, far away from the forlorn tasks of interviews, tours, recording, etc. The doorknob (or handle) to his escape ("through knorb") is his packed luggage ("this packymack").

Stanza two informs us that John will feel nearly thirty-five ("ne'er a thorty skive") when his plane slinks down for its night flight ("blink down"). Also, he will be free of authority ("a thorty") and will be able to save his sense of identity: "To save my . . . Ive" — both the good and the bad sides of his personality.

The first two lines of stanza three describe John's escape as being as swift as that of nimble Jack (of the nursery rhyme): "be nicky . . . but querry jump." The next two lines intimate that John's goal is connubial bliss: "I do but strive a hump."

Stanza four presents John talking to himself, mumbling over the intricate details of the mission. For example, he wonders which coat he's supposed to wear: "Am I the bairly oat?" — referring to his barley-colored coat. Then he makes a lusty joke about his sexual prowess: "With all your davey cockey/I'll always keep afloat."

Stanza five offers the most specific textual evidence for my interpretation. Epstein informs us in *A Cellarful of Noise* that the code name of the Lennons was "the Leslies"; George was Mr. "Hargreaves"; George's girlfriend Patti was Miss Bond. Both couples were to fly (together) from Luton to Amsterdam. The first two lines of this stanza make sense in such a context:

"Will I the baggy Dutch man" (meaning will I load bags at Amsterdam airport?").

"And haughty bygraves too" (George was said to have felt haughty over his fashion-model companion; he bragged to John that she resembled Brigitte Bardot).

Line three: "To all I give a limpage" — that is, John's disguise makes him look like an old man: a "limp age."

Line four: "To do what they will do" — which means that John will go along with the plan that involves them all.

Stanza six concerns the fans' wild response to the Beatles: "They rabble till they're tatter." John then admonishes his fans to stop screaming at all hours of the night: "Don't cream the midnight hour." The stanza closes with mention of other entertainers — i.e., Little Richard playing in Blackpool.

So far so good, but stanza seven through nine defy any structure that I can perceive. There is some surface meaning that emerges, however. We learn that someone named Ralphy has grown up to be a fatty ("Rephy grawn and gratty"). Also that Graddie is "large but small," and that she will not grant Ralphy a room to get drunk in ("Room to swig").

I wonder if the proposed trip chronicled in stanzas one through six did not trigger in John's mind an association with another Beatles' journey — the trek to Hamburg. The group's favorite bar in that city was the Gretel and Alphons ("Graddie and Rephy"?).

Stanza eight does have one verifiable Hamburg allusion: "Bilt." For it was *Bilt*, the leading German National newspaper, that reported on the Beatles opening of The Star Club. Unfortunately, the rest of the stanza remains an enigma.

Stanza nine touches on drinking again — "Ye bottle ginny" — and on sailing (the Beatles' final destination was Tahiti). The final stanza is a prayer for travellers, which supports my general interpretation. The Beatles wanted to replenish their souls and have what they craved: "Remplenish thou they cravie."

The final lines form a blasphemous benediction, while "God Speed" leaves us with the blessing for a safe journey.

Drawing Twenty-Five (p. 78)
This is a strange one — in that it doesn't illustrate the story with which it appears: "Victor Triumphs Again and Mrs. Weatherby Learns a Lesson."

Initially, one assumes the woman to be Mrs. Weatherby (though in the story she is described as "a typical . . . old hag," and this description hardly matches the drawing). We might figure that Victor is the long-necked male, but the woman's identity (and why Victor is kissing her) remains a mystery — as does Victor's upside-down position. The drawing is fun to look at; it simply is not connected to the story.

"Victor Triumphs Again and Mrs. Weatherby Learns a Lesson" (p. 79)
The Overview
In a small village ("Squirmly on the Slug"), vile rumors have been spread about by Mrs. Weatherby . . . against Victor Hardly. The gossip claims that Victor is holding Black Masses at his home, and that he desecrates the church cemetery.

The town becomes so alarmed that a group of thirty-two villagers sets an ambush for Victor at the graveyard. But although they wait for eight hours, Victor doesn't show — and the group wonders why.
The Key Themes
The harmful (and sometimes ludicrous) consequences of gossip in general. Also, the witchhunt mentality of any self-righteous group.
The Interpretation
This is one of the funniest stories in the book. From the title (written, appropriately, as a tabloid headline) to the very last line, we have sophisticated and biting satire.

The name of the village not only sets the tone of the story, but

73

formally indicts the citizens who live "Squirmly on the Slug." We are informed of the town's sexist patriarchy by the term "the inhabi-dads," and discover that Victor Hardly is one victim of the town's piteous gossip ("gossipity").

And the town gossip is, of course, Mrs. Weatherby: Joyce would have called her an "old mutthergoosip" (*FW* 623.4). Weatherby's claim is that Victor is "holding a Black Matt" at his "pad" (it's worth noting that Joyce also used "mat" for "mass," *FW* 366.8). Chances are Victor was seen shaking out a black doormat in front of his house; but nonetheless, Mrs. Weatherby spreads *her* version throughout the village.

Victor, however, doesn't try to stop the nasty rumor: he sim-ply isn't a leader. As a matter of fact, initiative is not his strong suit. Victor, alas, never takes the helm; he "never *halmed* nobody." He never *harmed* anyone, either, so all in all, Victor is an easy target. And so the witch-hunt grows until the town is all arms; that is, until "the whole village was alarming."

It makes sense that the myopic leaders of the local church would seize upon this innocent citizen, making him a scapegoat for their sins. Joyce, in fact, unites such narrow-minded evangels of the Gospel to the phenomenon of gossip itself: "gossiple" (*FW* 476.4).

Hiding out in ambush are the Parson (likened to a pre-packaged "Parcel") and the Vicar, both "noticeably amongst all the other *dead* things *lying* about." It is apt that living "dead" people who lie should also lie among the really dead people in the cemetery!

The conclusion of the tale is hilarious: these "dictionaries" (words without wisdom, or deflated dignitaries) wait for many hours before anyone notices "that nothing had happened." And, true to form, they fail to realize their own stupidity; indeed, they choose instead to continue trusting in their "reliable source" (old hag Weatherby — who, of course, is a "reliable sore").

Having gone through the story, we can now view the title as ironic; if Victor's full name were used, however, the truth of the tale would be revealed: "Victor Hardly Triumphs . . . "!

"I Remember Arnold" (p. 80)

The Overview

The closing poem of *In His Own Write* is an elegy. It consists of five four-line stanzas plus a closing couplet. The poem memorializes Kakky Hargreaves' childhood, and the day he was killed by a train.

The Key Themes

The ludicrous danger of life; and the fact that good elegies are hard to come by.

The Interpretation

"I Remember Arnold" is the first John Lennon poem ever to be published. It premiered in *Mersey Beat* on August 17, 1961. The poem is a mock elegy, with non sequiturs thrown in for good measure; to begin with, there is no "Arnold" mentioned in the poem itself! (a not-uncommon device — there is no "Bald Soprano" in Ionesco's play of the same name).

The first stanza states that Kakky Hargreaves is "Son of Mr. Vaughan." It is interesting to note that one of John's boyhood friends, Ivan, was indeed the son of one Mr. Vaughan.

The second stanza recalls Kakky's childhood: "He used to be so grundie" (foreshadowing Kakky's horrible death: "grundie" contains the words "run" and "die"). We also see an arrogant kid in the name Kakky ("Cocky"); and we hear about him riding his bike on a Sunday (also alerting us to his death, "Sundie").

The third stanza suddenly and inexplicably changes our boy into a girl, though "Kathy" remains a son to "Mr. May"! Regardless of Kakky's sex, however, one thing is certain: he/she is jokingly reliable, arriving "always dead on time."

The fifth stanza closes the elegy, but not before making us all aware that we too are as fragile as Kakky — or "Humpty dumpty." The unrhyming couplet jokes about death: "Bumble*dy* (die) Huble-*dy* (die) Humbley Bumdley *Tum* (tomb)." The "Thank you" seems to be an ironic compliment directed, perhaps, to whatever absurd god invented death.

Drawing Twenty-Six (p. 81)

John Lennon never liked to take himself too seriously; he was a poet, not a politician. And so, while the first drawing was of himself, vulnerable and afraid, dead Arnold (or Kakky, or Kathy), lying supine on a table, forms the visual equivalent of: "The End."

Chapter Three

A Spaniard In The Works: Reviewing the Reviews

(Or, Why Did Most Critics Have a Negative Opinion of John's Last Major Work?)

What the Critics Said

It is quite common for critics to freely and benevolently praise an author's first work, only to detest and lacerate that same author's second effort. Often this occurs irrespective of the quality of that work. Why? Is it because these critics feel compelled to quickly find fault with anyone who has already once received their bountiful blessing?

In the case of John Lennon, this predictable pattern had mitigating circumstances. Unlike the status of any ordinary "novice" writer, Lennon's debut and transition from unknown writer to published author coexisted with a Superstar Status (his fame being unprecedented, and virtually worldwide). Initially, John's Beatle-bandleader position was a pleasant novelty to the critics. It must have been fun and easy to give Lennon credit for *In His Own Write*. After all, the book's originality and sophistication was itself another novelty (since undoubtedly the critics assumed all "pop" musicians were toally illiterate).

Within the short space of one year, however, the novelty had worn off and reality was setting in — The Beatles were not a fad; they were a force, a movement that would wield an incredible influence around the world. It was symbolic of this phenomenon that on June 12, 1965, it was made public: The Beatles had been awarded "Membership of the Most Excellent Order of the British Empire." This investiture, as MBEs, was made by the Queen in Buckingham Palace on October 26, and was partially greeted with considerable outrage and anger by former recipients of this award — and the wrath of OBEs and BEMs as well. Similarly, *A Spaniard In The Works*, released June 24, 1965, received the resentment and jealousy of another group of "insiders," i.e., the critics.

John Wain's August 7 review for the *New Republic* best typifies the petty anger and condescending tone many critics would unload

77

upon Lennon's second, and last, major literary work. Wain, after citing a brief passage from the book, identifies the quotation as:

> " . . . the work of John Lennon; Esq., MBE, known wherever human beings walk the earth as the Writing Beatle. I didn't . . . read his first book . . . and I don't think I'll bother now, but this new one is worth a glance . . . because it will be read and absorbed by virtually the whole generation of adolescents in Britain and . . . America too."

To begin with, not only is failing to read an author's inaugural work exceedingly poor preparation on the part of a critic reviewing that author's *second* piece, but in this instance it becomes downright ridiculous. And that is because any book afforded the high esteem received by *In His Own Write* is simply not dismissable (without some attempt, at least, to reasonably argue the point).

It was obvious to me from the first line of this review that Wain refused even to accept John Lennon as a bona fide author (reviewing him instead solely through the mythos of the Beatles). Apparently both the collective success of the Beatles and the personal success of author Lennon served to intimidate and confuse Mr. Wain. Thus the only way Wain could appear as exempt from the mythos ("since the Beatles are a law unto themselves and will be followed anywhere they choose to go") was to simply rise above it all, casually stating (ho-hum) that he'd not even read (yawn) the Writing Beatle, (etc.).

Still, the real, elemental flaw of Wain's review of *A Spaniard In The Works* is his claim that it's only "worth a glance," and not for any literary reason per se, but because a lot of teenagers were going to read it! In short, Wain ignored the artifact entirely, choosing instead to share with us a personal reflection on the Beatles' popularity.

Now, there is some humor to be found in all this, and I think it's lodged somewhere in Wain's unconscious and contradictory critical stand:

> "The first thing any literate person will notice on reading through Mr. Lennon's book is that it all comes out of one source, namely the later work of James Joyce. Not only the determination to communicate almost exclusively in puns, but the equally determined smutty, blasphemous and subversive tone, are Joycean . . . . By crashing the barrier normally erected against the book, Mr. Lennon has, at one stroke, put the nonreader in touch with a central strand in the literary tradition of the last thirty years in every English-speaking country . . . . After an exposure to Lennon, the

present day adolescent will be able to take Joyce in comic-strip form."

Here Wain closely links Lennon to Joyce and directly states that John's writing puts the adolescent "nonreader" in touch with this most complex writer of modern literature. Yet Wain *still* refuses to actually give John any credit for such a feat; nor does he consider Lennon to be an innovative or noteworthy author in his own right. The truth is, most of this alleged "review" is essentially extolling the genius of Joyce (even as it altogether ignores the stylistic inventiveness of Lennon):

> "Mr. Lennon, coasting downhill with [the] huge gravitational pull [of Joyce's method], need provide nothing in the way of content except his automatic youthful irreverence. If, one day, he should decide to try to communicate something, we shall see whether he has any gifts . . . at the moment, there's no means of telling."

And so, according to Wain: All the pointed satire and verbal innovation of John Lennon is the result of "coasting downhill." The writing is proclaimed to be "automatic" — a reflex action, not the result of mental activity. Furthermore, while he admits Lennon can be safely compared to Joyce, he remains somehow ostensibly unable to "communicate"! This ludicrous opinion is then topped off by Wain's belief that the forty-nine examples of prose and poetry contained in John's two books do not provide us with any "means of telling" whether John even has "any gifts."

Unfortunately, Wain was not alone in his resentment of Lennon's literary achievements; witness Hilary Corke's review for *The Listener*, June 24:

> "It would be spectacularly ironic if it proved to be The Beatles who finally smuggled the understanding of poetic method over the populace-frontier, after generations of limp noisy failure from the radiant consciency boy-poets."

It's quite apparent that Corke is even more confused than Wain in regard to viewing Lennon as Beatle only — which is to say, *not* as author. In fact, Corke is asserting that *all* of the Beatles have actually written John's book! Notice further that the same idea that emerged in Wain is repeated here — that "pop star" Lennon has been able to do what "real" writers ("conscious" poets) have not: sell a complex literary style to the masses. And yet like Wain, Corke gives Lennon no quarter — no literary credit per se.

And Corke has the distinction of being even more direct than Wain in dismissing any value of sophistication to be found in Lennon's language:

> "John Lennon's trademark, in *A Spaniard In The Works* as in his earlier *John Lennon in his Own Write* [sic] is the thoroughly childish trick of misspelling common phrases to give them new meanings . . . . Five times out of six he misses."

As we discovered in *In His Own Write*, John does much more than simply "misspell" words to create "new" meaning. His writing style is highly varied, the dark humor being achieved through the subtle use of grammar and syntax, portmanteau and polyhedronic puns and an array of allusions, as well as by his accompanying drawings. As for Corke's ratio of John "missing" his mark "five times out of six," I believe Chapter Four will help establish that in fact Lennon was five times out of six right on target.

In addition to the Wain-Corke trend in reviewing *A Spaniard In The Works*, there may be found the more angry and brisk "putdown" approach, as in the July 15 review for *Best Sellers*:

> "[This book] is no better than his previously published *In His Own Write* and that is properly faint praise; it is conceivably much worse, too."

Then comes the following, thrown in apparently out of pure spite: "I don't blame the Library of Congress for not giving a number in time for it to be entered on the copyright page." ?!!

Along the same lines as the above is Francis Hope's review, August 13, for *New Statesman*:

> "John Lennon's jokes are simpler [than George MacBeth's in *A Doomsday Book*.] The endless half puns in which they lurk are about as funny as a nervous tic."

Fortunately, not all of the reviews are as off-the-wall as the four we've seen thus far. For instance, Phoebe Adams, writing for the *Atlantic Monthly* in August, only partially shares in the patronizing tone of the others:

> "John Lennon, the literate Beatle, has tossed off another book . . . Mr. Lennon's style is promiscuously derived . . . and

his point of view, when one has penetrated the linguistic brush pile, is tolerant exasperation with practically everything."

So far so bad: Once again Lennon is perceived not as a serious writer, but as a Beatle "tossing off" a book or two. His clever use of various stylistic devices remains unacknowledged; all linguistic complexity is swept into a "brush pile." Still, Adams does admit (and rightly, I believe) that:

"At his best, Mr. Lennon can achieve overtones of satire, parody, obscenity, political comment, and literary reminiscence in a single cannily distorted word."

The review in *The London Times Literary Supplement* is markedly different than the joyous report which accompanied the appearance of *In His Own Write*. However, unlike the out-of-hand attacks of other reviews, these negative, critical remarks are both specific and telling. That is to say, after first establishing that the book contains "faintly Thurberish line drawings and short prose lunacies" with "Joyce-like punnings," and that "much of it is very funny," the review continues:

"But there is one sadly unfunny element which was already present in the earlier volume and now seems to be getting out of hand. This is the sick (sic) humour typified in jokes about spastics, harelips, limps and humps . . . . A lot of people are not merely going to be not amused by this but will be unnecessarily hurt. Similarly there is a would-be comic vein of pointless destructiveness running through the book which is overworked till it just jars."

This charge of excessive and gratuitous violence is well-founded: John certainly exercises little restraint. He respects no boundaries, and all borders on the offensive; however the violence must be understood within the context of John Lennon's life experience at the time. I will fully elaborate upon this aspect of John's writing as part of the annotation in Chapter Four.

Not wishing the reader to conclude that *Spaniard* received only bad notices, I offer one evaluation that approaches full-throttle praise. It appeared in the *Virginia Quarterly Review*, the autumn issue:

"Yeah! Yeah! Yeah! The writer from the Beatles has done it

again. This second volume of satire in story and verse forms is as fresh and alive as *In His Own Write*. Lennon still rocks and rolls with the English language. Indeed, his style has become surer and richer, his subjects more literary, and his manner more spicy, without loss of his already established zest and buoyant playfulness . . . . In this volume his political attacks and his take-offs on literary standards assume an adult awareness and proffer mature fun . . . John Lennon has proven himself a writer of talent and bountiful imagination. No one is writing satire today with the flair that he has demonstrated in his first two books."

This perhaps overly effulgent appraisal still succeeds, I think, in establishing certain critically valid perspectives. One, John Lennon is rightly seen as "the writer from the Beatles" (not as a pop star dabbling in the writer's art). Second, this review correctly identifies the book's contents as "satire in story and verse forms" (not as "nonsense verse" or "doodles," but as true satire: the calculated use of sarcasm, irony, and keenness of wit in ridiculing vices, abuses, or evils of any kind). And third, the review maintains that Lennon did indeed become a better writer with a "surer and richer" style than before, and that he chose subjects generally "more literary" in nature for the "mature fun" of *A Spaniard In The Works*.

What the Critics Did Not Say

Assuming the critics were aware of the fact themselves, they failed to admit that their reviews were distorted by the biases they held against the *Beatles*. Basically the undercurrent running through almost every stated opinion was the mistaken notion that a "rocker" cannot be a writer. Also, the reviewers resented the enormous fame of Beatle John Lennon; they displaced this anger by lashing out at *A Spaniard In The Works*.

Unfortunately, this kind of myopia is still prevalent; it is a popular assumption that people in Rock-and-Roll are (ipso facto) either illiterate or simply not to be taken seriously as artists — that they are somehow noisy rebels bereft of legitimate genius. Yet Rock has produced some extraordinary and multifaceted artists whose collective impact may change this "traditional" bias; two who come to mind rather quickly are Paul Simon (credit his performance, screenplay and soundtrack for *One Trick Pony*) and the amazing David Bowie, superb in his Broadway debut in *Elephant Man*. (I personally find Bowie to be the most significant composer and performer to have emerged from Rock in many years. His style is that of a visionary, and ever-evolving; his stage presence is startling, and his persona is both unique and sophisticated.)

Ironically and painfully, John Lennon's death marked the first time anyone in Rock history was accorded the media attention and eulogizing usually associated with the assassination of a world leader. I think it's safe to say that at the same time, Rock-and-Roll music was (finally) taken seriously. But this was 1980, and the climate in 1965 was decidedly different.

If the critics failed to recognize the deepening of Lennon's style within *A Spaniard In The Works*, the proof of such a refinement will be found in Chapter Four.

So in a Few Words, What Does This All Mean?

John's second work didn't get a fair shake from the critics, even though we will see that *A Spaniard In The Works* contains the very best of The Literary Lennon. I should state at this point that the Lennon-Joyce connection no longer warrants exhaustive and direct cross-referencing with *Finnegans Wake* (as was done with *In His Own Write*). For emphasis only, rather general similarities will be highlighted when appropriate.

Chapter Four

Annotation of
A Spaniard In The Works

This chapter is organized in the same way as Chapter Two. And again, before we systematically progress through the book, we will first consider the work at large:

The Overview

John Lennon's second book consists of fifty-six items: eight mini-stories (ranging in length from three paragraphs to about seven-and-one-half pages); six poems (running from five stanzas to thirty stanzas); four special forms (one newspaper editorial, one gossip column, one letter to the editor and one television interview); and thirty-eight drawings (including several self-portraits and two Beatle portraits).

At a glance, this roster of selections appearing in *A Spaniard In The Works* may appear nearly identical to that of *In His Own Write* (see Chapter Two). Upon closer examination, however, a dramatic difference becomes obvious: with every selection, John has significantly increased the length of his writing.

To begin with, while there were fifteen stories in *In His Own Write* (or technically seven *more* than appeared in *A Spaniard In The Works*), the total number of pages taken for stories is about one-third larger in the second book — just over twenty-two pages to the former's fourteen-and-one-half pages. The single longest story in John's first book was two pages, while in *Spaniard* the longest story is almost four times that length. It is important to realize as well that not only are these stories longer, but (as we shall see) their language is consistently more complex (more density for your dollar!).

What of the poetry? On the surface, at least, there appears to be more of it in *In His Own Write* (eight poems to *Spaniard*'s six). And yet the longest poem in the first book contains ten stanzas (or forty lines), as compared to the thirty stanzas (or 121 lines) of *Spaniard*'s longest poem. In fact, all the poems in *Spaniard* are at least twice as long as their counterparts in John's earlier book, and several are three or four times longer! In fact, the total number of lines in *In His Own Write* is one hundred and fifteen, but there are nearly three-hundred lines in *A Spaniard In The Works* (296, to be precise).

There are five special forms in John's first venture, and four in the second. But true to the established pattern, the number of pages is (albeit only slightly) larger in *Spaniard*. And by the same token, there are more original drawings as well: there were twenty-six such drawings in *In His Own Write* (six requiring double-pages and twenty on single pages). *A Spaniard In The Works* boasts twelve additional drawings (or a total of thirty-eight, fifteen of which use double pages and twenty-one shown on single pages). Also, total pages using graphics in *Write* number thirty-two, while there are fifty-one such pages in *Spaniard*.

The only area that has been omitted from John's original format in *Write* is the play scene (though the television interview, "I Believe Boot . . . " in *Spaniard* does have scripted dialogue).

The Key Themes

Philip Norman in *Shout!* notes that John Lennon's depressions, those deep bouts of desperation, "were entirely separate from his outward success." That is, while the image John projected to the world appeared intact, inside his soul John felt trapped and suffocated by stardom. Norman also notes that a major "trough" of depression occurred in 1965, while Lennon was writing *A Spaniard In The Works*.

Musically there are two important analogs to this despair: the songs *Help!* and *You've Got To Hide Your Love Away*. In the *Playboy* interview (published January 1981), John gave us a summary of his emotional state at this time, and I believe it assists our understanding of the themes in *A Spaniard In The Works*:

> "When 'Help!' came out in '65, I was actually crying out for help. I didn't realize it at the time. But later, I knew I was really crying out for help. It was my fat Elvis period. You see the movie; He — I — is very fat, very insecure, and he's completely lost himself. Anyway I was fat and depressed and I *was* crying out for help.
>
> The Beatles thing had just gone beyond comprehension. We were smoking marijuana for breakfast . . . nobody could communicate with us, because we were just all glazed eyes . . . . In our own world."

You've Got To Hide Your Love Away strongly reflects the

emptiness of John's life at this time: As Norman puts it, the song is "sardonic and world weary."

Part of John's feelings of entrapment are definitely traceable to the business side of the Beatles circa 1965. Few people realize just how penurious the financial terms of the Beatles' contracts were — that is, until Brian Epstein's renegotiation in 1967. For five full years (1962–1967), the record company had the legal option to keep the Beatles (as Norman notes) "to the most niggardly contract that E.M.I.'s cheese-paring caution could devise." The royalty schedule would be laughable were it not for the minute sum the Beatles were stuck with for half a decade — Brian and the Beatles were literally dividing one penny for every double-sided record sold! In addition?! each individual Beatle's share was further reduced by Brian's own management contract — which gathered in twenty-five per cent of *all* Beatle earnings.

And so by 1965, the royalty schedule had increased by a scant three farthings. Now the farthing, folks, was (even in '62) so insignificant an amount that it had passed from general circulation. So here is John Lennon, leader of the world's First SuperGroup (which is more famous than any Combo in history), helplessly chained to a contract unfit for a beggar (much less a king)!

Another major influence on *A Spaniard In The Works* was the continually deteriorating marriage of John and Cynthia. When John wasn't literally away from home, he was so withdrawn inside himself that Cynthia could share very little with him. It's even a surprise to see her show up at all — in the drawing on page 91!

It's now safe to say that John Lennon endured a triple entrapment: he was caged by a record contract (which meant he had no real power over his future); he was imprisoned by his own fame (a distorting and destructive condition which caused him to prefer the haze of marijuana to reality); and he was tied to a woman he didn't love (making him seek fragmented affairs to compensate for his loneliness).

It was from just such a painful place that *A Spaniard In The Works* was born. Therefore it is not surprising that the themes of the book are intense alientation, emasculation, and utter hopelessness. And yet throughout *Spaniard* these themes are handled in a very funny way. Somehow this deluge of desperation helped refine Lennon's darkly comedic point of view. The result is often akin to Theatre of the Absurd, making us laugh at the general chaos of the world.

In *Spaniard* Lennon continues sharpshooting at the familiar targets found in *In His Own Write*: politics, Christianty, societal violence, television, personal betrayal, etc. Only now there is more (and much more) of a hard edge to the assault. Ultimately the result is a more provocative revelation of Lennon's inner state of mind.

Notes on the Front Cover. Only the Pp. edition retains the original cover. It is another fine photograph taken by Robert Freeman; only now John is "in character." That is to say, Lennon poses as "The Spaniard" (who is the protagonist of the book's first short story). It is a tongue-in-cheek photo of John in a cocked flamenco-style black hat, face half in shadow, one eye peering at us through a somber stare. His left arm is hidden under a reddish cape, and his right hand, covered inside a black glove, holds a large wrench.

The Pp. edition also has an inset, bottom left, that reads "His Second Book — John Lennon." The most recent Simon and Schuster hardback edition, *The Writings of John Lennon: In His Own Write, A Spaniard In The Works*, 1981 (hereinafter referred to as SS2) also displays this photo. However, it appears on the back cover and is competely black and white (without the red cape); and it has neither title nor inset.

Notes on the Back Cover. Unfortunately, John did not write another biography like "About the Awful" for his second book. Hence the original back cover (as on Pp.) consists of the Table of Contents. The Pp. version adds, in the left corner, "John's further adventures in literature and art."

"Title Page" (p. 83)
Our version places the title page *before* the first two drawings. However, both Pp. and SS2 more properly allow the drawings to introduce the reader to the book before the title page appears.

The title of John's second work is the same as that of the volume's lead story. As such, it takes an Absurdist tone — as Lennon's British heritage hardly qualifies him as "A Spaniard"!

But the book's title, *A Spaniard In The Works* also has a more decipherable aspect. For it is, in fact, John's take-off on the English phrase, "a spanner in the works." Now, the word "spanner" refers to any kind of wrench, and therefore the phrase is equivalent to the American euphemism of "throwing a monkey wrench into the works."

The photograph of John as "Spaniard," prominently displaying his monkey wrench, or spanner, thus neatly visualizes both meanings of the term. John's message is clear — his book is going to throw a large absurdist wrench into our neat preconceptions of the world.

Drawing One (p. 84)
This is the first of three self-portraits found in *A Spaniard In The Works*. It is also the first of two Beatle portraits. This fusion is

apropos, for John clearly views himself as Group Leader — the head of the Beatle body. But much has changed from the portraits found in *In His Own Write*.

To begin with: John is bald (the "mop top" image discarded completely). He is also seen with cauliflower ears and no teeth — rounding out the portrait of a man who feels old, helpless, and generally exhausted.

We further note that the Beatle body is no longer depicted as that of a dog (pp. 28–29), but is now the torso of a horse. I think John is saying here that the Beatles had graduated from "working like a dog" to working like — a workhorse. Indeed, this image accurately represents their output: by April of '65 the Beatles (in one form or another) had released (in the United Kingdom and America) eight singles, six Extended-Play records, and eight Long-Playing albums.

The final revealing feature of this combination Lennon/Beatle portrait is the feet. Earlier (p. 11) the Beatles were supported by four hands, each with individual fingers and nails; and each was shown as both relaxed and as offering the others maximum support (by being "feet-flat" on the ground). Now we witness a dramatic difference: the feet are claws — arched, sharply pointed, awkwardly drawn, and precariously and literally standing "on edge."

I find this first drawing highly indicative of John's state of mind at this period of his life. It stands in marked contrast to the happy-go-Beatles image that was common currency at the time. Significantly, only John Lennon could have revealed this shadow self to the public — though no one seemed to have perceived the pain behind the drawings.

Drawing Two (p. 85)

This is the second and final Beatle portrait in the book. The group is shorn of their hair and claustrophobically caged (they enjoyed at least some freedom of movement in "The Wrestling Dog," pp. 28–29). The head of the Beatle in the cage looks more like that of a shaved lion than John Lennon; I take the representation, then, to be a group symbol, herein portrayed as a defeated king in the musical jungle.

The Beatles are not only caged; they are now perfectly powerless to effect their freedom. And that is because the power rests with a grotesque gang: the bickering, stodgy board of E.M.I. directors. These corporate heads are your typical back-stabbers and scapegoaters (the three executives on your right are accusing one another, behind each other's backs, while the four on the left are accusing the Beatles of some nameless wrongdoing).

Taken together, Drawings One and Two establish a much harsher view of Beatlemania than did the first two drawings of *In His Own Write* (which, you will recall, also began with one self-portrait and one Beatle portrait).

Drawing Three (pp. 86--87)

This elongated creature very much resembles a drugged-out refugee from the Neville Club (p. 61). To me it simply represents the "strung out" feeling of John's spirit in 1965.

SS2 has the eye printed in green, and the figure in brown ink. Now I don't know on whose authority any or all of the SS2 "color" versions of John's drawings are based. Nor is it clear whether or not John's original illustrations were done in color, or whether John even approved of the SS2 choices.

The fact is, SS2 reprints *In His Own Write* using brown and blue ink (as in SS1), whereas *A Spaniard In The Works* is printed using brown, blue, and green. Irrespective of whose authority the color versions were produced under, I will comment on the aesthetic impact made by these colors on a drawing-by-drawing basis.

In this case, the green eye contributes slightly to the eeriness of the drawing; it's apt, but not necessary.

Drawing Four (pp. 88--89)

This bloated beast could be taken as a tongue-in-cheek self-portrait illustrating John's "fat Elvis" period (as could "The Fat Budgie," p. 99). However, I personally take it to be a companion piece to the former drawing. Drawing Three illustrates the "thin" of life; this is "the fat," the excess of fame, etc.

Also present in Drawing Four is a familiar stylistic technique of John's — the old eyeball-outside-of-the-face motif. And as before, the general effect is that the face appears to be both in profile and face-forward, simultaneously. Also, as in Drawing Three, SS2 colors the eyes green — which adds to the strange appearance.

Drawing Five (p. 91)

Here we have a rather pathetic procession — all the participants are seemingly destined to fall off the edge of the page. But our version, I think, is both a bit deceptive and the result of poor planning. In both the SS2 and Pp. editions, Drawing Five is (correctly) placed facing the Table of Contents; thus John's own characters are literally "drawing" us into the contents of the book. Our version places the Table of Contents for *Spaniard* next to that of *In His Own Write* — at the beginning of the volume (pp. 5–7).

If we look at the drawing itself, we may interpret the first four figures (from the right) as the Lennon family. John would be the guy whose hair is standing on end — an apparently recent escapee from the electric chair! Importantly, there are no saving graces, no birds "of potential" pulling back his hair as there was on p. 10. John is now being led by the hand — by a woman I take to be Cynthia Lennon. The woman is shown looking rather unhappy; she is ultra-conservative in hair style and dress.

Underneath the clasped hand of John and Cynthia is little Julian, age two (Julian was born April 23, 1963, while John was on tour). Julian is seen sitting on the family dog and reaching out for his mother; as mentioned previously, John was seldom home, and when he was, he was often depressed — and not reachable.

I view each of the remaining figures (behind John) as a "hanger-on" — an anybody or a nobody, trying to get close to Lennon. And I think the cannibal crouched on the ground, devouring some poor, minute creature, aptly summarizes the quality of friendship that John found available.

Drawing Six (pp. 92–93)

More than any other drawing in *A Spaniard In The Works*, this self-portrait graphically illustrates John Lennon's intense cry for help. On 92 we see a psychologist sitting calmly, intent on his client. He appears professionally self-contained, leaning on his knees in a posture of empathetic listening. John, however (on p. 93) looks absolutely crazed out of his mind — scared, screaming, jumping wildly into the air. The extreme contrasts within the drawing — and particularly, John's "insane" stance — make us laugh, but behind the picture is a serious plea. For it was here — in 1965 — that John was projecting himself into therapy. Five years later, in March of 1970, he would indeed immerse himself in Arthur Janov's Primal Scream Therapy.

Our version is different from both Pp. and SS2. In the former, John's figure is fully shaded; in the latter version, John is entirely in green! (I prefer SS2; it more graphically captures John "feeling nuts.") And so even before we come upon the text of the first story, we encounter six drawings which do much to introduce us to the tone and themes found in the book. This is twice the number of introductory drawings which opened *In His Own Write*.

Drawing Seven (pp. 94–95)

This is the first bona fide illustration in the book. As we learned in *Write*, John never felt that his illustrations had to accurately depict details of a given story, and this is no exception.

Initially, our attention is drawn to two old-fashioned cars (or "coaches") which are quite prominent. And yet we are told by the story that follows that no "coach of any description" is to be found at the Lord's castle — though there are horses aplenty. Moreover, the

"Spaniard" is a mechanic wielding a large wrench — although in the tale, he merely grooms and tends the stable horses. There is also no indication in the text that the Spaniard works in the nude! However in the drawing he's quite naked — albeit covered with a lot of body hair, quite strangely resembling Marian's *flies* on p. 18!

One further curiosity: the military stripes that are tattooed, apparently, onto his right arm. And you guessed it — no mention is made of these stripes in the story itself.

In spite of, or perhaps because of, the eccentricity of Drawing Seven, what is communicated is a feeling of displacement: we sense the complete bewilderment of a Spaniard living in Scotland!

"A Spaniard In The Works" (pp. 95–98)
The Overview

This is the story of Jesus El Pifco, a man who emigrates from Barcelona, Spain, to work as a handyman in the Highlands of Scotland. Jesus lives and works in the horse stables of a Scottish Lord. Soon he encounters, and falls in love with, the Lord's chambermaid. After the wedding ceremony, Jesus literally harnesses and then rides his new wife to the racetrack — for their honeymoon.

Alas — the honeymoon is interrupted by a phone call from Jesus's mother. She announces that she is leaving Barcelona in order to visit the newlyweds, who quickly return to the Lord's castle and inform their employer of Mrs. El Pifco's impending arrival. The Lord ponders the news — and then happily announces, "You're all fired!"

The Key Themes

God is dead. There is no escape from the chaos of the world. Women are chattel, and workers are always exploited by management.

The Interpretation

Let's begin with blasphemy: throughout this story, the concept of God is consistently reduced through the names of the characters. "Jesus El Pifco" means "Jesus The Fife" (if we pick up the echo from the root word "pifaro," or "fife" in Spanish). So, Jesus becomes a "little toot," taking after the small instrument. His nicknames "wee Jesus" and "wee dwarf" further reduce his stature, disqualifying him from any venerated or godly association. In fact, Jesus is described rather indelicately as "a garlic eating, stinking, little yellow greasy fascist bastard catholic Spaniard"! I should note further that a real company called "Pifco" was, in the early 1960s, regularly appearing in the transactions of the London Stock Exchange. And "Pifco" was found under the heading "Breweries and Distilleries"!

In this farcical tale it makes perfect sense that one Lord ("Jesus") should be hired by another Lord: the "Lord of the Asshole"

("Laird of McAnus")! It should be noted also that "Laird" is the regular Scottish form of Lord, and that the native form, "Lord," occasionally appeared as far back as the 15th century. John Lennon freely puns on both versions of the term.

Further: the term "Laird" likely suggests that McAnus is fat (sounds like "lard"). Certainly McAnus lives down to his "asshole" designation, for not only does he screw his maid at his late wife's wake, but he gives her crabs in the process.

From disenfranchised deities, we move on to mere mortals. The love interest in the story is a particulary grotesque figure. Her sexuality is blurred — not only by her male name, Patrick, but also by her "mass of naturally curly warts," her one eye, and leg braces. Jesus calls her "wee Spastic," because he can "spot a cripple anywhere." He also calls her "his sugar-boot" — possibly because she so "sweetly" accepts his wifebeating.

The hyperbolic ugliness of these characters communicates, I think, John's intense feelings of self-hatred. We would do well to recall the songs that prefigure the publication of *A Spaniard In The Works*: i.e., *I'll Cry Instead, No Reply*, and *I'm A Loser*, to mention just a few. Each of these songs comments on John's increasing sense of alienation and desperation. In *I'll Cry Instead*, John penned: "I have a chip on my shoulder that's bigger than my feet." In *No Reply*, a message of utter betrayal and rejection is painfully evident. But in *I'm A Loser*, John's glitter-shit syndrome is most directly verified: in the *Playboy* interview John is asked if this song was "a personal statement." John answers affirmatively: "Part of me suspects that I'm a loser and the other part of me thinks I'm God Almighty."

The story also contains Lennon's political humor. There is some justification, for example, that the Laird himself is a sendoff of former Prime Minister Sir Alec Douglas Home. I say this because the Laird, "that canny [not *un*canny!] old tin," is one "*whom* have a castle in the Highlads." And "Sir Alice Doubtless-*Whom*" (John's previous allusion to Sir Home, p. 122) was *in fact* a Scottish Laird quite famous for his opulent estate in the remote Highlands.

There are also several private gags lurking in Lennon's language. I take "Highlads" to be both a personal hello to the other three "*Lads* from Liverpool," as in "Hi, lads!" and also a reference to the Beatles' habit of "smoking marijuana for breakfast."

The pun "Barcelover," for Barcelona, could also be an inside snicker regarding John's May of '63 holiday to Spain with Brian Epstein. On this occasion Epstein finally declared his homosexual love for John, which (needless to say) John rejected.

Finally we find mention of the Beatles' first single, *My Bonnie* (recorded May, 1961, featuring Tony Sheridan), as well as the name of the Beatles' road manager, Mal Evans ("howevans").

John's puns on other names are more obvious and often very funny. For instance, Patrick leaves Jesus in "an agatha of Christy" — a perfectly subversive way of saying "an agony of Christ" even as it fortifies the story as a great "mystery." My own personal favorite is when Jesus speaks his native tongue for the first and only time, and his "gospel" turns out to be a slightly incoherent grouping of Spanish, Italian, and phonetic puns. Jesus utters, "qui bueno el franco senatro!" — which, roughly translated, or "rugby transplanted," means "Frank Sinatra is so good!" (An updated instance where John uses a personalized "global" language is seen in the lyric to *Sun King* on **Abbey Road**: "Cuestro obrigado tanta mucho que can eat it carousel.")

As one might expect, Lennon's indictment of marriage persists with a vengeance. John describes this "holy" union as a drug addict's dependency, numbing and deadly ("once morphia unitely in a love"), with the newlyweds carrying suitcases marked "his and hearse"! The sexism here is so hyperbolic, it become ludicrous: " . . . quickly harnessing his wife . . . he rode [her] at a steady trot . . . . 'We mustn't miss the first race my dear.' 'Not likely' snorted his newly wed wife breaking into a gullup." And this last word brings to mind a person easily tricked — that is, a gull — someone who's gullible.

There is much more to discover in this tale, so get to it! One thing is certainly clear: this inaugural story is structurally tighter, stylistically more assured, and generally better written than its counterpart in the first book: "Partly Dave," which opened *In His Own Write*.

Drawing Eight (p. 99)

This drawing dates back to the previous year, when Lennon gave permission for its use as a Christmas card in September of '64. Also the title itself, "The Fat Budgie," appeared earlier in *In His Own Write* — as "Fat Bourgies," in "Scene three Act one" (p. 41).

This is a funny drawing, particularly in the Pp. edition, where the Budgie is several times larger than in our edition. While SS2 also has the Budgie enlarged, there is a flaw: The bird is outlined in green. This is wrong for two reasons: First, although a parakeet could be green, the text of the poem establishes that Jeffrey (the bird in question) is yellow. And second, the use of green is a poor substitute for the black ink which, in the superior version, creates an immediate visual impact.

Most likely the "Fat Budgie" simply serves as an emblem of excess. For in this case, Jeffrey's gluttony has made it impossible for him to take flight. The natural abilities this bird once possessed have been destroyed.

94

"The Fat Budgie" (pp. 18--19)

The Overview

The action of this poem is best viewed in three parts: the speaker's introduction of the bird Jeffrey to the reader (the first two stanzas); a discussion of Budgie-haters, specifically of Uncle Arthur, who ate "the yellow brats" 'til his gluttony killed him (stanzas three to six); and a long description of the persona's own relationship with Jeffrey (pointing out Jeffrey's eating habits, weight problem, his singing and shitting, etc.).

The Key Themes

Transference: how easy it is to displace one's anger, and show aggression against someone who is helpless (i.e., a little yellow bird!). Also, the pet as a surrogate for human companionship.

The Interpretation

Lennon uses a very simple, fairytale-like lyric here in order to communicate maniacal violence. At first we assume that the persona (the speaker of the poem) is a small child: "I have a little budgie/He is my very pal." But a far more adult mentality is revealed by the end of the second stanza; we are told that the bird is named "after grandad/Who had a feathered brain"! The poem now becomes overtly violent; the speaker's attitude becomes increasingly ambivalent: "Some people don't like budgies/The little yellow brats" etc. And in stanzas four and five, a familiar "name game" motif pops up: the persona calls his uncle "Ronnie" — "Although his name was Arthur."

A potentially grave image comes immediately after we're told that Uncle Arthur "had been too greedy" (he ate a pet store's worth of budgies). And so "He died just like a zoo." Now, this could mean that animals are eaten up by cages that kill their will to live; it could also mean they are dished out to (inhumane stares of) strangers and spectators. Indeed, the doctors actually peer into Arthur's insides — quite a violation of privacy.

From stanzas seven to twelve we discover that our hero is hardly innocent of animal cruelty. He forcefeeds Jeffrey, stuffing eggs and toast into him with a spoon. He also finds it amusing that if Jeffrey gets any fatter, "He'll have to wear a crutch." Not to mention the line that (thankfully) does *not* appear in Lennon's "Imagine": "Imagine all the people/Laughing till they're sick"!

The topper comes when we finally learn that the persona is a middle-aged man who lives at home and who loves Jeffrey "more than daddie." So Lennon's intentionally puerile verse ultimately reveals the voice addressing us as that of a mental retard, a creature who rightfully belongs with the "Dwarts" of the following story.

Drawing Nine (pp. 102--103)

This, of course, is a picture of "Snore White and some Several

Dwarts." To be precise, there are 13 Dwarts, one dog, one spider, one bug, one palm tree, and one Snore Wife! Needless to say, there are many curiosities in this "busy" illustration.

For starters: Snore Wife bears a striking resemblance to Mrs. Weatherby (p. 78). She has more hair (or flies) than Jesus El Pifco (p. 95). And, unfortunately for her, she boasts the hump of Quasimodo! (This is a deformity not mentioned in the actual story.) Only in the SS2 version is the apple Snore Wife is holding colored green — which may suggest its poisonous contents.

The second most conspicuous figure (after Snore Wife) is third from the left — the fellow wearing three sets of glasses. Subsequent to the appearance of this drawing, this figure became directly associated with John Lennon — for two reasons. One would be the 1965 Signet paperback edition of John's writings, which features a cover photograph of John actually wearing three sets of glasses. Secondly, the **Walls And Bridges** album (released September 26, 1974) has a photo of John wearing no less than *five* pairs of glasses! I don't know why John is posed in this way, or whether the photographers were aware of this illustration in *A Spaniard In The Works*. But I do know one fact is clear: John's glasses (as pictured on the front cover of Yoko Ono's **Season Of Glass**) have passed into our vocabulary as the one singular symbol of the man himself.

From here on it becomes harder to spot motifs in the crowd, but with a little scrutiny we can spot the following: the Beatle "body" from p. 85 has temporarily escaped from its corporate cage, and is now standing at the foot of the man with three pairs of glasses. Also, we see yet another cannibal-on-all-fours, as on p. 91; this time he's crawling behind Snore Wife's right foot. We can also pick out a bizarre character reminiscent of one of the druggies at "Neville Club" (the figure above the dog is going in three directions at once, just like the character on p. 61).

All in all, the members of this motley crew are standing around without apparent purpose; some are pointing right, some left, and some are reaching out while not apparently touching. This innovative illustration sets the tone for the tale that follows.

"Snore Wife and some Several Dwarts" (pp. 104--105)
The Overview

In a "sneaky" forest there lived eight dwarts. One day, upon their return from working in a diamond mine, they found Snore Wife asleep in Grumpty's bed.

Now at the same instant, in a castle not far away, a Wicked Queen is consulting her magic mirror. She is observed by Miss Cradock and Father Cradock — the latter dismissing her consultation as "just a face she's going through."

Meanwhile, Snore Wife is happily accepted into the Dwart household. Suddenly they hear someone below selling apples, but at present no one is interested in buying any. A few days later the same apple vendor returns, and Snore Wife does purchase one.

We then discover that the vendor was really the Wicked Queen, that her apples were poisoned, and that Miss Cradock is really a handsome Prince (who promptly eats both the Queen and her mirror!).

The Prince moves in with the Dwarts, but he doesn't marry Snore Wife. And . . . they all "lived happily ever [after] until they died."

The Key Themes

Modern-day Princes are *not* into marriage.

The Interpretation

Obviously, this is a parody of fairy-tales in general and of "Snow White and the Seven Dwarfs" (with a touch of "Goldilocks and the Three Bears") in particular. But aside from the basic burlesque of these two fairytales, Lennon builds in a layer of humor based on private associations.

For example: we're told the Dwarts "all dug about in a diamond mind ["mine"] which was rich beyond compere ["compare"]. And this line, in addition to its literal meaning, also connotes Beatle history; the "Cavern Club" is where the Beatles dug about, turning that dark cave into a diamond mine of a career. Their success exceeded even the astute prediction made by Bob Wooler, in 1961 in an article called "Well Now — Dig This!" — for the August 31 issue of *Mersey Beat*. Bob Wooler was indeed called "compere" by the Beatles (the French word for "godfather"); Wooler promoted the Beatles and other Beat groups years before Beatlemania.

Another inside joke occurs when the Wicked Queen consults "her daily mirror." She asks, "Whom is de fairy in the land," and the reply comes: "Cassandle!" Now, what the reader doesn't realize is that Casandra was a real gossip columnist for the tabloid *The Daily Mirror*. Hence John Lennon is here publicly attacking the "manhood" of one of England's better-known personalities; he goes even further by producing a parody of Casandra's own column later on in *Spaniard* (see pp. 142–143).

By now we are able to recognize certain stylistic motifs which have carried over from *In His Own Write*. One such motif is the listing of names. In "Randolf's Party" (p. 31) there was a list of sixteen names, including "Harold?" In "The Famous Five Through Woenow Abbey" (pp. 34–35) we saw a list of ten names, including "Craig?" — and "On Safairy with Whide Hunter" (pp. 64–65) closed with a list of six names. So we are not surprised to find another list, this time of eight names, in "Snore Wife" — including the name "Alice?" (It seems that John enjoyed representing tentativeness of identity by adding a question mark.)

It should be pointed out that other modern authors, particularly James Joyce and Samuel Beckett, were notorious for their list-making. However, these literary lights would take their lists all the way to the breaking point: "exhaustive enumeration," to use Hugh Kenner's phrase. For instance, Joyce names over 300 rivers in one section of *Finnegans Wake*! And so by comparison, Lennon's lists are short and to the point.

Now, many of the names in "Snore Wife" are puns that draw on the names of the dwarfs in Walt Disney's animated version of "Snow White": i.e., "Sneezy" becomes "Sleezy," and so on. In fact, Disney's influence on Lennon dates back to 1963, when John nicked the opening lines for *Do You Want To Know A Secret?* from certain lines of dialogue he remembered in Disney's "Cinderella." Also, John uses the Disney dwarfs' "Heigh Ho" song; only here it's twisted so that the Dwarts are singing as they're coming home. If this is a reflection of John's attitude towards work, we see it again when the *irk*some aspect of the Dwarts' labor is economically suggested by using "wirk" for *work*.

Throughout John's parody, he adds touches worthy of Ionesco and of the Theatre of the Absurd — i.e., "Father Cradock turns round slowly from the book he is eating and explains that it is just a face she is going through"! Or, "Sick to death of this elephant I am . . . sick to death of it eating like an elephant all over the place"! The fact that Snore Wife is called "Wife" throughout the tale (but is never married) is also absurd.

Last, we note how John infuses scatological innuendo into this fairytale. The Wicked Queen's poison is more than just "arsnic" — it's also the product of "arsenickers" (or "ass-knickers")! There's sexual innuendo too, as when Grumpy "didn't seem to mine ["mind"] finding a woman in his bed! So all in all, this story is a rollicking send-up of all fairy tales, written in a deft and beguiling style.

"The Singularge Experience of Miss Anne Duffield" (pp. 106--115)
The Overview

The extremely convoluted action of this story becomes easier to follow when the tale is divided into nine scenes:

Scene One (pp. 106--108). It is the end of March ("Marge") 1892; the opening action takes place in a London flat on Baker Street ("Bugger Street"). Sherlock Holmes ("Shamrock Womlbs") and Dr. Watson ("Doctored Whopper") have just had their lunch interrupted by a phone call. Holmes answers, and then tells Watson what he already knows — that Mr. Oxo Whitney has escaped from prison. At that moment Mr. Whitney knocks on the door, then enters in a frantic state. Holmes asks him for a cigarette, but before Whitney can answer, Holmes has kicked him to the floor and commences to beat the shit out of him.

Scene Two (last two lines of p. 108 — first line of p. 110). Mary Atkins, a prostitute, is seen primping before a mirror. Soon she moves into an armchair to read the newspaper ("Jack the Ripper Strikes Again" is the headline). Her pimp, Sydney Aspinall, makes a surprise entrance, then quickly leads Mary downstairs into a cab — to chase after a car. Both Sydney and Mary point out tourist sites to the cab driver as they go around in circles.

Scene Three (second through ninth lines of p. 110). Holmes is seen explaining to Watson that Jack the Ripper is not only a murderer, but also a sex pervert. Watson asks Holmes how he knows this; Holmes replies, "I have seen the film."

Scene Four (line 10, p. 110 — line 12, p. 111). That evening Inspector Basil makes an unexpected visit to discuss Jack the Ripper with Holmes. After the Inspector has a drink and a few sandwiches ("sam leeches"), he asks Holmes "Guess who's out of jail?" Holmes shouts "Oxo Whitney!"

Scene Five (line 13--line 24, p. 111). Meanwhile in Chelsea ("Chelthea"), Jack the Ripper waits in the shadows for his next victim. His knife is poised to reap revenge against prostitutes, for giving him venereal disease.

Scene Six (line 25, p. 111--line 8, p. 114). Mary Atkins is now back home, primping (once again) before her mirror. And as she talks to herself, she attributes the recent bad "business" to her "hump." Mary then takes a cab to her hangout (Nat's Cafe). After awhile, a high-class gentleman (Jack the Ripper) asks her, "How much?" And the two head down the avenue.

Scene Seven (line 9--end of p. 114). Sydney the pimp is seen explaining to Sherlock just what a good woman Mary was, but Holmes only wants specifics on her untimely death. Sydney exits and Watson asks Sherlock "What happened to Oxo Whitney?" Holmes replies, "That's a question."

Scene Eight (last line of p. 114--line 16 of p. 115). The next morning Watson fixes Sherlock his usual breakfast, only to discover that Sherlock has already left the flat. Watson waits; he calls some friends for information, but all to no avail.

The story concludes a week later when Watson is shocked by Holmes's dishevelled appearance ("dishovelled apeerless"). Watson asks Holmes "Where have you been?" The answer arrives only after Holmes has recuperated, at which time he tells Watson a story that to this day Watson can't remember.

The Key Themes

Life is an unsolved, and unsolvable, murder mystery (clues to its understanding are hopelessly confusing, even to a master sleuth).

The Interpretation

This is a fullscale parody on Sir Conan Doyle's wonderful *Adventure of Sherlock Holmes*. The tale's title, "The Singularge Experience of Miss Anne Duffield," certainly has that detective-case-study ring to it. But, as in Ionesco's play *The Bald Soprano* (which contains no bald soprano) or John's poem "I Remember Arnold" (p. 80, which never mentions "Arnold" outside the title), this longest of Lennon's short stories has no Anne Duffield! What the story does have is a density of puns that creates a rather hilarious version of Sherlock and Dr. Watson.

For one thing, John's language gives rise to uncertainty regarding Sherlock's sexuality. Now, even his name ("Shamrock *Womlbs*") testifies to this ambiguity: he may have the luck of a shamrock, but we suspect also that his "rocks are a sham" (and what is a man doing with a *womb*?).

Still, Sherlock tries to pull off a macho image: he doesn't merely stand, but "studs" in front of the fire — "casting an occasional gland." In addition, his pipe is definitely a sexual object, for we see Sherlock "puffing deeply in his wife." His preoccupation with sex is also apparent when John calls Jack the Ripper "Jock" the "Nipple." And also when Watson addresses Sherlock and Basil as "genitalmen"!

Sherlock's macho posturing, however, is undermined by his frequent farting and his "cloacal obsession" (H.G. Wells' term, used to describe James Joyce's literary interest in defecation and general bathroom behavior). Holmes receives a "tele*phart*" (his own fart exploding along with the sound of the phone ringing). The resulting smell is so offensive that Holmes "turds" instead of "turns" to Watson! Instead of Holmes simply saying to the Inspector that "the button on his waistcoat is missing," he says "the *buttock* on his waist*box* is misting."

The final touch to Sherlock's strange sexuality is the fact that he draws fake eyebrows on his forehead with his "eyepencil"! Certainly John wanted our great detective to be completely deflated, which transforms the story from a mystery into a farce.

On the other hand, highly sophisticated humor is found in John's additional descriptions of Sherlock. To begin with, he is portrayed as resembling various birds; he has a "thought*fowl* face;" his nostrils are like ostriches ("nostriches"); and his eyebrows are like feathers ("tufted brows").

The truth is, it's amazing just how many details about Sherlock and the other characters we elicit from Lennon's compact language. We observe, for example, Sherlock's "smirk" through the "smoke" as he sits puffing his pile of tobacco ("smirking his pile").

The character of Watson is well-developed and generally acts as a foil to Sherlock. That is to say, Holmes is stalky while Watson is rotund; Holmes is flippant, Watson somber, etc. As usual, John's pun on Watson's name provides us information about this character's appearance. Thus from the name alone, "Dr. Whopper," we learn that he is as fat and round as an all-American hamburger. (By the way, John was addicted to "Whopper" burgers for years!)

More importantly, however, we discover that of the two members of this detective duo, Watson is the serious one. For instance, Watson doesn't just "interpose" into a conversation, but rather "interpolls" into one. That is, Watson takes a poll of opinion as well as mentally consulting the files of "Interpol" (the *Inter*national *Pol*ice Organization). Watson is truly the embodiment of reserve and civility (he doesn't "implore" — that would be pushy; he tells us, "I imply").

All of this Watsonian gravity is perfect, for it heightens the irony and the humor by having the entire story told to us via Watson's straightforward delivery. The tale was, in fact, nosily recorded into Watson's notebook, one that he cornered away, but recovered: "I find it recornered in my nosebook."

Minor characters (such as Mary Atkins) are handled quite effectively. Mary's unanchored personality and her illusionary beauty is captured very succinctly: "Mary . . . pruned herselves in the mirrage." Hence the mirror only gives her a mirage of her appearance (her real prostituted body is shrunken like a prune; she wears dentures; and apparently she is "humped" by either pregnancy or deformity). The mirror does reflect one truth of Mary's life — her rage ("mir-rage").

The first scene in which Mary appears (p. 109) also contains a structural surprise — a travelogue counterpart to "Liddypool" (p. 56). "Liddypool," you recall, gave us a tourist's view of Liverpool, whereas this scene offers a guided tour of Central London.

The cabbie — a "scab" laborer who ignores the ongoing transporation strike, hence a "scabbie" — calls out "Whitehall." Whitehall is the main street leading into Trafalgar Square, but here is also being used as an obscene reference to Mary, "White hole mate!" The two best images in this section, I think, are those of the Changing of the Guards (Lennon aptly capturing the truth of this event by calling it "the Chasing of the Guards" by tourists) and the Statue of Eros in Piccadilly Circus ("the statue of Eric in Picanniny Surplass"). Actually, it's a statue of the Angel of Christian Charity, and not a statue of Eros, that perpetually flies over the center of Piccadilly Circus — but this is a common mistake. John seems to have visualized this famous landmark of London as being peopled by many unemployed and denigrated Blacks ("piccaninnies in surplus"), thus adding some political reality to this popular tourist site.

Mary's scenes also bring back a motif found first in Lennon's "bio" for *In His Own Write* and then in "Good Night Nigel" (p. 22) — the sound of laughter described as a dog's gutteral barking: "she shrieked laughing arf arfily."

The Inspector is both a ghostly figure ("In*spectre*") and a rather flat one, used primarily to keep the entangled plot going; Sydney Aspinall serves a similar function, but is given at least some literary dimension as an allusion to Neil Aspinall, who, as the Beatles' first road manager and driver, ferried the touring group around to "places of interest" all over England.

In conclusion, I consider "The Singularge Experience of Miss Anne Duffield" to be a very fine parody which indeed qualifies as one of the very best prose pieces in *A Spaniard In The Works*.

Drawing Ten (p. 106)

Technically, the preceding tale has more illustrations than any other of John's 35 stories appearing in either *Write* or *Spaniard*. This first drawing consists of a magnifying glass (the emblem of Sherlock) set upon the word "Singular." John's pun, "singularge," works because the tale isn't about one singular experience, but is in fact a largescale canvas. Thus the letters under the glass, "large," are duly enlarged — to create the magnifying effect.

Drawing Eleven (p. 107)

Here, of course, is Sherlock and Watson. Watson is depicted, and rightly so, as a small, subservient, child, clutching the hand of his mentor. Sherlock's eccentricity is apparent by the little "wings" on his hat, the nearly webbed shape of his cape, and by his large hump (not mentioned in the text).

A nice touch to this second illustration is the fact that Sherlock and Watson are wearing watches that tell different times. This visually conveys and typifies the differing personalities and points of view between these two friends.

Drawing Twelve (pp. 112--113)

Apparently just for the fun of it, John has made each of his three drawings depicting Sherlock and Watson look entirely different. This one reveals a rather gargantuan Sherlock (in stark contrast to the pole-thin portrayal in Drawing Eleven, p. 107). Watson is of Munchkin size here, shown without both his glasses and his clothes!

There is a slightly sinister aspect to this drawing, for Sherlock looks as if he might smash Watson to bits! SS2 adds some contrast to this scene by outlining Watson in green and Sherlock in brown.

As per John's trademark, there is no one scene in the story which corresponds to this drawing.

Drawing Thirteen (p. 115)

Perhaps this final illustration for "The Singularge Experience of Miss Anne Duffield" attempts to reveal Sherlock in his "dishevelled" look?! After all, Sherlock now wears glasses, has lots of hair sticking out of his cap, and boasts a full mustache and beard!

Unfortunately, our version almost completely blurs Watson's head and face, while in Pp. and SS2, Watson is clearly visisble in wire-rimmed spectacles, dark mustache, and shaved head — with a sort of "five o'clock shadow" giving it a patchy appearance.

"The Faulty Bagnose" (pp. 116--118)

The Overview

This is a poem in seven stanzas and 35 lines. It is best divided into three sections: the narrator's introduction of the preacher, who then begins a sermon from the pulpit (Stanza One); the narrator's historical review of religious freedom (contrasting the Pilgrims to modern-day Britons) in Stanzas Two and Three; and finally, a long prayer that comments on Holy Communion (the bread, the wine) and which concludes with a general chastisement against religious intolerance (Stanzas Four through Seven).

The Key Themes

Christianity viewed as a harshly judgmental, hypocritical, and virtually incoherent belief system.

The Interpretation

The erratic pattern of thought and action in "The Faulty Bagnose" makes it a confusing poem at best. Still, even given its fragmented development and obscure references, some central ideas come through.

First of all, I take the poem as a whole to be an attack against Christianity. The title reads, to my mind anyway, as "The Fault Finding and Faulty Bag of Noise."

The central figure is the Mungle. ("Mungle" is a real word meaning "a stick for stirring." Here it could be used to mean a preacher, i.e., one who stirs the ideas of a congregation.) Knowing this, the first line can now be interpreted as "Softly softly, reads the preacher" ("Threads" refers to the preacher's eyes threading through the Bible, and, of course, it also contains the word "reads"). The next four lines of the stanza constitute the preacher's sermon:

> "Thinner thorn behaviour street
> Whorg canteell whorth bee asbin?
> Cam we so all complete
> With all our faulty bagnose?"

Or, paraphrased:

> "Sinner, thou torn, behave, save our street
> What organization can tell who's worth being a has-been?

103

Came we all so complete
With all our fault-finding bag of noise?"

Admittedly, even with a paraphrase, this "sermon" remains muddled and vague (which may have been John's actual intent). There is, however, much greater clarity in the next stanza, which tells of the Pilgrims who sailed far away ("awoy" is "away" — it also echoes the phrase "ship ahoy!") in order to escape the religious persecution of King George III ("Reli*george*"). Some fell by the wayside, some on the dockside ("Sam feels on the waysock-side"), while others — after such a long voyage — only wanted to be curled on a girl ("and somforbe on a gurled").

Stanza Three clearly indicts Christian indoctrination in general, for the modern Mungle "tells us what to do" ("tells us wop to doo"). The Mungle treats the congregation like a baby who is suckling the scriptures of omnipotent Jesus ("Omnipple to our jew").

The remainder of the poem is a montage of various rituals and prayers, i.e., "Bless the communion bread" ("bless thee loaf he eating;" "loaf" also makes the "host" an "oaf"!). The Mungle is then asked to exercise more faith and bless the kitchen ("Good Mungle blaith our meathalls"). Finally, the congregation asks permission to get drunk (from the intoxicating influence of Communion wine) and to stagger around the room ("Staggerboon undie some grapeload").

The last stanza partly parodies the Lord's Prayer ("Give us this day our daily bread") becoming "Give us *thisbe* our daily tit." (This line also contains an obscure allusion. For John actually played "Thisbe" in an edited scene from Shakespeare's *A Midsummer Night's Dream*, May 6, 1964. The event was broadcast on the television show "Around the World.") Other fragments of scripture are also parodied, i.e., Joseph's "coat of many colors" is rendered "a goat of many coloureds."

The entire poem concludes with a strange invocation to the heavens: "Wiberneth all beneath unravelled," hitting home with a final angry assault: "And not so MUCH OF YER FAULTY BAGNOSE!"

Drawing Fourteen (pp. 116–117)

This bizarre illustration seems to say that behind the honest, naked exterior of the Mungle is a chained or enslaved congregation. Perhaps since the King of England has, more than once, been politically shackled by the Church, John has one chained figure wearing a crown (p. 116).

This drawing also suggests that the modern Mungle is also the music industry Mogul. I believe that John shows this by having the caged Beatle body (p. 85) tied up behind the corporate preacher (p.

117).

SS2 has both the Royal "prisoner" and the Beatle "convict" outlined in green (which appropriately creates a bolder visual separation between Mungle and slaves).

Drawing Fifteen (p. 119)

This is not an illustration, but rather a self-contained cartoon. It simply shows one of life's typical frustrations, i.e., the taking of a photograph.

The humor is derived from the father unconsciously blocking the photographer's subject, the baby that dad is holding. So dad continues to "coo to baby" — to get a good pose — even as he makes it impossible for the photo to be taken! While this goes on, mother simply stands back (looking fatter than father), and the pint-sized photographer is positively stymied.

Drawing Sixteen (pp. 120--121)

This drawing continues the theme of "blocked vision" found in Drawing Fifteen. However, in this rendition, the subject has been parlayed into a political cartoon.

We see a blind man (p. 120) casting a "blind vote," while another blind man (p. 121) apparently wants to steal him blind (of a vote)! This scene serves as an introduction to the next tale, which deals specifically with the General Election in England.

For some unknown reason, Pp. fails to print the "X" of blind man no. 1. This is a significant oversight, as the "X" is symbolic of the ignorance and illiteracy of the voting population.

Drawing Seventeen (p. 122)

This drawing effectively conveys the notion that it's useless to divide the government into two parties, when in fact the parties are Siamese twins joined at the belly! The sharp teeth on both parties signify the cannibalistic potential of modern-day politics.

"We must not forget . . . . . the General Erection" (pp. 122–123)
The Overview

This is John Lennon's account of England's general election, held mid-October, 1964. It is written as a newspaper editorial and therefore contains no plot per se, but is simply a review of the election results. It is the first of five special forms in *A Spaniard In The Works*.
The Key Themes

The usual political arena: scandals, lies, meaningless shifts of power, ridiculous promises, grim social realities that are chronically ignored, etc. etcicero.

The Interpretation

This piece is easily deciphered when one is first made aware of the actual campaigns and election results of the 1964 general election. For example, this editorial opens:

"Azue orl gnome, Harassed Wilsod
won the General Erection, with a
very small marjorie over the
Torchies. Thus pudding the Laboring Parly back into powell
after a large abscess."

Now John has brilliantly condensed much of the election right here in the first two sentences. "Azue orl gnome" works not only as a phonetic pun — "as you all know him," but also as a subtle comment upon Wilson's personality, physique, and campaign.

For a start, the election of Harold Wilson, who at age 48 was the youngest Prime Minister of the century, rode to a successful outcome "on a tide of stupendously opportune verbal gimmickry" — as Philip Norman tells us in *Shout!* So it makes sense that John's first three words reflect this "verbal gimmickry." Wilson had promised "a dynamic, expanding, confident, above-all purposive Britain." Hence, a "bright blue" future — "azure." Furthermore, Wilson was a short man; "orl" is a small tree, and a "gnome," of course, is one of a race of diminutive spirits fabled to be the guardians of earth's treasures.

Typifying the election as an "erection" brings home the idea that for politicians, nothing gets your rocks off like votes! The "Torchies" are the "Tories" or Conservative Party (Wilson represented the Labour Party), and it's true that Wilson won with a small majority ("marjorie") of just four Parliamentary seats.

The second sentence is also historically accurate: "Thus pudding the Labouring Partly back into powell after a large abcess" — or, "Thus putting the Labour Party back into power after a long absence." The fact is, the Labour Party had indeed been laboring, in part at least, to get back into power after some 13 years. And "powell" for "power" refers to Mr. Enoch Powell, a Tory Cabinet Minister from Wolverhampton South-West, who sustained his position of power because the swing vote to Labour was only 0.9 percent against him in the election.

By the way: "Pudding" for "putting" works well when you remember that in England, pudding is a form of stuffed sausage — an apt metaphor for stuffing new leaders into the old stomach of the previous administration. Using "abcess" for "absence" comically refers to the New Socialism of Harold Wilson's government, which would work to establish socialized medical services (including dentistry) in Britain.

106

I think you can see that inside the polyhedronic prose is a rather straightforward narrative; and so far, it's all factual. However, the complete truthfulness of Lennon's account fails in the third sentence (whether by design or by accident): We're told, and correctly so, that Wilson's election required the backing of the Trade Unions, headed by Frank Cousins ("the barking of the Trade Unions, heady by Frank Cunnings"). But we're also informed that Cunnings " . . . noun has a SAFE SEAT in Nuneating . . . and Frank (only 62) Bowels hasn't." The fact is, Frank Cousins (leader of the Transport and General Workers Union) was appointed by Wilson to the post of Minister of Technology, whereas Frank Bowles (who *was* 62 years old at the time of the election) was *re-elected* to his Labour Party seat, representing Nuneaton.

The second paragraph opens with a quotation that is attributed to former Prime Minister Sir Alec Douglas Home ("Sir Alice Doubtless-Whom"), who allegedly was "bitterly disappointed." John simply uses this quote in order to poke fun at the Scottish Laird and his wealth (and political indifference): "smirking on his 500,000 acre estate in Scotland." The real Sir Home did issue a statement immediately after he had offered up his resignation, but is was hardly indifferent; he made it quite clear that he would lead the Tories in opposition.

Thus the third paragraph rightly establishes that the Tories, now the official opposition ("now in apperition"), must convince the country that they still have "the capable qualities of such disable men" as "the very late Harrods McMillion"! You might recall from "You Might Well Arsk" (p. 57) that Harold Macmillan resigned as Prime Minister due to the fallout of the Keeler scandal. Lennon himself alludes to this in the next sentence, "What, you arsk, happened to Answerme Enos (ex Prim Minicar)." "Answerme" refers to the official interrogation and investigation of John Profumo in the House of Commons; "Answer me!" "Enose" is an obscure word meaning "to choke" or "to hamper" which, by luck or design, fits well into this "scandal" section.

But Lennon's language is even more precise in its political punning, i.e., "The very *late* Harrods McMillion" tells us a great deal. First, it was the opinion of many that Harold Macmillan was literally "very late" in resigning as Prime Minister (a year to 18 months too late). The "McMillion" refers to the fact that Macmillan, as Prime Minister, headed the Tory or Conservative Party and, as the *London Times* has it (October, 1964): "Conservatives provide the image that succeeds electorially in . . . affluent areas." "That Suez pudding" alludes to the delicate and complex politics regarding who exactly had control over the Suez Canal, a hot controversy during Macmillan's administration.

107

The editorial concludes with more specific election results, i.e., "the great roles played out by Huge Foot and Dingie" refers to the new ministerial appointments of Sir Hugh Foot (Minister of State for Foreign Affairs) and of Mr. Dingle Foot (Solicitor General). The line "We must not forget Joke Grimmace (LIB)" comments on the jokingly small number of parliamentary seats held by the Liberal Party. During this general election, the Liberal Party saw only four gains and two losses — including "J. Grimond," representing Orkney and Zetland (thus giving the Liberals a total of nine seats).

John throws in some silliness as well: "G.P. Ostmen" looks official or "political" enough, but "G.P.O." simply stands for "General Post Office," and therefore "G. Postman" needs good shoes ("clogs") to keep the yuletide mail from "clogging" up ("we must not forget to Post Early for Christsake")!

"Lastly but not priest," Lennon leaves us with an ominous note regarding nuclear war. The general election results were published in the *London Times*, primarily on October 16 and 17, 1964. October 16 also marked the day that China announced the testing of a nuclear bomb. Harold Wilson's eagerness to arm Britain, coupled with the growing threat of world atomic warfare, led John to close with "We must not forget to put the clocks back when we all get bombed"!

It is important to realize that "The General Erection" is structurally and stylistically a vast improvement over the one-liners of "You Might Well Arsk." Here John convincingly demonstrates a proficiency with biting, subtle political satire. His attacks are streamlined and specific; they generally reveal a steady hand and a thought-provoking point of view.

Drawing Eighteen (p. 123)

Obviously Mrs. Wilson did not appear nude on television to "show her toilets"! What John indicts with this illustration is the Labour Party's general TV blitz during the campaign. T.A.M. (Television Audience Measurement) was reporting in the *Times* that "The Labour Party achieved the highest national viewing figure among . . . party political broadcasts."

John blatantly portrays the wife of the new Prime Minister as the quintessential dingbat, kneeling before a shitpot throne-of-a-husband. Thus Lennon's summation of the British "General Erection" is concisely rendered in this drawing — with a "Vote for Harold" sign placed directly over the toilet!

Drawing Nineteen (pp. 124–125)

This is a picture of war. Specifically, we observe 23 people fighting — with spiked clubs, closed fists, swords, knives, hand grenades, and guns. These warmongers are kicking, swinging, jumping, falling, and running – all to inflict bodily harm to each other!

Such a crowd scene of chaotic violence effectively serves to introduce the next tale – of a British Declaration of War.

"Benjaman Distasteful" (pp. 124--125)
The Overview

The scene is set in Parliament. We are told by an unidentified narrator that Benjaman has just stopped speaking (while a spy is summarily removed). We then hear part of Benjaman's message: a declaration of war! The narrator looks around the House of Commons for a reaction before launching into a speech that compliments Benjaman and supports the idea of war.

But to the narrator's surprise, Benjaman is *not* pleased. (Even so, the narrator is nonetheless impressed by Ben's great knowledge, and he is further convinced that Ben will have no strong opposition.)

Benjaman continues speaking, only to put down the narrator (who in frustration asks Benjaman, "Why – why?"). The scene abruptly closes with "To this day I'll never know."

The Key Themes

War is forged in a jumble of words.

The Interpretation

At a glance (or even a pause), this piece reads incoherently; this, I believe, is the point. The Parliament (whose very name means to "parlay" ideas into policy) no longer houses humane and civilized oratory; it now sets the stage for vague but militaristic messages.

Benjamin Disraeli (Prime Minister during 1868 and 1874--1880) is used here to represent British Imperialism. His speech is both deadly and a breach of truth: "his grave flow of speach". Ben has a spy lugged off, as he could see the spy peek-a-booing behind his scarf and cigarette ("lug off a cigarf he knew where peeky boon").

Benjaman's actual speech is typically weasel-worded: "It were all nok," he says, meaning "It was all not O.K., or naught." Benjaman simply wants to wrap up a war ("warp") and start another Crusade after the Holy Grail ("grale regrowth"). Furthermore, he wants to replenish Her Majesty's troops ("replenishamatsaty troop") and have harlots either readily wed or else ready for warfare ("and harlas a wedreally to fight").

The narrator is hardly the voice of reason, for he rejoins "I say get a battlyard pussload, ye scrurry navvy" (meaning, "fill the Royal fleet with prostitutes").

All of a sudden Benjaman turns against our narrator, telling him "it's a pretty poor show when somebody of my stature has to be placed or deposited on the same level as you, young slave." – Or, "its a pritty poreshow when somebottle of my statue has to place yongslave on my deposite."

The narrator's squeal of "Why — why?" is all anyone can ask regarding war, but I hope it's not "THE END" — as this piece unhappily concludes.

"The Wumberlog (or The Magic Dog)" (pp. 126–133)

The Overview

This is by far the longest poem that John Lennon ever wrote. The poem consists of 30 stanzas (121 lines)! "The Wumberlog" is the poignant story of a lonely little boy who dies of a broken heart (after his only friend, his Uncle Joe, passes away).

The structure of the poem is the boy's journey towards his reunion with Uncle Joe. In Stanzas One–Four the boy prepares for his departure; he packs his clothes, notebooks, food and money, and imagines who he'll meet. Stanzas Five–Seven introduce a Curlew (who leaves the scene almost instantly) and the Magic Dog. The Magic Dog stays just long enough to give the boy an enchanted boat. It's this boat that will transport the boy to "the land where all the secrets hid."

In Stanzas Eight–Fourteen the Wumberlog (a "highly feathered species" of bird) joins the boating boy (to guide him, just in case he's gotten "lost at sea"). The boy's initial fear abates when the Wumberlog tells him "I friendly — always."

Stanza Fifteen forms the crucial transition from dreamworld to Underworld:

> "And soon the land came interview,
> A 'tastic sight for sure,
> An island with an eye to see
> To guide you into shore."

Stanzas Sixteen–Twenty feature a welcoming party. Here the boy meets and converses with a tree, a thing, and an apple (as well as being reunited with the Magic Dog and the Curlew). In Stanzas 21–22, the boy restates his mission: " 'Where are all the peoble, please,/ Wot live when they are dead?' " A carrot tells him he must first "eat a plate of me" — a rather whimsical rite of passage into this fantastic island.

Stanzas 23–27 bring the boy closer and closer to "the wondrous peoble." But as he approaches his destination, he notices that these people are literally burying each other:

> "In fact they took it turns apiece
> To lay down in the ground
> And shove the soil upon the heads
> Of all their friends around."

Stanzas 28–29 finally reunite the boy with his beloved Uncle Joe. Joe is sad the boy has found him, but the boy is happy to share the grave with his only friend. The poem concludes with Stanza 30,

110

as the boy and his uncle, together now for eternity, bid the world "a fond goodbye."

The Key Themes

Death viewed as a homecoming: the final family reunion.

The Interpretation

Both stylistically and imaginistically, this poem is the direct precursor to the lyrics of three important songs: *Tomorrow Never Knows*, August 1966; *Strawberry Fields Forever*, February 1967; and *Lucy In The Sky With Diamonds*, June 1967. The motif of "floating downstream" comes together (in this poem) for the first time with the image of picturing "yourself in a boat on a river" while traveling to some eternal Elysian Field.

The actual plot of the poem is based upon rather traditional mythology. It was commonly believed by the Ancient Greeks that upon death, the spirit journeys to the underworld — to Hades. This voyage is taken in a boat or ferry, with a Guide, upon the River Styx. In John's version, the boat docks at the Elysian Fields, the everlasting dwelling place of righteous souls . . . where the inhabitants live with their heads sticking out of the ground.

Now Lennon's reworking of myth is humorous — very tongue-in-cheek. We smile when we see the boy pack his food stamps ("voucher") as he anticipates encountering some magical dwarfs under a tree. (You probably recall Lennon's Buddha-Under-A-Tree-Awaiting-Enlightenment motif, used in "I Sat Belonely," p. 66.) There is also the private allusion to the daily "giggles" that the Beatles were experiencing from that harassed substance known as marijuana ("The larfing leaping Harrist*weed*").

Most striking are the lines quite similar to a phrase in *Strawberry Fields Forever* —

> "I would, if only, but
> You see — well — yes, oh dear,
> The thing is — "

— lines which are transformed by the song into the following:

> "That is, you can't, you know, tune in —
> But it's all right —
> That is, I think it's not too bad."

Such calculated tentativeness is found throughout this poem *and* in John's song. In the poem, reality is ever shifting; is the Wumberlog the same creature as the Magic Dog? Is the Curlew really the Wumberlog? Who is Thorpy Grumphlap? In fact, during the boy's trip many creatures enter and then disappear without explanation or warning!

Whatever seriousness the poem builds to, John (as usual) subverts:

"With just their heads above the ground
They bade a fond goodbye,
With all the people shouting out
'Heres mud into your eye!'
(And there certainly was.)"

Unfortunately, John could become embarrassed by his own "heavy" or serious side; he used Ringo's phrase *Tomorrow Never Knows* to take the edge off the philosophy in that song, and the title *Yer Blues* certainly undercuts the notion that this is a "real" blues tune. Had John been less reticent on this count, perhaps "The Wumberlog" might have had a more potent, and thus more satisfying, message.

Drawing Twenty (p. 128)

Here we see a scene which was omitted from "The Wumberlog," in which the Magic Dog apparently is approaching the gates to Elysium.

SS2 colors the walls (as well as the Magic Dog) in green; the text, however, states that the Magic Dog is "all black."

Drawing Twenty-One (p. 131)

Here the "little boy" of the poem is depicted (without explanation) as a fully grown, mature man. He sits in the boat without oars, and with the Wumberlog standing on his head (presumably "guiding" the boat).

In the background is a large fish, blowing a fountain of water into the air from its blowhole. Both Pp. and SS2 have the boat shaded in.

Drawing Twenty-Two (pp. 132--133)

This is the last illustration for "The Wumberlog." It seems to accurately depict the "diggers" putting each other to rest . . . in the ground. If viewed outside the context of the poem, it could suggest the Beatles being buried alive by the "flowers" of fame, the love of their fans: a macabre twist to life being no bed of roses. In fact, there are four people being buried here, not merely two (as in the text).

Drawing Twenty-Three (p. 134)

This hilariously funny soul is none other than Araminta Ditch. She sits (or slumps) in a strange posture indeed, unmindful of her nakedness — which, according to the story, is her perpetual condition. (She is "conti*nude*.") Arminta is dangling a dwarfish man from her left hand; more than likely, the man is either Fred or Richard in the text. It hardly matters, though; the point is that Araminta totally eclipses her peers.

The Overview

This is the story of Araminta — the woman who could not stop laughing. The action begins as we follow Araminta through a typical day: she rises from bed laughing; she laughs through breakfast and the morning paper; she howls on the bus going to work, etc.

The scene switches focus to the reactions of various people to Araminta's perpetual laughter. Her boyfriend Fred says it causes his family and himself "tribulation and embarrassment;" Araminta, of course, finds Fred's remark laughable. And Araminta's neighbor Mrs. Camsby says she'll go insane if Araminta doesn't stop! (Mirth provoking madness?!)

Soon the local folks begin holding meetings to discuss ways to "quell this mirth." Richard (another boyfriend) testifies that Araminta is driving him to drink. Mrs. Camsby then suggests to the Vicar that he "exercise" (exorcize) it out of her — after which the story again switches focus. We now find Araminta herself seeking help, from Reverend Lionel Hughes. She tells him "The trouble with the people around here is that they have forgotten how to laugh." The Reverend is powerless to help, and Araminta angrily departs.

The tale concludes with Araminta having outlived all of her detractors. And at eighty years of age, she finally laughs herself happily into death.

The Key Themes

"The trouble with people . . . is that they have forgotten, I repeat, how to laugh."

The Interpretation

You've probably noticed that this story is structurally quite similar to "Victor Triumphs Again and Mrs. Weatherby Learns a Lesson" (p. 79, *In His Own Write*). Here we see yet another Innocent persecuted by town and clergy. The difference between the two stories is in the characters: Araminta is a protagonist of significantly greater depth than Victor Hardly. For Araminta Ditch is actually a "Holy Clown" or "Wise Fool." As such, she's truly alive, authentic, and attuned to Truth: nothing is more honest, human, or liberating than laughter. Araminta, then, is a kind of sage, "larfing as usual with that in*sage* larf." But to people who live solely by habit, having lost the solace of spontaneity, Araminta is just a fool — that is, she's completely "insage" (insane).

All the "dead" people around Araminta are clearly threatened by her unbridled, unwavering and totally joyous mode of expression. "I hope she's not all larfing at me," her defensive neighbor laments — never wondering how she herself could share in Araminta's happiness. Interestingly, Lennon's language itself informs us that Araminta's enemies are in need of enlightenment; i.e., the bus conductor

113

diagnoses Aramina's laughter as the result of drunkenness (he and the passengers think she's "*pub*bled"). However, John makes us see that the conductor himself is mistaken: he's a "*con*doctor"!

Araminta's laughter may be viewed as a metaphor for artistic or existential freedom: certainly those without it are often baffled or angered by those who have it. "Thy lafter causes sitch tribulation," says Fred, her puerile boyfriend ("boyfred"). His use of vaulted biblical language reveals his puritanical, overly zealous reaction to Araminta's sweet laughter. But Araminta correctly categorizes Fred's outburst as just so much fetid air ("outburp").

John takes all the citizens of Araminta's community to task with just one word: "neighbores." That is to say, they are both braying and boring! And Araminta's (other) boyfriend, Richard, hardly fares better than Fred, and probably worse: he's both a "boyfiend" and a "Turd"!

The truth is, all but Araminta have lost a healthy perspective on life; with our heroine, at least, there's "a certain insight left." This makes Araminta a problem, and the townsfolk decide that something has to be done: "Obvouslieg samting hed tow be doon." Their words reveal how this "obvious league" ("obvouslieg") wants to keep Araminta in check — or in "tow" — in order to effect her doom ("doon"). But Araminta, of course, has the last laugh!

It should be noted here that John Lennon's mother, Julia, may have influenced the point of view in this story. She was said to have found humor in almost everything. Furthermore, she often embarrassed family and friends by her uncompromising and iconoclastic behavior, i.e., wearing panties on her head as a hat, or donning eyeglasses without lenses, etc.

I feel that behind the ludicrous surface of this tale is the smiling soul of a Buddha (or, at the very least, the winsome wit of a Shakespearian court jester).

Drawing Twenty-Four (p. 139)
Apparently this is a drawing of Araminta's cats! In the story we're told that Mrs. Cramsby (a neighbor) took care of them "whilst Araminta was at work."

Pp. has both of the cats shaded in a light grey, whereas SS2 colors the seated cat green (with brown eyes) and the standing cat grey (with green eyes).

Drawing Twenty-Five (pp. 140--141)
This is yet another self-contained cartoon. Both characters are "buskers," or street performers, and both play the trumpet to survive. It's a funny scene, however, for John includes such novelty items as a sign on a sighted man and dark glasses on a blind man's

dog. Lennon loved to capture ludicrousness, and here he does a fine job of it.

"Cassandle" (pp. 142–143)

The Overview

This is the second "special" format found in *A Spaniard In The Works* (the first being "We must not forget . . . the General Erection," pp. 121–123). "Cassandle" is a parody of Casandra's column appearing in *The Daily Mirror*. As such it has no plot per se, but rather consists of three short commentaries. In "You all know me" (p. 142) Casandra laments his telephone service; in "The way I see it" (p. 142) he attacks the Beatles; and in "Koms der revolution" (p. 143) he lodges his complaint against caviar!

The Key Themes

Gossip columnists are egocentric idiots.

The Interpretation

The critic for the *London Times Literary Supplement* found this selection to be "a wholly untactful parody of Casandra." The *Times* may have a point, for John does venture to describe the real Casandra as "yer borein' owld gassbag," and "a bald old get with glasses"! Furthermore, John's assault on Casandra's character began even earlier in *Spaniard*, for in "Snore Wife" (p. 104) he is called "de fairy in the land"!

Tactless or not, Lennon successfully indicts all yellow press journalism – those gossipy tabloids with their "Kiss And Tell" ("Cass-an-dle") commentaries. John's pointed pen aims to puncture the megalomaniacal posturing of such "writers."

For example, in "You all know me" (a perfectly arrogant headline), Cassandle refers to himself no less than 14 times – and the column itself only has about 15 lines! Thus all we hear about is "my telephone . . . my Aunt Besst . . . my famous column with a picture of me" – etc. et circular!

In "The way I see it," we have a variation of the structure of "A Letter" (p. 39). In the earlier entry, a "fan" praises the Beatles; here John himself (disguised as Casandra) brutally characterizes the Beatles as "these incredible sleasy backward, bad, deaf monkeys, parsing as entertainers, with their FLOPTOPPED hair." By the way, this section of "Cassandle" is in fact Joycean: Joyce also wrote "letters" (using a pseudonym) to "attack" his own work:

> "*A Litter to Mr. James Joyce*
> Dear Mister Germ's Choice,
> in gutter dispear I am taking my
> pen toilet you know that I have
> been reading . . . your 'Work In
> Progress' [*Finnegans Wake*]

You must not stink I am attempting to ridicul . . . but I am so
disturd by my inhumility to on-
thorstand most of the impsloca-
tions constrained in your work
that . . . I am writing you, dear
mysterre Shame's Voice, to let
you no how bad I feeloxerab out
it all.

Please froggive my t'Emeritus
and any inconvince that may have
been caused by this litter.

Yours very tass
Vladimir Dixon"!

Returning to "The way I see it," this section of "Cassandle"
also echoes Field Marshal Lord Montgomery's often-quoted remark
that "a good smell ["spell"] in the Army would cure them." (Montgomery made his first appearance in *In His Own Write* in "Scene
three Act one," p. 40.) So John definitely has some fun criticizing
the critics in this portion of "Cassandle."

Finally, there's "Kom der revolution." The headline sounds as if
some serious political statement is about to be made; alas, it's only
about 1) a show-dog who loves caviar, and 2) Casandra himself, who
doesn't!

Drawing Twenty-Six (p. 143)

Both SS2 and Pp. have made a fine aesthetic choice with this
"inset photo" of Casandra. The inset is placed above "Kom der
revolution," and *all* the copy is pushed upon *one* page, making
"Cassandle" look more like a tabloid. But a truly special touch is the
full-page blowup of the inset, which appears directly opposite the
column. Needless to say, Casandra's egoism is much more graphically
featured in SS2 and Pp. than in our version.

Drawing Twenty-Seven (p. 144)

This is a very straightforward drawing of "The National Health
Cow." It stands, however, as the penultimate addition to Lennon's
considerably large menagerie. Chances are you might not have realized that thus far in *Write* and *Spaniard*, Lennon's gallery of animals
has included drawings of dogs (John's favorite animal), cats, birds
(budgies, parrots, Wumberlogs, etc.), flies (creatures often over-
looked by most artists!), snakes, elephants, giraffes, rhinos, frogs,
horses, spiders, bugs, and even a fish — not to mention the herd of
sheep coming into view very soon — see pp. 156–157!

The only conspicuous aspect of this cow? Her udders are in fact
disposable bottles!

"The National Health Cow" (pp. 144–145)

The Overview

This is a poem in five stanzas and 20 lines. It tells the story of a man who strolls into a farmyard looking to milk "the cow with glasses." This cow appears, and she's quite relieved to be milked, as she hasn't been "milked for days."

The lad asks the cow why she's been ignored, and she replies, " 'perhaps it's 'cause/MY milk comes out in bottles.' " The poem abruptly ends when the boy kills the cow with a brick!

The Key Themes

Life is short and violence long.

The Interpretation

Ah, yes — shades of "Good Dog Nigel" (pp. 22–23) and "Randolf's Party" (p. 31) from *In His Own Write*. That is to say, their structures are similar: an innocent tone is established, the reader's empathy is engaged, and then BAM! Somebody, or some animal, is KILLED! — just like that, and apparently from out of nowhere. Now *this* variation of the structure is a bit more ominous than its predecessors; this time we have a premeditated murderer.

The farmyard is clearly "cased out" (our killer waiting until "no-one was about"). Our culprit has even patterned out the cow's footsteps, "Treading past the troubles" (with "troubles" suggesting previous knowledge). Furthermore, he calls out to one particular cow (having apparently done this once or twice before, as the cow is not startled or suspicious). And just as this poor cow's discomfort is relieved, our killer strikes "in a tick," and "The cow fell dead all sudden."

John's black humor is heightened here, as it is in "Nigel," by an almost fairytale style in the verse. Given Lennon's "swallowed rage" during this period of his life, this kind of instant death must have heartily appealed to John's sardonic side.

Drawing Twenty-Eight (p. 146)

Apparently this is a picture of the editor who handles complaints for the *London Times*. He is seen angrily barking into a telephone (hardly the diplomat here), standing below a sign proclaiming "Readers Letters" ("Readers Lettuce").

This illustration captures the "tone" of the piece that follows, but it is somewhat misleading: the "editor" appears only in a footnote to the letter in question.

"Readers Lettuce" (p. 147)

The Overview

This is the third special format to appear in *A Spaniard In The Works*. It's a "letter to the editor," and it concerns an article that theoretically appeared in the *Sunday Times*. (Of interest: *Mersey Beat*'s mailbag was called "Readers Letters.")

The letter (in response to the article) features Jennifer Cough's defense of the Honorable Gentleman Norman Ccough (no relation!) from the attack of one Mr. Mothballs. Jennifer cites Mr. Ccough's various worldwide organizations, his humanitarian speech at the Assembly of Natives, and his unprecedented "Blessed Old Widows" Charter, etc. Jennifer also asserts that Mr. Mothballs has "taken leave of his senses" if he believes Indonesia will attack Australia. Her letter closes with Jennifer's personal request for a photo of Mr. Ccough.

The piece formally concludes with the editor's rather pointless footnote.

The Interpretation

This letter is calculated to appear quite convoluted in its indignation; it stands as a layman's self-important attempt at a "critical" style. Lennon's pun on the corresondent's name quickly reveals Jennifer's letter to be a farce: "Jennifarse." Indeed, we suspect that this letter is simply an irate wife's defense of her husband. (Tagging on "no relations" after her signature probably refers to her present sexual status with hubby!) Of course, Mothballs charges that Ccough is impotent ("social impurdent"); Mothballs' very name, however, confirms his *own* lack of sexual prowess!

The language is very clever; i.e., "Indo*negro*" reflects Mothballs' prejudice against people of color. (He also assumes that predominantly "white" Australia is the target of "black" Indonesia.)

This humorous epistle adds variety to the book (though *In His Own Write*'s "A Letter," p. 39, is more interesting – no doubt due to the Beatle history it incorporates). Both our version and the others (SS2 and Pp.) do an effective job of making the print look like a poorly typed letter (thus adding a visual touch quite appropriate to this piece).

"Silly Norman" (pp. 148–151)
The Overview

This story begins with Norman burning his Christmas presents in the fireplace. He is, in fact, quite baffled that he is the recipient of so many letters and parcels; (not only does he get more and more each year, but they're from people he doesn't even know!).

Norman decides to take a break and enjoy his favorite snack – a cup of tea with chocolate cookies. Norman goes to the sink to get water for the tea and finds (to his dismay) that there isn't any; he fails to realize the pipes are frozen. So Norman figures he'll go next door. He bundles up, goes outside, and (to his amazement) he finds there are no houses in sight! Norman falls to the ground, fearing that God has destroyed the earth.

Norman's mother arrives! She's somewhat confused by her son's hysteria. He tells her that God has ended the world, whereupon she calmly informs him that no one has *ever* lived near him (and that Norman himself always claimed he preferred privacy). Norman praises his mom and admits it was silly of him to forget. And so mother and son, arms linked, walk back into the house.

Once inside, they discover the tap is on, and so they prepare tea. The tale closes with a little prayer that tells us no matter how dark life becomes, God's light will always shine through.

The Key Themes

The delicate balance between sanity and insanity; the fear of isolation and our attendant terror when we believe we're alone. Also, the balm of companionship (and the healing power of a mother's solicitous love).

The Interpretation

In "Forewords and Afterwords," I state that "Silly Norman" is the single most difficult of Lennon's stories. Now I can be more precise: "Silly Norman" forms the most significant, fully sustained and thorough use of polyhedronic prose in all of Lennon's work. John's verbal innovation is nowhere keener, nor does his sense of absurdity ever appear more elemental and raw.

Because of the complexity of "Silly Norman," and the need to establish clearly its literal meaning, I believe the story warrants a complete, word-for-word paraphrase. From this foundation I will proceed to highlight particularly difficult and comedic aspects of this singularly extraordinary story.

Silly Norman

" 'I really don't know what to make
of these,' said Norman, as he sorted
through his Christmas post. 'It seems
that I get more letters and parcels
than (what) I know people, it surprises
me more and more each year, as more of
these parcels keep coming. I really
don't know who all they [every] body
are — sending it; all this.' He
climbed quietly to the fire, shoving

119

a few more rubbish on. 'It's come to a
pretty part when I don't even know where
they came from.' Norman [re] cooped, on
steady keel, and promptly went into the
kitchen to put up the kettle on. 'I
might as well make me a cup of tea. I
might as well have a chocolate cookie as
well, while I do nod [off].' So saying
so he marched off to that teapot and
takes it to that sink: but to his great
surprise — what! — but no water. 'Good
Harolds! what's all of this going on?
Do my eyes deceive me? Am I not looking
at my own sink under ice, and there be no
water?' He was quite right, lo! the
water didn't no, appear, try as he might.

Of course we all know why this water does
not come, because the tanks they are all
freezed up, all of them, they're all freezed up. Norman did not know that, for
Norman he's a silly man — yes — Norman
is so soft. 'OH deary me! Oh woe is me,
what can I do, there are no waters to
make a cup of tea, and my mother, she's
after coming pretty soon too. I shall
have to go next door, perhaps they might
all have tea.' So Norman he gently puts
his hat and coat on, making sure to wrap
himself up like his mommy tells him,
brush behind the ears, and out of the
front he goes. To his true amazement, he
finds not a house, not a house in sight!
What on earth is happening? — why —
there is not a house to be seen, not anywhere for miles about. 'Good God, which
art in heaven, hallowed [humbled] be thy
Norm[an]! Is this not the end of the world?
Surely to gossip, I am not the last man on

earth?' He fell suddenly to the ground
weeping and wailing crying [and drizzling]
to the Lord above to save him or just
spare a friend or two. 'I will give of all
my worldly possessions, all my foreign
stamps, all my classical records, all
my fave rave pictures of Humpty Little-
sod (the great nothing). All these,
wondrous Sailor up above, I offer you
if only you will save me!'

Norman's mother, who you remember was
coming to tea, was shocked when she
came across him lying on the floor,
thus crying. 'My dear Norman!' she
screeched, 'What in God's name are you
doing, why are you carrying on this way?'
She jogged slightly over to her own son,
with a worried look in her eye. 'Please
don't carry on like this my son, tell
Mother what's the matter.' Norman
raised himself slowly and sadly looked
at her. 'Cannot you see, mother, God
has end[ed] the world. I only went to
get some water, and then it didn't work,
so I went to go, next to try a neighbor
and I saw what had happened — God had
ended the world. I saw nothing —
everywhere there were no neighbors. Oh
Mother what is happening?' Norman's
mother took one long look at him with a
disbelieving expression on her face.
'My God! Norman what are you talking
about son? Don't you [re]member that
there have been nobody living here,
ever? Remember when, the day [we] first
moved in, how you'd say — "Thank heaven
there are no people about this place, I
want to be alone?" Have you forgotten all

this?' Norman looked up at his mom (still crying) with tears in his eye, saying — 'Mother, thou art the one, the power of attorney, for heaven's sake, amen. Thank you dear mother, I had truly forgotten. I am a silly Norman!' They both linked arms and walks brightly to the house.

'Fancy me forgetting that nobody lives around here, mother! Fancy me forgetting that!' They each laughed together as they headed for the kitchen — and lo! — the water runs again (the sunbeams had done it), and they both had tea, both of them. Which just shows you —

> 'However black you two may be
> In time they'll pass away
> Have faith and trust in BBC —
> God's light make bright your day!

AMEN (and Michaelmas dentist.)

Now that the entire tale is reduced to its purely denotative level, we can more easily zero in on its rich connotative aspects. First, Norman is actually an international or composite character — an Everyman, rather than a single personality. Thus Norman's speech patterns continually lapse into or fuse with different dialects: West Indian ("woot tow mak of these"); Irish ("mither . . . she arther coming"); German ("Doe mein ice desleeve me"); French ("surplizeses moi moor et moor") etc. Furthermore, Lennon also employs common English slang ("wogged" is drived from "golliwog," and "wog" is somewhat the British equivalent for "nigger." A golliwog doll looks like a racist caricature of a Black minstrel). There is also "pop" slang ("fave rave") and parodied biblical language, i.e., "Goody Griff, which artery in Heffer harold by thy norm." By the way, James Joyce also played on these opening lines of the Lord's Prayer, i.e., "Oura vatars that arred in Himmal haloed be her eve, her singtime sung, her rill be run, unhemmed as it is uneven"! (*FW* 599.05; 104.2–3).

John's elastic language tells us about Norman all right, but the story is about all of us. For the key conflict in the tale is the archetypal, human fear of total isolation, of feeling like an "ignormed man" or a "no man" (John, of course, went on to elaborate this theme many times in his music: *Nowhere Man, Isolation, I'm Scared, Cold Turkey*, etc.). Edward Albee, one of America's most superlative dramatists, also dealt with this same nameless terror; in 1966 it formed the spiritual spine of his Pulitzer Prize winning play, *A Delicate Balance*.

In both Lennon's story and Albee's play, this elemental fear seems "silly" at first (because we are never given concrete reasons to justify its horrendous impact on the central characters). And yet, this nameless terror is very real to Norman, and becomes actually frightening when experienced onstage in Albee's play; and soon we begin to suspect that we also have such terrors hidden in us. In other words, to be human is to be both powerful and helpless — in short, to experience a curious cohabitation of applied rationality and irrational fear.

Norman's fear is assuaged by a metaphorical "mother." Now, it makes sense that John's Everyman would truly yearn for "mother," since Lennon himself lost his real mother *twice* (as a child, when Julia left him to be raised by his Aunt Mimi; and in his early teens, by Julia's untimely death. It's also not surprising to learn that John's most frequently used term of endearment for Yoko was "mother").

In this story, however, "mother" is a very ambivalent figure indeed: she is "Muddle" as well as "mother." In fact, this tale embodies an emotional dilemma commonly referred to as the Madonna/Whore complex — a dichotomy which Norman reflects by praising his mother (pedestalizing her) on the one hand, while Lennon describes her as a common tart on the other. (She's seen as some "toots" on the street, combing her hair: "Norman's mother, who you remembrane, was a *combing tooty*.")

Even with all of Norman's pain and emotional vacillation, "Silly Norman" manages to formally conclude on the upbeat. Mom arrives, bringing nurturing companionship with her; she, in fact, brings laughter back to her son. The tap water runs again; the sun shines; and a lovely tea is prepared and enjoyed. Still (in typical Lennon fashion), a subverting footnote is offered — just in case we forget how "gossip" turns into "goosestep."

The closing verse is difficult to interpret, but for me it is saying one of two things. First, that no matter how depressed one becomes (like a "black tower" in Liverpool), in time the depression passes away ("bassaway," since the bass approximates our being "low"). And secondly, on a somewhat lighter note, if we trust in media (the all-seeing Eye of the *B*ritish *B*roadcasting *C*orporation), "God" will bless us.

A variation on this interpretation is that no matter how many

Beat groups vie for audiences, TV will eventually make live performances passe. (The "Tower" Ballroom was the largest venue in the "Pool," meaning Liverpool and environs, i.e., Blackpool; it may also be "black" because the Beatles performed with Little Richard at The Tower in 1962.)

Irrespective of the above interpretation, John's final word is hardly reassuring, for both God (that Great "Riff" or "Grief" in the sky, i.e., "Griff") and the BBC will make "amends" ("amens") with the Nazi-like moguls seated in the hotseat ("dentist" chair)!

Drawing Twenty-Nine (p. 149)

This is a portrait of Silly Norman, standing in all his anthropological glory! Importantly, our Everyman is being *touched* by someone; almost all of John's drawings show people "reaching for" others, but never actually making contact.

The most surprising version of this drawing is in the Pp. edition: Norman is completely black! This comes as a real shock (particularly if you've only seen our version), even though there is textually some justification for it (the "wog" pun and the repeated use of "Moor").

SS2 offers a surprise of a different color: Norman is completely green! However, there is no justification that textually warrants this choice. And yet, the original Jonathan Cape first edition of *A Spaniard In The Works* has Norman in green, so it's possible that John stipulated to such a coloration.

The little man and tiny dog appear in the drawing, though neither one is mentioned in the story itself.

Drawing Thirty (p. 152)

This is a portrait of Mr. Boris Morris, whose rather meager exploits are chronicled in the next story. Here Boris is attempting to look gallant — by offering a single flower to his (unseen) hostess. His "charming" image is tainted, however, by this turned head and closed eyes — suggesting that Boris' true status is that of a charlatan.

For some reason, Pp. depicts Mr. Boris Morris as Black. The SS2 version stops short of Pp. by making Boris' skin dark gray. Yet all that the text provides us is the fact that Boris is Jewish!

"Mr. Boris Morris" (pp. 152–153)

The Overview

This is the story of Boris, "a man of great reknown," whose fame hinges on his ability to crash posh parties. Once he infiltrates a "do," Boris mingles — taking unflattering (and hopefully compromising) photographs of the guests. He does this at the garden party of Miss Pearl Staines, and at the yearly Oriental Fete. However, when he attempts to repeat his act at a masquerade party (The Hunt Ball), a guest reaps revenge by shooting Boris in the face.

The tale closes with Boris standing in his bathroom, musing in the mirror about how he must "fix this blob of mine," i.e., his poor face! His wife concurs, and the story abruptly halts.

The Key Themes

We all prefer wearing masks (our public persona, a tailored appearance) to cover our naked faces.

The Interpretation

There is something admirable about Mr. Boris Morris; at least he attempts (via candid photos, "candy shots") to reveal the "truth" hidden behind party confections. For instance, our first hostess is allegedly a "polished pearl," inviting her guests to a sumptuous garden party. The truth is, this event is run by a "stained" woman with her garden party resembling a refuse dump ("Miss Staines . . . garbage partly").

Boris' presence is a thorn to the mask-makers, for he enjoys asking questions that reveal reality; i.e., Miss Staines' facade of generosity is cut short with Boris' question, "how come you never invited your sister to the do?"

Facades fall by the wayside as Lennon's language gleefully reveals the paltry face behind the ornate mask. In one case a Duke is duped by his very name, reducing his titled nobility to the occupational standing of a lowly hospital orderly, i.e., "The Dupe of Bedpan." Another aristocratic front, The Annual Oriental Fete, is rendered as "anyearly jap festival," clearly exposing the token nature of the event.

Needless to say, Boris' behavior arouses anger among the elite. Thus we are not surprised when (after Boris shows up at the classy "Hunt Ball") he is indeed "hunted" down by a guest and shot. It is also not shocking that the other high-falutin' guests mistake Boris' bloody, disfigured face for "a clever mask" — for when one is accustomed to lies, the truth can seem quite unreal.

Boris remains undaunted as the story closes; he ponders how to fix his face, so he can again infiltrate the high society scene. Unfortunately, Boris's wife is too stupid or self-involved to realize what her husband's escapades are all about. She thinks he's "putting on" a face to please her!

One final note: The *London Times Literary Supplement* stated that this story (plus other selections in *A Spaniard In The Works*) suffers from a "kind of insensitive wit that allows the author, no doubt, unconsciously, again and again to indulge in the old anti-semitic game of writing 'jew' with a small 'j.' " I feel this charge is without foundation, since Lennon only used "Jew" (whether in upper or lower cases) in an *integral* way, both in his stories and in his poetry.

125

For example, in "A Spaniard In The Works" the word "Jew" is used simply as a phonetic pun to bring out Jesus' Spanish accent (hence "news" is written as "jews," p. 98. Furthermore, "jews," in this instance, is not capitalized because "news" wouldn't require capitalization). In "The Faulty Bagnose," the line "Omnipentent to our Jesus" is rendered "Oamnipple to our jew" (p. 117). Here the lowercase usage is justified because the speaker, a Protestant preacher (and not a Rabbi of Judaism) is underplaying Jesus' Jewish heritage.

Finally, in "Mr. Boris Morris" Boris is referred to by others as "the jew with a view"! But in this story Boris's Jewish background is pivotal to the action. First it helps explain why he is banned from posh parties, by showing the "lowercase" station these party guests attribute to Jews in general and to Boris in particular; and then it confirms that Boris has a "view" that threatens the false front of high society.

"Bernice's Sheep" (pp. 154--155)
The Overview
This is a poem in five stanzas and twenty-five lines. There is no clear storyline per se, but rather loosely constructed reveries occurring in Bernice's half-awake, half-asleep mind.

In Stanza One we learn that Bernice has a "heavy heart" from "all the troubles of the world. Stanza Two informs us of Bernice's painful task (slaughtering cows all day) and how she seeks her sheep for comfort. Stanza Three further details Bernice's work as we see her crouching to churn butter in her own basement room ("cronching our batter/My own bassoon").

Stanza Four identifies Bernice's great fear — that her heifer's firstborn will somehow be nabbed ("nabbie by furburn"). The final stanza reveals Bernice's bolstered courage as she proclaims that she will "seize" and protect her sheep.
The Key Themes
None clearly emerge in this poem.
The Interpretation
The *London Times Literary Supplement* called "Bernice's Sheep" the "best and dottiest of all [the] nonsense verses." For me this poem is the "Churly Morn" (p. 76) of *A Spaniard In The Works* — the most incoherent.

While a remotely plausible sequence of events may be traced in "Bernice's Sheep," in the end nothing truly makes sense. In fact, interpreting this poem is like trying to fathom the ramblings of a delirious dreamer. I realize, of course, that the poem begins coherently enough, with the traditional bedtime prayer "Now I lay me down to sleep." Also I admit there are some fairly straightforward portmanteaus in the first stanza, i.e., "Brattling" suggests "rattling" with the persistence of a "brat."

Yet the remainder of the poem is quite opaque:

> "I slapter counting one be one
> Till I can cow nomore this day
> Till bethny hard aches leave we
> Elbing my ethbreeds
> Dear Griff's son."

This could be paraphrased as:

> "I slaughter, counting one by one
> Till I can count cows no more this day
> Till beefy heartaches leave me
> Helping my other breeds;
> Dear God's son."

The "other breeds" are her sheep, the "lambs" of God ("Dear Griff's son").

Yet none of the next three stanzas are nearly as decipherable as the first two (and they require a considerable stretch of mind!). In particular, the final stanza is the most baffling. We can establish only that Stanza Five directly counters Stanza One. For in the former, Bernice is found "with hefty-heart and much saddened," but in the latter she is now depicted "with lightly loaf and great larfter."

All in all, I feel this poem offers the reader an excursion into the joys of creative confusion (but not much else).

Drawing Thirty-One (pp. 156–157)

Of course, this is a picture of "Bernice's Sheep." Pp. has the grazing field in black, whereas SS2 has it appropriately in green. The most conspicuous aspect of the drawing is that one of the sheep is floating in the air (perhaps the lamb of God ascending to heaven?!).

"Last Will and Testicle" (pp. 158–160)

The Overview

This tale opens with the reading of the will of one "Barrold Reginald Bunker-Harquart." From the will, we learn that its chief benefactor, thirteen-year-old Elsie, must be entombed in a box until her 21st birthday. A carpenter is sought out to customize the "casket," and Barrold's niece Elsie is duly encased.

Old Nanny Harriette places the boxed Elsie in the garden and charges the "curious" an admission fee. After three years Elsie's skin has greatly deteriorated and her visage becomes frozen in a sickly grin. Thereafter fewer people come to call," the Nanny having raised the admission price.

On the eve of Elsie's 21st birthday, Old Nanny Harriette brings the box inside to warm by the fire. Unfortunately, the box bursts into flames, completely incinerating Elsie. The family doctor is summoned the next monring, but his only concern is sexually assaulting Old Nanny. The story abruptly closes with a "paying guest" stating that '90% of more accidents are caused by burning children in the house'!

The Key Themes

Don't wait for fortune; chances are that no matter what you do, you'll still die impoverished!

The Interpretation

"Last Will and Testicle" is written in a rather straightforward style, both its plot and language easy to follow. The result is a simply hilarious story.

John produces the "actual" document for several reasons: the Will serves as a springboard for satire (it's a lot of fun to have such a somber manuscript held up to ridicule); also, the artifact of the Will introduces us to characters and central conflict. And certainly the Will adds visual novelty: the type font approximates florid calligraphy.

From the farcical premise of Uncle Barrold having his "nice niece" entombed for eight years ("to be carried out as I lie in the ground getting eaten"), we move to the family's execution of the Will. Surely everyone even remotely related to this family is certifiable for Bedlam! To begin with, Old Nanny Harriette's tears, after the reading of the Will, is not due to the horror of the decree, but is in response to Elsie's big foot! (She fears it will cause problems having a box made to fit Elsie.) Later on, the Doctor's scheme of tying a microphone to Elsie's mouth does little to help her communicate (as Nanny usually turns off the speaker)!

Throughout the tale Lennon punctuates this bizarre action with equally bizarre platitudes, i.e., "Children should be seized and not hard"! In the end, a thoroughly insensitive world has been convincingly created. People are so turned around that they fail to connect — they have no sense of direction. And so . . . Welcome to Planet Earth!

Drawing Thirty-Two (p. 161)

This is Elsie, apparently getting a "fitting" for her "box." She looks quite mad: which is to say she looks ready to begin her eight-year entombment. You'll note that the labels on the box are contradictory (which in this tale, also makes sense!).

Drawing Thirty-Three (pp. 162–163)

Elsie again (note her *foot*!); this seems to be a second fitting (for the box). As before, there is visual contradiction: she faces the wrong way, based on the signs.

SS2 and Pp. darken in the ground, so there is more contrast here than in our version.

Drawing Thirty-Four (p. 164)

This is a portrait of "Our Dad" (the subject of the next poem). He looks positively Cycloptic and fat, and is adorned with only an imbecilic smile. SS2 further punctuates his strangeness by coloring him green (Pp. has him shaded in grey). The text informs us he has a "hook" hand (echoes of *In His Own Write*'s "Little Bobby," p. 72), though it is not visible in the drawing.

"Our Dad" (pp. 165–167).

The Overview

This is the final poem of the major works of John Lennon. Structurally it consists of 18 stanzas and 72 lines. The plot is as follows: Dad decides he's not wanted by his family, so he starts to pack his belongings (Stanzas One–Eight). His farewell scene begins (Stanzas Eight–Nine) but is immediately interrupted by an argument with his sons regarding Mom (Stanzas Ten–Twelve). Dad's final farewell is the subject of Stanzas Thirteen–Fourteen.

Stanzas Fifteen–Eighteen chronicle the aftermath of dad's departure. First, the vulturous sons hurry to find any valuables dad might have left behind; in Stanza Sixteen they seize money and dad's pension book. The sons then plan a party (Stanza Seventeen). The poem concludes with a statement — the family will never hear from "Our Dad" again.

The Key Themes

Inside every horrible family are horrible family members.

The Interpretation

Here John Lennon appears to be expressing a considerable amount of rage against his own father. In fact, the opening stanza could be taken quite literally as autobiography:

> "It wasn't long before old dad
> Was cumbersome — a drag
> He seemed to get the message and
> Began to pack his bag."

Fred Lennon married Julia in 1938; he went off to sea (as ship waiter) in 1939, returned briefly in 1940, and then left for good. So indeed, "it wasn't long" before John's real dad "packed his bag." Undoubtedly John's personal appraisal of his father's character is reflected in such lines as "Yer stupid bastard . . . Yer shrivelled little clown! . . . The slimy little jew" (here "jew" is used in a deliberately offensive way, used to suggest a Shylock or traditionally penurious person).

The second stanza also is very close to being pure autobiography: in 1965, a quarter of a century after Fred's abandonment of wife and child, the senior Mr. Lennon showed up (to get money from his famous son):

" 'You don't want me around," he said,
'I'm old and crippled too.'
We didn't have the heart to say
'You're bloody right it's true.' "

When Fred Lennon actually arrived at his son's mansion, it's true that John "didn't have the heart" to say what he really felt. He simply slammed the door in his father's face. It was the last time father and son would ever "see" each other again. Nevertheless, Fred Lennon managed to eventually extract some "guilt" money from his son (John had his accountants provide a small pension for "Our Dad"). In addition, Fred also made some money from the sale of his life story and a record called "That's My Life," released December, 1965.

As for the poem itself — it must be remembered that dad and family are generally quite fictionalized. To begin with, we have an unspecified number of sons telling the tale. Also, dad's occupation is none other than pimp (to his wife!) — "ponce," in Stanza Twelve, is British slang for "pimp." Furthermore, dad's not only off to the "workhouse," he also leaves money behind!

The language of the poem is simple throughout, except for Stanza Three's "tatty klied" (which I take to mean dad's "ratty, tattered pride"). The term, out of context, also tells us "daddy lied."

Overall we can safely say that the harsh humor of "Our Dad" has roots in John Lennon's personal experience. The sarcastic ending — which asserts that dad will "remain in our hearts — a buddy friend and pal" — masks the deep loss John felt over both his father and mother. This repressed anger finally was released five years later, in "Mother."

"Mother you had me, I never had you . . .
Father you left me, I never left you . . .
Mother don't go . . .
Daddy come home . . . "

Drawing Thirty-Five (pp. 168--169)

This is the comedy of topsy-turveydom, i.e., a tankful of humans being fed their ration of fish! In SS2, the fish are green; in Pp. they're shaded grey. Perhaps the message of this drawing is that people live their lives in a circumspect way, either wildly competing for the means to survive, or else passively waiting for others to take care of them.

Drawing Thirty-Six (p. 170)

This is a portrait of a religious talk show host on BBC television. (In the *Lennon Play* he's named "the Reverend Felix Hyacinth

Smythe"). The name of the show is "I Believe, Boot . . . " and the drawing depicts the Reverend in an appropriately inviting pose, that of a "pal" inviting conversation.

Both the Pp. and SS2 versions are preferable to ours, because they significantly enlarge the drawing (thus the Reverend seems much more intimate, almost as if he's interviewing the reader). SS2 also has the Reverend's eyes in green (an apt touch, since he is prone to fits of jealousy).

"I Believe, Boot . . . " (pp. 171–173).

The Overview

This is the fourth and final special form in *A Spaniard In The Works*. Its format is that of a television transcript of the Reverend's interview with Mr. Wabooba. The sequence of action in the show may be summarized as follows:

1) The Reverend presents a sermonette, then introduces Mr. Wabooba.
2) The Reverend makes a racist remark, which causes Wabooba to come back with one of his own.
3) The Reverend tries a non sequitur (to confuse his guest).
4) Wabooba charges God with racial discrimination.
5) The Reverend answers in an obscure parable (another smoke-screen).
6) Wabooba says the parable is irrelevant, so the Reverend tries another one.
7) Wabooba indicts the Church for greed and hypocrisy.
8) The Reverend blames the Catholic Church (exempting the Church of England).
9) Wabooba calls the Reverend a "Christian Imperialist."

Their argument momentarily de-escalates with Wabooba forgiving the Reverend, and vice versa. Then the interview fades out "on suitable Christian captions."

The Key Themes

The racism and financial self-aggrandizement found in the Christian Church.

The Interpretation

The *London Times Literary Supplement* found "I Believe, Boot . . . " to be "a firstrate concluding satire," and indeed it is a fine way to close the book. Here John's hand is steady and his message incisive.

The Reverend's sermonette sets the tone for this piece. From the Reverend's own words we learn he is a clergyman who is unable to answer the most rudimentary of theological questions, i.e., "What is sin?" Yet he is undaunted by his ignorance and just keeps talking in circles, begging the question(s). In fact, the Reverend's mute mind turns a definition into a "*deaf*inition"!

To the ever-popular question "Why does God bring misery into the world?" the Reverend is again evasive — this time citing scripture ("God walks in such mysterious ways"). Stylistically, we notice a phrase John had used in *In His Own Write*: "slowly but slowly" ("No Flies on Frank," p. 21; "Liddypool," p. 56). Here the phrase effectively conveys the pointlessness of pursuing a road to Godly perfection. Once the sermon concludes, Mr. Wabooba is introduced.

Now the *Lennon Play* provides a full name for our guest: Mr. Aka Walla Wabooba (supposedly from the London suburb of Clapham East). In any case the Reverend begins interviewing Wabooba with a racial slur ("may I call you Wog?"). The Reverend's antagonism is a prod to Wabooba's own racism (hence a "*prod*lem" arises).

We witness, throughout the course of the interview, how neither participant makes any headway with the other; each is entombed by a self-sealed premise. For Wabooba, Fats Waller is truly a holy name (Waller representing the genius of Black people and indirectly pointing the way out of the ghetto through his role as entertainer). And, for the Reverend, Mickey Most, an English record producer, is part of the Holy Trinity!

As we've come to expect by now, Lennon's language contains some hilarious puns. For example, "The Archbishop of Canterbury" is rendered "de Arch bitter of Canterbubble"! This brings out the sourness of sermons and the ephemerality of religious power groups ("Canterbury," England's second city and seat of ecclesiastical power, is here a mere "bubble").

"I Believe, Boot . . . " also confronts a basic contradiction in Christendom, i.e., its amassing of personal wealth while parishoners are left to suffer in poverty. As stated before, however, the Reverend sidesteps all serious criticism of institutional Christianity — in this case by scapegoating Catholicism.

This selection contains moments of sheer Theater of the Absurd (quite apropos to the subject at hand):

> "Rev. . . . can you hallucinate? (He
> colours)
> Mr. W. 'I can.' (Colouring too)

Or, when the show is over:

> "FADE OUT ON SUITABLE CHRISTIAN
> CAPTIONS" etc.

In closing, we would do well to remember that John Lennon's awareness of racial tension in England was always acute (*In His Own Write*'s opening story introduces the theme). Unfortunately, the riots throughout Britain in 1981, particularly in Liverpool, testify that Black people everywhere are still oppressed and hated by White majorities.

Drawing Thirty-Seven (p. 173)

This is a curious drawing, in that today's reader gets an immediate flashback: the cover of *Two Virgins* (released November, 1968). Also, what is illustrated here does not appear to be "I Believe, Boot . . . " but instead seems to be Adam and Eve (in all their unadorned glory). An overdressed man of the cloth is leering at them, and in his hand is "That Book" — obviously the Bible, which has done so much (instilling sexual fear and guilt!) . . . for so many (generations).

The *Two Virgins* association will be carried on in another of John's drawings for "A Short Essay on Macrobiotics" *(see Chapter Six)*.

Drawing Thirty-Eight (pp. 174--175)

Sad but true: this officially concludes the major literary works of John Lennon. This drawing is a bit more upbeat than the one which closes *In His Own Write* (the corpse of Kakky, p. 81). Here, at least, we have two *living* persons!

I admit that John's closing message is hardly optimistic. It seems to say "We must be submissive to the seats of power" (a theme that opened *A Spaniard In The Works*).

SS2 and Pp. do not print "The End" under the chair, as does our version, they leave it for the following page. From this point, then, we move into a new beginning: an investigation of the Minor Works of John Lennon.

Part II
The Minor Works

Chapter Five

From Juvenilia
to *In His Own Write*

One of the curious things about writers is that their literary gifts can be revealed virtually at any point in their lifetimes. For instance, Eugene Ionesco, who is believed by some to be one of the finest comedic playwrights since Aristophanes, penned his first play, *The Bald Soprano*, at age thirty-six. Dylan Thomas wrote his first great poem — one that brought him to the attention of major critics — at the rosy age of 18 (the poem was "The Force That Through The Green Fuse Drives the Flower"); T.S. Eliot's first book of poetry, *Prufrock and Other Observations* (a volume of profoundly beautiful and probing work) was written, in the main, when the author was just twenty-two.

Another interesting aspect of writers is that they may start off in one genre, only to find their real abilities lie in another. To wit: Edward Albee had already written several mediocre novels when, at age thirty, he authored his first play *(The Zoo Story)*. The play, of course, was absolutely brilliant, and Albee would henceforth claim dramaturgy as his rightful home.

Regarding John Lennon — I will chronicle his literary output through five writing periods (elementary school, high school, college, *Mersey Beat*, and Beatle Fan Club).

Elementary School Writing

John Lennon's literary ability, and the foundations of his original style, date back to early childhood. His penchant for wordplay can actually be traced to his Dovedale Primary School days (in fact, John was reading at age four-and-a-half). Thus Lennon was already writing stories, verses, and making drawings while he was in elementary school; mature use of these talents would provide the basic format for both his major books.

Of John's writing style at Dovedale, his teachers recall one conspicuous aspect — his unorthodox spelling. Phillip Norman states the matter rather succinctly: "He changed almost every word into another one like it," citing "funds" becoming "fun" as an example. Needless to say, this "talent" for misspelling developed into the polyhedronic style of his mature writing.

Whenever John, as a young boy, attended some exciting event (such as the annual Christmas Pantomime at Liverpool's Empire Stadium), he would be inspired to record the experience in the form of prose, poetry, and cartoons. Technically John began forming his literary work into "books" at the tender age of seven! We even have the title of one of these collections of writing: *Sport and Speed Illustrated*. Now, it is not clear whether any of the contents of *Sport and Speed Illustrated* still exist. Phillip Norman tells us in the preface to *Shout* that John's Aunt Mimi still has "a bureau drawer [containing] the little drawings and verses, written on the blue, ruled paper of childhood." This sounds more like Dovedale material than any high school work, but unfortunately for us, Norman doesn't clarify the matter.

Probably the main point worth remembering about this initial period is that Lennon's creative urges first found expression in writing and graphic art, *not* in music. Also, Lennon's literary bent was (from the very beginning) fused with his drawing ability.

High School Writing

At the age of twelve, John Lennon entered Quarry Bank Grammar School — and a very fertile period of writing began. During these years John's stories, verses, illustrations and cartoons were carefully collected into exercise notebooks. Unlike the material from *Sport and Speed Illustrated* (which was either lost or is still part of Mimi's "bureau"), we *do* have two extant poems from these Quarry Bank books: "The Tales of Hermit Fred," and "The Land of Lunapots."

Both of these poems originally came from exercise books which had been confiscated by a Quarry Bank teacher. Bill Harry (founder and editor of *Mersey Beat*) attempted to locate the teacher and recover the books, but to no avail.

The poems were published for the first time in *Mersey Beat*'s 68th issue, February 27, 1964:

The Tale of Hermit Fred

The wandering Hermit Fred am I
With candle stick bun
I nit spaghetti apple pie
And crum do I have fun

I peel old bagpipes for my wife
And cut all negroes hair
As breathing is my very life
To stop I do not dare

This is an example of Lennon as true nonsense poet (a la Edward Lear). There are no double entendres, simply the joy of sound and the fun of creating a pointless plot. Later, in 1967, Lennon would produce a lyric, *What's The News Mary Jane?* — which was quite similar in its nonsense style:

She looks as an African Queen
She eating her chapatis and cream
She tastes as Mongolian lamb
She coming from Aldebaran

(Chorus) What a shame Mary Jane
Had a pain at the party
What a shame Mary Jane
What a shame Mary Jane
Had a pain at the party

In particular, one line in "Tales of Hermit Fred" —

"With candle stick bun
I nit spaghetti apple pie"

is clearly echoed in *What The News Mary Jane?*:

"She'd like to be married with Yetty
He grooving such cookie spaghetti"

And, interestingly enough, *What's The News Mary Jane?* (of which there are *two* recordings by the Beatles) was almost released as a single in 1968.

The Land of Lunapots

T'was custard time and as I
Snuffed at the haggis pie pie
The noodles ran about my plunk
Which rode my wyrtle uncle drunk
T'was not the dreaded thrilling thud
That made the porridge taste like mud
T'was Wilburs graftiens graffen Bing

139

That makes black pudding want to sing
For them in music can be heard
Like the dying cough of a humming bird
The lowland chick astound agasted
Wonder how long it lasted
In this land of Lunapots
I who sail the earth in paper yachts

This poem was strongly influenced by Lewis Carroll's "Jabberwocky." The opening line of Lennon's poem, "T'was custard time and as I . . . " suggests Carroll's " 'Twas brillig and the . . . . " Also we notice Carrollesque words like "wyrtle" and "graftiens" appearing the poem.

Even Carroll's warning "Beware the Jabberwock . . . the Jubjub bird . . . " is reflected in Lennon's "T'was not the dreaded thrilling thud . . . the haggis pie pie." The most interesting image, however, is the following:

"In this land of Lunapots
I who sail the earth in paper yachts"

What strikes us is that "paper yachts" is a precursor to the "newspaper taxis" of *Lucy In The Sky With Diamonds*.

One sad truth about the Quarry Bank years is that so many of John's earliest works were both produced and lost during this time. Not only did most of Lennon's confiscated exercise books never resurface, but on the home front, Aunt Mimi personally destroyed much of John's writing. In the *Rolling Stone* interviews John remarked upon this period and his Aunt Mimi's actions:

"I got fuckin' lost in being at high school. I used to say to me Aunt 'You throw my fuckin' poetry out, and you'll regret it when I'm famous,' and she threw the bastard stuff out. I never forgave her for not treating me like a fuckin' genius . . . . "

One exercise book, however, was confiscated by teachers, made the rounds among the school staff, and then was returned to John at the end of the term. We even know the name of this book: it was *The Daily Howl*. Unfortunately John later lost the book himself and tried in vain to find it for three years. *The Daily Howl* was at last located by Rod Murray (a former Liverpool Art College chum) in Rod's own flat in Gambier Terrace — a location now famous for its many Beatle rehearsal sessions.

Bill Harry rounds out the *Howl*'s odyssey by confirming that "arrangements were made for the return of the books to John." I note here that because of the fragmented accounts regarding *The Daily Howl*, it is not certain if *Howl* consisted of one or several "books" — Harry uses the plural; Lennon uses the singular. Whatever the case, we can be fairly certain that this lost work finally found its way back into John's hands by the early months of 1964.

Of *The Daily Howl*'s contents, it is known to have been filled with stories, poems, and cartoons. We're lucky that *Mersey Beat* conducted an interview with John regarding *The Daily Howl*, for no other source has ever investigated this book. The interview was published in *Mersey Beat* July 30, 1964, and it opens with John discussing the origins of *The Daily Howl*:

> " 'I wrote most of the stuff years ago and most of it isn't very good — but it means alot to me, I spent years filling that book up."

(From Norman's research we can surmise that a significant amount of *The Daily Howl* was penned "in the last forty mintues of every [school] day, in the unsupervised 'prep' period.")

Lennon also informed Bill Harry at this time: "You can print any of the items in *MB*, but explain that they were written a long time ago." John's interest in tracing his other juvenilia was then expressed: "I'd appreciate it if you can trace where the poems came from ["The Tales of Hermit Fred" and "The Land of Lunapots"], as there may be some more of my writings there."

Now, it's unclear why *Mersey Beat*, having received John's express permission, did *not* go ahead and publish any items from *The Daily Howl* (perhaps the book was again lost, or maybe legal complications arose). Whatever the reason, today what we know of its specific contents comes to us only through the recollections of Bill Turner. Turner was a friend of John's while still at Quarry Bank Grammar School, and his remembrances appeared in the March 12, 1964 issue of *Mersey Beat*. From that article, simply called "The Daily Howl," we learn the following:

1) Just as John said that the contents of *In His Own Write* had originally been written "to read among my friends," Bill Turner confirms that *The Daily Howl* was penned mainly for John's best friend at Quarry Bank, Pete Shotton.

2) Not surprisingly, we learn that John's stories were often based on the high school "rages" at the time, i.e., the Liverpudlian fascination with American frontier figures like Davy Crockett. In fact, one of the two story titles Turner supplied for *The Daily Howl* reflects this — "The Story of Davy Crutch-Head"!

141

3) Another source of inspiration for John's writing came from current hit records. Lennon enjoyed taking popular song titles and playfully planting them in his stories. For instance, the song called *Suddenly There Was A Valley* was rendered "Suddenly there was a valet who rode up riding."!

4) John Lennon's earliest use of "Special Forms" can be traced to *The Daily Howl*. Here, John included a format of weather reports, i.e., "Tomorrow will be Muggy, followed by Tuggy, Wuggy and Thuggy"! What's fascinating about this quotation is that *many* years later, after the Beatles had long since disbanded, and after John had recorded several brilliant solo albums, this line miraculously resurfaces. For when John Lennon was guesting on WNEW, FM, New York, promoting the soon-to-be-released **Walls And Bridges** album, late September, 1974, he had several occasions to give *real* weather reports. So, as you've undoubtedly guessed, while John was on the air, he threw in the above line from *The Daily Howl*! (Well over two decades from its original appearance in John's Quarry Book notebook!) John added "Tomorrow will be Sunny, followed by Money, Tune-y, Wennie . . . . Tomorrow will be just the same as today, only different"!

5) The *Daily Howl* often featured curious reoccurring motifs such as "Wigan Pier." Turner states that John had an "obsession" with this term: "forever Wigan Pier kept cropping up." In particular, this phrase appeared repeatedly in one story, "A Carrot in a Potato Mine." At first I assumed "Wigan Pier" was an example of a private joke of John's, but a letter from Bill Harry informed me otherwise: "The names of Lancashire towns have always amused Liverpudlians and are the object of much humour. Just the mention of one of them can send a Scouser into paroxysms of laughter. We joke about 'Wigan, Accrington' — which used to have a good football team called Accrington Stanley — and 'Scunthorpe' (this also explains why the latter towns, Accrington and Scunthorpe, pop up in the 'Classified Ads' that John submitted to *Mersey Beat*)."

6) Finally, thanks to Turner, we have a unique footnote regarding one of John's "favorite cartoons" in *The Daily Howl*. It's noteworthy not simply because it details a drawing from this "lost" work, but also because this cartoon was the original inspiration for a cartoon appearing in *A Spaniard In The Works* (Drawing Twenty-Five, p. 140):

> "One of his [John's] favorite cartoons was a bus stop scene. I remember he wrote under the sign, which said, 'Bus Stop — Why?' And he had a flying pancake at the top of the cartoon and *below it there was a blind man wearing glasses leading along a blind dog — also wearing glasses*" [Italics are mine.]

Though no one has ever mentioned it, I believe John's title, *The Daily Howl*, is a takeoff of Allen Ginsberg's Beat Generation Anthem, *Howl*, which was written in 1956 and in which a circle of Liverpudlians held an avid interest.

Also, one last footnote is supplied by John Lennon himself. In the one and only book review Lennon ever wrote (published in 1973 and discussed in detail later in this chapter) he states:

> "One of my earlier efforts at writing was a 'newspaper' called the Daily Howl. I would write it at night, then take it to school and read it aloud to my friends; looking at it now it seems strangely similar to The Goon Show! Even the title had 'highly esteemed' before it!"

So now we know that (technically) the full name of this work is *The Highly Esteemed Daily Howl*. Also, we have evidence that this work was still in John's mind in 1973 and that it can be compared in style and tone to the wonderfully surreal and wacky humor of "The Goon Show."

College Writing

John Lennon left Quarry Bank in July of 1957 and went on to Liverpool Art College. On the surface, one might expect these so-called college years to be a time when The Literary Lennon was flourishing. But the facts deny such an assumption.

To begin with, John never really wanted to go to college (but rather "gave in" to his Aunt's urgings and thought "Well, what the hell"). Second, Lennon seldom attended classes and almost never did his assignments. Third, this was "Art" college, and thus not one that would develop John's literary talent. Fourth, and most crucial of all, *music* had become the dominant interest in Lennon's life.

What we do know of this period is that John's notebooks were essentially artist's "sketch books" (though, apparently, his portraits and caricatures of tutors were accompanied by prose descriptions and, sometimes, short verses). Arthur Ballard, a fine abstract painter in his own right, and John's tutor in the intermediate course, once found an unidentified sketchbook of John's in his classroom. Inside its pages he discovered the same wildly comic caricatures and non-realistic portraits which later appeared in *In His Own Write* and *A Spaniard In The Works*. Ballard was quite impressed and, in fact, is quoted by Norman as having found Lennon's work "the wittiest thing I'd ever seen in my life."

Well, needless to say, John (who seldom displayed his work for class critique) must have been surprised when Ballard used his drawings as models of free interpretations of human subjects! Sadly, Ballard may have been the *only* professor to have seen the humor and brilliance of Lennon's visual point of view (others found him talentless and just generally too eccentric).

One interesting aspect of Ballard's teaching style is that he hated lecturing in stodgy classrooms, preferring instead the intimacy of a small back room in a pub called Ye Cracke. John would spend considerable time in Ye Cracke, for it was an Art College hangout (and Lennon was soon performing here during student lunch breaks).

Ye Cracke is also memorable because its back room was where Bill Harry made firsthand acquaintance with the poetry of John Lennon:

> "We were sitting beneath a panoramic black and white engraving of 'The Death of Nelson' and I mentioned to John that I'd heard he was a poet. He seemed embarrassed and mumbled something. I told him I was genuinely interested in reading what he'd written and he took a scrap of paper from his pocket and handed it to me."

Harry's recollection of this introduction to the literary side of Lennon is recorded in *Mersey Beat: The Beginnings of the Beatles* (1977) and reveals an astute critical eye as he continues:

> "It was something totally different from what I'd expected. The American Beat Generation poets were the 'thing' at the time and most student poetry was a pastiche of Ginsberg, Ferlinghetti and Corso. John's poem, a piece of pure rustic wackiness concerning a farmer, had freshness and originality in its sheer lunacy. There was an Englishness to John's piece which was to forecast the rise of the Liverpool Poets and indicated the breakaway by creative Liverpool people in the various arts from the American influence which so dominated the thinking of the time."

Unfortunately, John's "farmer" poem has (more than likely) disappeared forever. As was mentioned earlier, John's university career was rather haphazard, and by 1960 he left college for good. Lennon was now off with the Beatles to perform in Hamburg for the first time (their homecoming gig at Litherland Town Hall, December 27, 1960, marks the point at which their future greatness was apparent to all in attendance). Of course, John's commitment to the Beatles had affected his college work long before the Hamburg departure. For instance, The Silver Beatles were touring Scotland with Johnny Gentle when John was supposed to have been at college taking major exams!

Beyond any doubt, *Mersey Beat: The Beginnings of the Beatles* (1977), edited by Bill Harry, remains the single most valuable resource regarding the writings of John Lennon before *In His Own Write*. Indeed, credit should be given to Bill Harry on at least four counts: One, for singlehandedly creating *Mersey Beat* (the finest historical publication in existence chronicling the Beatles' rise to fame). Two, for personally encouraging John to keep writing in his original style. Three, for providing an uncensored forum for Lennon's literary work. And finally, for giving us a facsimile edition featuring *Mersey Beat*s from July 1961 to November 1964.

The Beatles had an intimate involvement with *Mersey Beat* from its inception. Harry tells us "The Beatles were the most frequent visitors to the office, answering the phone, helping with the typing and providing spiritual support." More particularly, Harry informs us that when he told John Lennon that *Mersey Beat* would provide him with a regular column for his original writing, John "eagerly brought in a huge bundle of his poems and stories." Alas! *All* of this "huge bundle" of The Literary Lennon was lost when *Mersey Beat* moved into its new offices! It's painful to ponder the large amount of work that vanished at this time. Certainly most of the Quarry Bank exercise books, probably all his college work, and conceivably even Dovedale material were among the items in this pile. But no use dwelling over this loss, for we still have some fine uncollected work from this period.

Bill Harry, in a reminiscence written exclusively for readers of *The Literary Lennon*, further elaborates on the contemporary literary scene and John's writing:

> What was the intellectual climate at Liverpool College of Art when I attended it with John? Apart from being on the Student's Union Committee, I was also in charge of the Film Society and the type of films I booked included Cocteau's "Orphee" and the Bunuel/Dali films "L'Age d'Or" and "Un Chien Andaleau."
>
> In Britain, a literary movement called 'The Angry Young Men' contrasted American Beat Generation writers. The popular books were Colin Wilson's *The Outsider*, Salinger's *Catcher In The Rye* and Kerouac's *On The Road*. A book called *Protest* was a collection of works by both the Angry Young British writers and the Beat poets and authors. I remember one story by John Clellan Holmes in which a man sat on a tube train with a newspaper in which he had torn two eye holes through which he stared at the other

145

passengers. This reminded me strongly of John Lennon's macabre sense of humour. I also obtained some City Lights books with poems by Corso and Ferlinghetti. My favourite poem at the time was Ginsberg's "Howl." Despite this interest in the exciting American movement, I particularly favoured starting a Liverpool group of creative writers and artists to explore our own local environment.

In Liverpool at the time, we had a coffee bar scene — among the hang-outs were The Jacaranda, The Studio Club and Streates. The Studio was run by one of the art school models and Streates was the venue for the poets and 'bohemians."

The artists who impressed us at this time were Modigliani and Van Gogh; the Van Gogh influence was particularly evident in Stuart Sutcliffe's early work. The leading lights at the Streates poetry readings were Phil Tasker (a Dylan Thomas lover) and Roger McGough. Together with the manager of Streates, I organised the North's first-ever "Poetry To Jazz" concert at the Crane Theatre.

Both John and Stuart were in different classes than I, but we used to get together in the college canteen, Ye Cracke pub in Rice Street, and at students' flats in nearby Huskisson Street.

During evenings at Ye Cracke, I suggested a name for our movement — "The Dissenters" — and the main people involved were Stuart, John and Rod Murray. I was aware at this time of John's rebellious nature and of the escapades he got up to with his close friend Jeff Mohammed.

John's sense of humour betrayed a cruel streak, as he seemed to be very amused by jokes about cripples and spastics. It was also the time of the sick joke. Two that went the rounds included: "Mummy, Mummy, Daddy's fallen over the cliff!" "Don't make me laugh, my lips are chapped" and "Mrs. Johnson, can Johnny come out and play baseball with us?" "But you know he's a quadruple amputee." "Yeah, but we just wanna use him for third base."

When I finally got John to show me his poems, I was impressed by the Englishness of them. There was no evidence of the Beat Generation influence.

One poet who did capitalise on the Beat Generation type poets by emulating them was a writer from the South of England, Royston Ellis, and we went to one of his readings at Liverpool University. John liked him and they got together to back him at a poetry-to-Beat reading at the Jacaranda. Later, they took him back to the Gambier Terrace flat where he introduced them to soft drugs such as purple hearts and benzedrine, which could be obtained by breaking open a Vick inhaler and chewing the contents (a "spit ball"). There were also Bronchipacs, tablets for bronchitis, which, if you chewed twice the normal dose, sent you on a "high."

Rod and John shared the Gambier Terrace flat. Students often got together to share a flat near the art college. Stuart had one in Percy Street and I rented one with a couple of students in Upper Duke Street, although I continued to live at home.

In many cases, as happened to me, the other members reneged on the rent, leaving one person to pay the balance for them all.

When I started *Mersey Beat* and got John to write "On The Dubious Origin Of Beatles," he seemed, once again, initially embarrassed about showing his work. He gave it to me on two scraps of paper in the Jacaranda and seemed surprised that I loved it. He spelt Paul's surname as "McCartrey," which confused me and led to several mis-spellings of Paul's surname in *Mersey Beat*. Once it was published and he discovered the positive response, he came into the office one day with a huge bundle of material. Poems, short stories, mini-articles, together with illustrations. I told him that I'd publish them regularly as a column. I chose the name Beatcomber myself, as I loved the humour of J.B. Morton's Beachcomber column in the *Daily Express* newspaper. There was a degree of political content in John's work and he mangled the political names, particularly that of Harold McMillan, and I remember reading through all of the material and thinking that one of his biggest influences must have been Stanley Unwin's fractured English.

Another personal favourite of mine at the time was Edward Leacock's "Nonsense Novels" and John's material also reminded me of this, particularly the short stories.

There were no exercise books among the bundle of writings that John handed to me but they were on lined pieces of paper, obviously torn out of exercise books and, on reflection, John could have selected the pieces he liked from his various Daily Howl books and presented them to me. I placed them all in the top left hand drawer of my desk.

At the time I was still attending art college. John and Stu had left. I'd rented a tiny room on the top floor of a building in Renshaw Street for £5 a week from David Land, a wine merchant.

The complete office equipment comprised one secondhand

office desk, a broken swivel chair, a typewriter, phone and wastebin. My girlfriend Virginia was the only fulltime member of staff. It was gruelling turning out a fortnightly paper because I had to do all the layouts, collect the advertising, write all the copy, correct the proofs at the printers and deliver the copies myself, in addition to attending to my college work. Virginia did the accounts, handled all phone enquiries and ran the office in my absence. We went to gigs seven nights a week, also to lunchtime gigs and often worked a 100 hour week. Naturally, with such pressure, typo's were inevitable. In addition, there was further pressure because we had no money or working capital to start with, apart from £50. Virginia was paid £5 per week and I took no money at first and had to survive on a small grant.

David Land offered us a complete first floor with two offices at a generous rent and we moved to the floor below. Virginia took charge of the move while I spent several lunchtimes interviewing groups at the Cavern sessions. When it was time to get a new issue together I dipped into my drawer to select a new Lennon piece for Beatcomber and couldn't find anything. I asked Virginia where the bundle of papers were and she told me that she had noticed a pile of scrap paper in my drawer which she had put in the wastebin, along with some rubbish. The dustbinmen had taken away the stuff a few days previously. I was horrorstruck! We obviously had to let John Know and met him that night at the Blue Angel. When we told him he broke down and cried on Virginia's shoulder. He got over it, we had a few drinks and had no option but to accept the situation.

However, it kept preying on my mind. One afternoon I came into the office and Virginia told me that two girls had dropped by with a couple of John's poems: "The Land Of The Lunapots" and "Tales Of Hermit Fred." She said the girls had told her that the poems had been given to them by a teacher at Quarry Bank School who had told them that he'd confiscated exercise books from John and still retained the copies. Unfortunately, the girls hadn't left their names or addresses so I couldn't contact them to discover the identity of the teacher. I tried to find out who he was by calling the school but they were on Summer holiday. I published the poems and decided to find out if any more of John's works could be traced. I made enquiries and was told that John had left a copy of The Daily Howl behind him in the Gambier Terrace flat. No students lived there now. This was some time after I'd left the college. I found that Rod Murray had also left and no one seemed to know his whereabouts. I continued my enquiries and eventually discovered that Rod had moved to Princess Avenue, so I sought out the house and rang the bell. Rod answered. I never got as far as the doorstep but he told me that he did have a copy of The Daily Howl but refused to give it to me to enable me to return it to John as he felt that The Beatles were earning enough money and he should be paid for handing over the book. His main contention, which I could sympathise with, was that John had left him to pay the full rent for the Gambier Terrace flat. I contacted Brian Epstein's office to tell them where The Daily Howl was and suggested that they negotiate with Rod to obtain it for John. They put their solicitor Rex Makin onto it and he did obtain the book. I believe that Rod was given a nominal sum to reimburse him for the flat money.

Now that John is gone I often wonder if I'm the only person who read and studied that bundle of material. I've heard that hypnotists can put people into a trance and make them remember items from books they read many years previously, that through hypnotism a photographic memory could be tapped. What if, I think, a hypnotist put me into a trance and took me back all those years ago? Could he drag from the recesses of my subconscious mind that bundle of work that John had written?

Issue One of *Mersey Beat*, which debuted July 6, 1961, contained, right on the front page, a commissioned piece by John Lennon. It was written in response to Bill Harry's request for an article on the origins of the Beatles. What John produced was the following:

BEING A SHORT DIVERSION
ON THE
DUBIOUS ORIGINS OF BEATLES

Translated from the John Lennon

Once upon a time there were three little boys called John, George and Paul, by name christened. They decided to get together because they were the getting together type. When they were together they wondered what for after all, what for? So all of a sudden they all grew guitars and formed a noise. Funnily enough, no one was interested, least of all the three little men. So-o-o-o on discovering a fourth little even littler man called

Stuart Sutcliffe running about them they said, quote 'Sonny get a bass guitar and you will be alright' and he did — but he wasn't alright because he couldn't play it. So they sat on him with comfort 'til he could play. Still there was no beat, and a kindly old aged man said, quote 'Thou hast not drums!' We had no drums! they coffed. So a series of drums came and went and came.

Suddenly, in Scotland, touring with Johnny Gentle, the group (called the Beatles called) discovered they had not a very nice sound — because they had no amplifiers. They got some. Many people ask what are Beatles? Why Beatles? Ugh. Beatles, how did the name arrive? So we will tell you. It came in a vision — a man appeared on a flaming pie and said unto them 'From this day on you are Beatles with an 'A.' Thank you, Mister Man, they said, thanking him.

And then a man with a beard cut off said — will you go to Germany (Hamburg) and play mighty rock for the peasants for money? And we said we would play mighty anything for money.

But before we could go we had to grow a drummer, so we grew one in West Derby in a club called Some Casbah and his trouble was Pete Best. We called 'Hello, Pete, come off to Germany!' 'Yes!' Zooooom. After a few months, Peter and Paul (who is called McArtrey, son of Jim McArtrey, his father) lit a Kino (cinema) and the German police said 'Bad Beatles, you must go home and light your English cinemas.' Zooooom, half a group. But even before this, the Gestapo had taken my friend little George Harrison (of Speke) away because he was only twelve and too young to vote in Germany; but after two months in England he grew eighteen, and the Gestapoes said 'you can come.' So suddenly all back in Liverpool Village were many groups playing in grey suits and Jim said 'Why have you no grey suits?' 'We don't like them, Jim' we said speaking to Jim. After playing in the clubs a bit, everyone said 'Go to Germany!' So we are. Zooooom. Stuart gone. Zoom zoom John (of Woolton) George (of Speke) Peter and Paul zoom zoom. All of them gone.

Thank you club members, from John and George (what are friends).

Again, it's to Bill Harry's credit that this funny chronicle of John's was not censored in any way. Initially, John himself had suspected that Harry would want something written in a more conventional style, but was relieved and pleased to get nothing but approval and encouragement from Harry.

What's perhaps most intriguing is the fact that, at this time, the Beatles were still a quintet: John, Paul, George, Pete, and Stu! While the article contains some "real" history (the Hamburg "burning" incident is here, later covered in "A Letter," p. 39), generally a tongue-in-cheek account is presented. It should be mentioned, however, that readers weren't quite sure what was to be believed as fact: the McCartney misspelling ("McArtrey") persisted for several issues!

What is important is that from this article, we can observe John's prose style is well on its way to attaining the caliber of *In His Own Write*. The piece stands as a delightful example of John's early work (with hints of things to come).

The first poem of Lennon's to be published was "I Remember Arnold" — in the August 17, 1961 issue of *Mersey Beat*. The poem elicited considerable positive reaction from the *Mersey Beat* readership (the poem also had a bizarre photograph of the Beatles above the title when originally published). If you recall, "I Remember Arnold" closed John's maiden book, *In His Own Write* (p. 80).

"Around and About" was the title of John's inaugural work as "Beatcomber," which premiered September 14, 1961. Harry informs us that "Beatcomber" was a pun Harry himself devised as a send up of "Beachcomber," a humor column in the *Daily Express*. John's title for this piece was itself a takeoff on *Mersey Beat*'s column "Mersey Roundabout" (a roving news report of Beat group activity in the "Pool"). This selection was later significantly edited and retitled "Liddypool" for inclusion into *In His Own Write* (p. 56). Below is the complete, unexpurgated text:

Around And About, By Beatcomber

Reviving the old tradition of Judro Bathing is slowly but slowly dancing in Liddypool once more. Had you remembering these owld custard of Boldy Street blowing? The Peer Hat is very popularce for sun eating and Boots for Nude Brighter is handys when sailing. We are not happy with her Queen Victorious Monologue, but Walky Through Gallery is goodly when the rain and Sit Georgie House is black (and white from the little pilgrims flying from Hellsy College). Talk Hall is very histerical with old things wot are fakes and King Anne never slept there I tell you. Shout Airborne is handly for planes if you like (no longer government patrolled) and the L.C.C.C. (Liddypool Cha Cha Cha) are doing a great thing. The Mersy Boat is selling another three copies to some go home foreigners who went home.

A little guide to entertain may be of some helpless, so here it is:

> The Casbin — Stricktly no members only.
> The Sheates — The Bohernia of Liddypool.
> The Jackarandy — Membrains only.
> La Locantry — Next to La Grafty.
> La Matumba — For a cheap heal.
> The Pheolix — Also Bohumbert.
> El Camunal — Bald Stream.
> The Dodd Spot — Watch out for details.

These are but to name a few of the few with so little for so many, we'll fight 'em in the streets, so to Speke. We've been engaged for 43 years and he still smokes. I am an unmurdered mother of 19 years, am I pensionable? My dog bites me when I bite it. There is a lot to do in Liddypool, but not all convenience.

The edited portion begins with "A little guide to entertain," and ends "My dog bites me when I bite it." Perhaps the reason this section was cut out of *In His Own Write* is that its references were thought to be strictly "in-house" jokes among readers of *Mersey Beat*. Yet this wouldn't be a very forceful reason, as I think the *entire* piece is all but incomprehensible to any non-Liverpudlian.

We're fortunate that in *Beatlefan* recently, Bill Harry provided some helpful annotations to John's writing in *Mersey Beat*. To begin with, Harry clarifies John's "Liverpool Guide," revealing that it is a direct parody of an "Entertainment Guide" featured in early issues of *Mersey Beat* (i.e., "The Casbah — Haymans Green: Streates — Mount Pleasant: The Odd Spot, 89 Bold St. Watch announcements for opening dates: The Jacaranda — Slater Street, Members Only: La Cabala — Bold Street . . . ").

In a letter, Harry adds this information: "Liverpudlians have a habit of adding a 'y' to things spoken in conversation, or an 'ie'. The Caste Iron Shore is referred to as 'the cassie,' someone called Walter is always 'Wally.' John would use 'Jacarandy' in this sense. Note 'La Locantry' — this is adding the 'y' to a club name, as in the case of Jacarandy, purely for the way it sounds."

Below, I've added a brief historical context for a few of the clubs:

1) "The Casbin — Stricktly no members only." This alludes to the "Casbah Coffee Club" in Hayman's Green, which was actually the redecorated cellar of Pete Best's family home! It opened in 1958 with the "Quarry Men" (John, Paul, George and Ken Browne) as its resident band. Later "The Fabulous Beatles" would have its first "return" engagement "Direct from Hamburg" at the Casbah early in 1961 (Pete Best was now officially the Beatles' drummer). The name "Casbin" suggests "Cash Bin" and "Has Been"! Also, as this was a real local club, John plays with its "small time" status in the line "Stricktly no members only"!

2) "The Jackarandy — Membrains only." This refers to the Jacaranda Coffee Bar run by Allan Williams (he was to become the Beatles' first manager). The "Jac" ("*Jack* — arandy") was John Lennon's, and fellow Art College Students' ("mem*brains*") hangout. It was also the meeting ground for Beat groups (Rory Storm and the Hurricanes or Cass and the Casanovas, who were among the regulars). Furthermore, it was in the Jacaranda that John and Stu Sutcliff painted an original mural. Before this rare item was painted over, it was seen by an American art professor, who was quite impressed by its style and execution.

The article closes with a funny and fragmented flurry of Dear Abbyesque letters, to wit: "I am an unmurdered mother of 19 years, am I pensionable?" ("I am an unmarried woman, age 19, am I pardonable?")

John Lennon's next Beatcomber piece, published August 23, 1962, offers us the tale of "Small Sam." This story is noteworthy because, unlike "Around And About" and Lennon's final Beatcomber, "On Safairy with Whide Hunter" (September 6, 1962), "Small Sam" was *not* a part of *In His Own Write*. Eventually John decided "Small Sam" should be included in *A Spaniard In The Works* (and specifically asked Bill Harry to send him a copy of the tale for that purpose). For whatever reason, it was left out of *Spaniard*, too, so it remains a tasty uncollected work. By now, "Beatcomber" was featured as a headline, and the story's title as a byline:

BEATCOMBER

Small Sam

Once upon a Tom there was a small
little Stan, who was very small.

"You are very small Stan," they said.

"I am only little," replied Stan answering, feeling very small. Who could blame him, for Stan was only small?

"You must be small Stan," people were oft heard to cry, noticing how extremely very small Stan was in fact. But being small (Stan was small) had its condensations. Who else but Stan (the small) could wear all those small clothes?

Stan was highly regarded by everyone (for Stan was small and little). However, one day Stan saw an adverse in the Mersey Bean for "Club you quickly grow your boots." So on that very day Small Stan (by name called) purchased a pair of the very same. So now when Stan passes by, folks say "Is not that small Stan wearing a pair of those clubs you quickly grow you boots?"

And it is.

This story's opening should sound familiar, as "Once upon a Tom" is the identical opening to *In His Own Write*'s "The Wrestling Dog" (p. 28). The remainder of the tale, however, is quite unique.

Basically, "Small Sam" derives its humor from the incremental repetition of Sam's diminuitive size. Sam's real sense of smallness, however, is due to his club foot; that is, until he sees an advertisement in *Mersey Beat* (for boots with a raised heel to compensate for the "short leg" from the club foot). So, just as publishing in *Mersey Beat* raised John Lennon's self-esteem, so too, an ad published in *Mersey Beat* raises Small Sam's self-esteem!

As was previously mentioned, "On Safairy with Whide Hunter" was the final installment of Beatcomber. Although John says (in the table of contents to *In His Own Write*) that it was "written in conjugal with Paul," this story was originally published *solely* under the banner of Beatcomber. Aside from minor spelling changes, i.e., "Otumbath" to "Otumba," "maybe" to "Mable," "Doctrine" to

"Doctorine," "stop" to "Stob," it remains identical to the version found in *In His Own Write*.

The other writing forum that *Mersey Beat* provided John Lennon was the "Classified Ads" section. Here, if John shelled out 4d a word, he could construct and maintain personal messages and private jokes:

"HOT LIPS, missed you Friday, RED NOSE"
"RED NOSE, missed you Friday, HOT LIPS"
"ACCRINGTON welcomes HOT LIPS AND RED NOSE"
"Whistling Jock Lennon wishes to contact HOT NOSE"
"RED SCUNTHORPE wishes to jock HOT ACCRINGTON"
                                               (August 17, 1961)

In *Beatlefan*, Bill Harry delighted his readers by revealing the following: "Comparing the Classified Ads column in the book [*Mersey Beat: The Beginnings of the Beatles*, p. 20] with the original column from Page 2 of Issue No. 6, I noticed that the column had been edited and missed out this item:

'BUT, ON SALE — Chord formations of flute, oboe, and against harpsichord form. Underlead, playfullode — TWUGGER.'

Many people believe, and still do, that TWUGGER was John Lennon."

Harry continued to note that words such as 'playfullode' "were similar to those created by humorist Stanley Unwin who appeared regularly on British radio and television in the 60s. I'm convinced that he must have been John Lennon's main influence in his creative writing. American readers may be familiar with Stanley as he starred in Gerry & Sylvia Anderson's 'Secret Service' live-action/puppet series."

Of the above ads I note the Lancashire towns, Accrington and Scunthorpe, provided by Lennon to automatically crack up Scousers. Also, John's reference to himself as "Jock" Lennon. Harry's letter asserts that John "put Jock Lennon in just for the sound" but "Jock" still connotes a macho rocker (John would use the term "Jock" seven years later, in a Beatle Fan Club message).

"HEAR BOB WOOLER SING with the Beatles at Aintree
  Institute"
"HEAR BOB BEATLE at the Woolerstute"
"WANTED! Talented rock for newly formed"
                                               (September 14, 1961)

This second series of ads features Bob Wooler, the true compere of the Beatles (having *personally* introduced the Beatles over *three hundred* times at Liverpool venues!). While many have subsequently laid claim to being "the fifth beatle," Bob Wooler is the *only man* ever referred to in print as a "Beatle" by the leader of the Beatles himself! Also, unlike America's Murry the K (who simply seized the slogan "fifth Beatle" and rode the Beatle bandwagon with a vengeance in 1964), Bob Wooler, since 1960, significantly and consistently contributed to the Beatles' success; he pitched them to promoters; he wrote articulate and critically sensitive articles about them for *Mersey Beat*; he turned the Beatles on to his personal record collection of vintage American Rock-and-Roll (which *really* inspired and helped shape the Beatle sound); and he *never* used his association with the Beatles for personal gain or fame. It's about time that Bob Wooler gets the credit he deserves, as an important friend and first-mover of Rock-and-Roll music in Liverpool.

Returning to the ads . . . when Stu Sutcliff wrote to John from Hamburg saying that a mutual friend, Jurgen Vollmer, a friend of Stu's German fiancee, Astrid Kirchherr, was soon to holiday in Paris, John took out the following series of ads in *Mersey Beat*:

"Happy XMAS – Jurgen"
"Hello from Norman Lennon Vollmer"
"FROLICHE FUSSBODEN – Herr Vollmer"
"GOOD MORNING Jurgrow, from George"

(December 14, 1961)

There is a touching memento of Lennon's association with Jurgen that is still readily available: **Rock 'N' Roll**, which was first released February 17, 1975 in America. For the album's cover, featuring John in his early Hamburg days, was photographed by none other than Jurgen Vollmer.

In July of 1982, I asked Jurgen for his recollections of these Classified Ads. To our mutual surprise, Jurgen had *never* heard about them! Jurgen did remember that, as a gift, John had given him a subscription to *Mersey Beat*. But Jurgen had only thumbed through the issues, focusing particulary on the photos of Liverpool rockers (Jurgen's own pictures of the Beatles in Hamburg were first seen in *Mersey Beat* and are, of course, now available in his book *Rock N Roll Times*, 1982).

So, over twenty years after John Lennon had originally written his messages to Jurgen, Jurgen read them for the first time! He was just delighted when I pointed them out in *Mersey Beat: The Beginning of the Beatles* (p. 26). In particular, he laughed out loud when he read:

"Froliche Fussboden — Herr Vollmer"
a line that translates into perfect nonsense as "Happy Floor — Mister Vollmer"!

Returning to Jurgen and John's friend Stu Sutcliff, John wrote many letters to his friend and often included poetry. However, the only published example is found in Hunter Davies' "authorized biography" of the Beatles. (The version below is based on the holograph, *not* Davies' printed version):

> "I remember a time when everyone
> I loved hated me
> because I hated them so what
> So what so fucking what
> I remember a time when belly
> buttons were knee high
> when only shitting was dirty
> and everything else clean & beautiful
> I can't remember anything
> without a sadness
> So deep that it hardly
> becomes known to me
> So deep that its tears leave me a spectator
> of my own STU*PIDITY*
> And so I go rambling
> on with a hey nonny
> nonny nonny no"

Though this is awkwardly written and only half-serious, some of John's real pain is still apparent. It makes one wonder whether any of the other serious poems which John wrote to Stu were more honest and direct in expressing his rage and hurt. Someday, I hope such poems resurface.

Fan Club Writing

The Beatles, wishing to reward their loyal fans, decided that every year they would issue a special Christmas record (only available to members of the Official Beatle Fan Club). As a result, from 1963--1969, seven such records were diligently pressed (the complete series is available on the Apple release, *From Then To Us*).

In the November/December, 1977, edition of *Beatles Unlimited* (a Beatle bi-monthly publication from Holland), a "complete text" of the seven Beatle Christmas Fan Club Messages was printed. It must be understood that *Beatles Unlimited*'s text is *not* a "reprint" of *any* of the original scripts used by the Beatles. Rather, their text is an "oral transcript" created by careful listening. As such, it is not surprising that a few minor discrepancies came up when the text I derived from my own listening was compared to their published version. At any rate, I've combined the best of both in the text below.

The original "song" was recorded October 20, 1963, and because of its strong stylistic similarities to other Lennon writing, I have attributed its authorship to Beatle John (he also sings "lead" on the tune).

On the record, the Beatles begin by singing, a cappella, the traditional English Christmas carol, "Good King Wenceslas." Below I provide the "correct" version, followed by the Lennon version:

> "Good King Wenceslas looked out,
> On the feast of Stephen,
> When the snow lay round about,
> Deep and crisp and even.
>
> Brightly shone the moon that night,
> Though the frost was cruel,
> When a poor man came in sight,
> Gathering winter fuel."

And now Lennon:

> "Cooking Wenceslas flew down,
> On the feast of Stephen,
> As the slow ray round about,
> Deep and crisp and crispy.
>
> Brightly show the boot last night,
> On the moss-ty crue-el,
> Henry Hall and David Lloyd,
> Betty Grable too!"

After this song, John comes on saying "Hello, this is John speaking with his voice!" He capsulizes the year and concludes: "I'd like to say thank you to all the Beatle people who have written to me during the year, and everyone who sent me gifts and cards for my birthday (which I am trying to forget) in October. I'd love to reply personally to everyone, but I just haven't enough pens, in the meantime . . . [John then sings the following to the tune of "Happy Birthday"]:

"Gary Crimble to you,
Gary Mimple to you,
Getty Baybull dear Christmas,
Happy Birthday me too!"

To my knowledge, this chapter now contains all of the available writings of John Lennon — from childhood up until the publication of *In His Own Write*. Chapter Six will present a similar compilation of the literary works appearing after *In His Own Write*.

Chapter Six

From "The Toy Boy"
to "A Love Letter"

The Final Writings of John Lennon

A short time after the appearance of *In His Own Write*, an American Beatle magazine claimed to have published original writing by the Beatles. Supposedly, the Beatles collaborated on a group biography, "This Is Our Life!" as well as authoring individual bios, i.e., "John's Story; By John Lennon." Immediately following the title of the former piece the editors added, "You may need a translator for the 'Liddypool' lingo, but your struggle will be well rewarded." After the title "John's Story; By John Lennon," nothing was added.

There is no reason to believe that *any* of the Beatles wrote *any* of these articles. In fact, it's highly probable that the material was part of some Beatle publicist's ghost-written copy (or else completely unauthorized writing served up by some enterprising editors).

The text of "John's Story" is rather trite stylistically, and offers only lies about childhood and career, i.e., "This is John Lennon. I think I must have had a happy, contented childhood, because I don't remember anything special about it . . . I think I lived a life of uninterrupted calm"!! Or how about, "One day our big break came with an offer to appear at The Star Club in Hamburg." Now why *this* gig, the Beatles' fourth Hamburg stint, April 13, 1962, should be considered the "big break" is anybody's guess! Later "John" says he saw Ringo for the *first* time at the Beatles' "third" Star Club date (whereas John Lennon not only knew Ringo years earlier, but the Beatles had actually recorded a record with him in the fall of 1960! Etc. ad nauseum . . .).

The truth is, the *first* uncollected original writing by John Lennon was published after both *In His Own Write* and *A Spaniard In The Works*. It is "The Toy Boy" which surfaced, without fanfare, in the December 1965 issue of *McCalls* (p. 68). In fact, this most important poem not only appeared "without fanfare," but arrived virtually unnoticed by anyone. (Even the cover of this issue of *McCalls* does not mention that John's work is inside!) Needless to say, no one has ever written about, much less studied, "The Toy Boy".

161

The Overview

This is the *second* longest poem in the published writings of John Lennon. It consists of eight stanzas and 80 lines (*Spaniard*'s "The Wumberlog," pp. 126–133, is the longest poem, at 30 stanzas and 121 lines).

The opening of the story is told from the point of view of toys living in a young boy's bedroom. Ralph, the Elephant, holds court on the question of whether or not the *boy* is alive! Testimony in the boy's favor is given by Sydney, the Shoe, and by an unnamed Rocking Horse. But Ralph rejects their observations and calls for a quick vote.

The other toys rebel, stating that if the boy is alive he will awaken in the morning. Thus at 8:00 a.m. the clock rings and all the toys become immobile. The point of view switches to that of the boy, as *he* now ponders whether or not the *toys* are alive! He decides they are and informs both of his parents of his discovery. His parents, however, promptly whisk him off to a psychiatrist — who certifies the boy as insane. The poem then closes with a simple "There you are."

The Key Themes

Children's perceptions are not prejudiced by adult concepts of "impossibility." Therefore, children easily entertain and accept the "marvelous" in life, whereas adults limit their experience to certain "facts." Also, parents often punish their children for perceiving anything outside of the parents' immediate reality (in short, they fail to take their children's life experiences seriously).

The Interpretation

From a writing standpoint, "The Toy Boy" is undoubtedly *the most finely crafted poem of all John Lennnon's published work.* It is as captivating and delightfully witty as any of the children's verses in T.S. Eliot's *Old Possum's Book of Practical Cats* (1940). Unlike Eliot, however, Lennon's alleged children's verse incorporates an adult's pointed and rather sardonic point of view.

Thematically, "The Toy Boy" reflects James Thurber's celebrated "The Unicorn in the Garden," from *Fables of Our Time* (1939). For in that fable, a man's wife is certified as insane simply because of her correct perception of what others deem impossible: she sees a Unicorn! As for plot and theme in "The Toy Boy," I believe both are derived from a very personal source — John's own experiences of unreality and isolation, both in childhood and in his Beatle persona.

For instance, in the *Rolling Stone* interviews, John revealed the following about his childhood (italics are my own):

> "I used to think I must be a genius but *nobody's no-tired* . . . I used to think it when I was a kid, writing me poetry and doing me paintings. I didn't become something when the Beatles made it, or when you heard about me, I've been like this all me life . . . I was different. *Why didn't anybody notice me?*"

In *John Lennon: In His Own Words* (1981) he states further:

> "There was something wrong with me, I thought, because *I seemed to see things other people didn't see.* I thought I was crazy or an egomaniac for *claiming to see things other people didn't see* . . . It was scary as a child, because *there was nobody to relate to.* Neither my Auntie nor my friends *nor anybody could ever see what I did* . . . . It was very, very scary."

This is precisely the plight of "The Toy Boy" — *no one sees him*; no one validates his perceptions. Not only is he treated like a defective toy by his parents, but the boy's own "playthings" doubt his very existence; he is *completely* alone. It should be pointed out that the poignancy of this poem is significantly heightened in *Mc-Calls'* original layout. For none other than Robert Freeman was responsible for the unusually tender color photograph of John Lennon that accompanied the poem (you will recall that Freeman did the fine cover photography for both **Meet The Beatles** and **Rubber Soul**, *In His Own Write*, and for *A Spaniard In The Works*).

Freeman's touching portrait of John for "The Toy Boy" shows Lennon sitting on the floor, sans glasses, looking as vulnerable as "The Toy Boy" himself. His left arm is around a large seated, stuffed Teddy Bear, and both "boy" and Bear are in a room unobstructed by furniture or decoration (so that one's focus is *solely* on John and his stuffed companion). Given the tens of thousands of photographs taken of "Beatle" John Lennon, this one stands as an *exceptionally rare* and sensitive view of the *real* John's feelings: fragile and fairy-tale soft.

As was discussed in Chapter Four, 1965 was John's "Fat Elvis" period; thus, by this time the Beatle fame felt like a prolonged projection of an "unreal" self (an image only, not John's actual personality). Add to that Lennon's constant drug use, etc., his lousy EMI contract, his deteriorating marriage . . . and John must have thought of himself as a mere boy, tossed about by various malevolent forces.

The poem is filled with disarming and charming rhymes, i.e.,

"This was Ralph the Elephant/Talking loud and eloquent." There are also funny double entendres: " 'Unfair, unfair!' the Toys all said/ Shoes and Hats have got no head!" I think the most telling section, however, is John's tongue-in-cheek portrait of artists (via the Clock):

> "I will not chime unless I'm heard!"
> He was an *artiste*, so you see —
> He didn't like to chime for free!

The story closes with the boy being betrayed and feeling "small." We'd do well to listen to Lennon's musical analogue to these painful experiences — *You've Got To Hide Your Love Away*. For that song, recorded no later than March, 1965, explores similar feelings of isolation, and therefore deepens our response to "The Toy Boy."

The next two tales, "Jock and Yono" and "Once Upon A Pool-table" were recorded Fall 1968, and released December 20 on the Beatles Annual Christmas Message record. It is important to realize that by 1968 the Beatles were so psychologically "disbanded" that their Fan Club messages were recorded *separately* (and then edited to sound as if all parties were present).

In creating a text for both of these stories, I have used three sources. First, I have again consulted *Beatles Unlimited*'s version published in 1977. Second, I incorporated a "new" version which appeared in 1982 (as part of a classy deluxe "Record Book" inserted in the album **John Lennon — Limited Edition** on Bag Records). Third, I used my own ears to verify the final condition of the text.

"Jock and Yono" has a particularly significant place in the works of *The Literary Lennon*: First, the piece remains the *only* example of John's writings that documents the abuse and harassment suffered by John and Yoko as a result of their celebrated courtship ("Jock And Yono" also *precedes* any Lennon music chronicling their experience; *The Ballad Of John And Yoko* was recorded April 22, 1969); second, "Jock and Yono" is the *only* uncollected writing John thought important enough to bring up in the *Rolling Stone* interviews. Here John remembers how Paul and George mistreated Yoko (Ringo was the exception; he accepted John and his new love without judgment or malice):

> "You can quote Paul . . . . He said many times that at first he hated Yoko and then he got to like her . . . . It's too late for me, I'm for Yoko . . . and George, shit, insulted her right to her face in the Apple office . . . and we both sat through it, and I didn't hit him, I don't know why . . . I couldn't believe it you know. And they . . .

sat there with their wives, like a fucking jury and judged us."

John then goes on to quote a line straight out of "Jock and Yono," the story which was his revenge against the onslaught of Paul and George:

"The only thing I did [as a defense against their verbal attacks] was write that piece about 'some of our beast friends' in my usual way, because I was never honest enough. I always had to write in that gobbledegook."

With John's recollection as a backdrop, we are ready to read "Jock and Yono" (I have chosen to present this piece as a "poem," based upon John's phraseology, and also because I believe it adds to the reader's understanding. I readily admit, however, that the original could have been written in pure prose form).

JOCK AND YONO
By John Lennon

Once upon a time there were two balloons
Called Jock and Yono —
They were strictly in love,
Bound to happen,
Livin' in years . . .
(They were together, man)
Unfortunate timetable
They seem to have previous experience,
Which kept calling them one way or another
(You know how it is)
But they battled on against overwhelming oddities
(Including some of their beast friends)
Being in love they cloong together even more, man,
But some of the poisonousmonsters of
Outratedbusloadyshitthrowers
Did stick, slightly,
And they occasionally had to resort
To the dry cleaners —
Luckily this did not kill them
And they weren't banned from the Olympic games . . .

They lived hopefully ever after
(And who could blame them?)

You will remember that John, in August of 1961, joked about his machismo by referring to himself as "Jock" Lennon in *Mersey Beat*'s Classified Ads. Seven years later he uses "Jock" again, now as a pun on his pugilistic urge to beat up his "friends." John cleverly reveals and conceals in this piece. For example, the buoyant love they shared (childlike in its innocence) is well reflected in the image of John and Yoko as "two balloons." Yet it may also conceal a charge made against them — of being as oversexed and as crazy as two "balling loons." The phrase "bound to happen" on record sounds like the phonetic pun "*band* to happen" (which could connote that John and Yoko not only "banded" together as lovers and artists, but also that they were "bound" to be "banned." In short, their destiny was to be together, regardless of the consequences).

Throughout "Jock and Yono" the parenthetical remarks personalize John's battle against the Beatle bigots and anonymous attackers: "(They were together, man)" "(You know how it is)" etc. But Lennon saves his most pointed phrases to describe his oppressors. Thus the Beatles become "their *beast* friends" (from "best" to "beast" is like from "friend" to "fiend"). Lennon's run-on term, "outratedbusloadyshitthrowers" is particularly well turned.

Actually, the above phrase is composed of three units. The first is a phonetic pun for "outdated." This not only indicts people as being obsolete and passe, but also asserts that people have lost love, being literally "out of dating." "Outrated" itself implies criticism, "rating" John and Yoko, and these self-styled "raters" are "outraged" at the celebrated romance. Thus "busloady" refers to the average and anonymous people, crowded on buses, who spread ugly, gossipy rumors on their way to work. John suggests most of these people are drunk or on drugs ("loaded"). The third part of the terms, "shitthrowers," is self-explanatory; however, John's pronunciation also approximates "hip throwers" (which refers to all those critics who conceive of themselves as "hip," but who only throw the public cheap comments — shot from the hip!).

The narrative line concludes on an upbeat note ("They lived hopefully ever after"); and, seemingly speaking only to other lovers and believers among the readers (or listeners), John asks the simple question, "And who could blame them?"

"Once Upon A Pooltable" differs from "Jock and Yono" in that it appears to be solely a soundsensical work. While admittedly there is plenty of linguistic experimentation present, none of it develops into a coherent point of view. This piece is particularly difficult to transcribe because John uses various dialects, muddy overdubbing, intrusive noises and partially pronounced words in his performance.

It is interesting to note that the "new" text, inserted into **John**

Lennon — Limited Edition, is *twice* as long as the commercially available version. The Fan Club message ends with George yelling "Cut!" which could imply that John's "story" was arbitrarily edited. **John Lennon — Limited Edition** offers no explanation as to the added length of its transcription, so I have no way to verify its authenticity.

I will first present a text to the recorded version found on **From Then To You**, give a brief interpretation, then offer the "long" version without further critical comment (I will state here that this latter version appears totally consistent, stylistically, with the undisputed portion of "Pooltable").

In order to create some semblance of order, I've used a free verse format (attempting to link meaningful clusters of words):

> ONCE UPON A POOLTABLE
> by John Lennon
>
> Once upon a pooltable
> There limped a shorthaired butcher's boy
> By the way of Ostergrad did comes
> (In sentenC'estpoolarrowick airport)
>
> Herr father was in an along story cut short
> (In the middle of his lifesentence)
> We're indebted to the colloquial office
> "For its immediate disposal, our Honorwitz"
> Including, I might add,
> "Hoc Virtallo Virttutembe"
> On the other handbag, I mean to say,
> "L'Amouray nous sommes toujours realistic"
> (Rictly speaking)
>
> For this film is about
> An hourglass houseboat
> The full meaning of Winchester Cathedral
> Defies description
> (Their loss was our Gainsborough nil)
>
> The sound of a manservatile
> Defectively lasting
> (Bared up in a wellbusy Gailydale time)
> How close can yer
> GettysburganddeviatoryCounciloriginally
> A birdbath feeling . . . .

Well, Laities and Gentlenuns, here goes! The most conspicuous aspect of this piece is its multilinguality: German, Russian, Latin and French all swirl in John's sentences. For instance, "Ostergrad" combines two languages: "Oster" is German for "East," and "grad" is Russian for "city." Latin appears in the guise of a logical fallacy, "Ad Hoc Virtallo Virttutembe."

The predominant nonEnglish language used, however, is French. Why? Don't ask moi! But if you're going to call an airport a "cesspool" you might as well say it in French: C'estpool ("*It is* a (cess) pool"!).

The only line almost entirely in French (spoken I might add in a very demotic pronunciation) is "L'amour nous sommes toujours realistic," which translates roughly into "Love to us is always realistic" (that doesn't explain anything, I know, but "There you are")!

Taken out of context, some of the phrases are funny — for instance, "Herr Father" (John pronounces "her" as "Herr"; "Herr is German for "Mister," but also connotes respect or honor) is also "heir" to and "indebted to the colloquial office"! Now, that office houses informal or regional conversation; in short, it may be the place where all of the tale's dialects originate. Herr Father's speech includes a Germanesque term, "Honorwitz" (which also is ironical English for "Honor-wits").

Throughout this hopelessly convoluted "story" are such playful paradoxes as "an a*long* story cut *short* ("In the *middle* of his *life sentence*"), or "Their *loss* was our *Gains*borough *nil*" (the end of which sounds like the score of a soccer game!). Whatever John's intent, "Once Upon A Pooltable" remains a curious and off-the-wall example of Lennon soundsense.

ONCE UPON A POOLTABLE
(continued)

Sort of dissattisfiedthe founder
(Was a bricklayer)
i.
Thelooked into each others eyeballs
Thir tongue clenched minds grasping
At each others whatsits
This was elimentary and the beginning
Of a new line
(Only now it is an old one already —
See how it ages, be on your very askey?)
Known as a briefcase of malaria
To reign over us,
"God Save The Queen,"

(A HARD WORD)
Perhaps she is right to say, "tape it,"
But it's not the same is it??? Taping is
Tapingisstapingodpolerotiniouslyaboutaswell-
sangthingelseon earth do dwell
A scarlet little child
Who is lost to us all in his approach
To humaniteatimetable to kepp up with
Hisownhearse
(Feel a little sick myself)

WITH A CAPITI MY. to whom it may

The next item, "A Short Essay On Macrobiotics," completed by John November 7, 1968, is *not* really an essay at all. It is probably best described as a pictograph plug for *Harmony*, a magazine specializing in macrobiotic diets then being sold in "Greg's" health food store in London. It consists of eight small gesture sketches, accompanied by a few gragmented sentences.

The text, particularly when read without its associated drawings, is puerile and rather awkward. In fact, the single run-on sentence is almost completely monosyllabic and undoubtedly was dashed off without any thought of literary values. Thus, it should be taken simply as a whimsical favor done for Lennon's friend, Greg. The thirty-eight words of the "essay" extol the virtues of a rice diet and, of course, the need for people to subscribe to *Harmony*.

What makes this piece at all interesting? — the miniature illustrations. They include the only "cartoon" versions of the infamous nude photos used on **Two Virgins** (released in America November 11, 1968); also, when John uses "I" in the text, the drawing shows John *and* Yoko, revealing Lennon's complete involvement with his Ocean Child (John *first* performed onstage with Yoko at the Rolling Stones' Rock and Roll Circus Concert December 11, 1968. Later, of course, on **Imagine**, John would declare "I just believe in me, Yoko and me, that's reality."). "A Short Essay On Macrobiotics," complete with illustrations, can be found in *Lennon Remembers* (personally, I prefer the Penguin Books edition, reprinted in 1980, as it's a larger reproduction than those found in either the Popular Library or original Straight Arrow Book's versions).

"This Is My Story Both Humble And True" is John Lennon's last published poem; it was completed in February of 1969. The poem was conceived as part of *John Lennon/Bag One* (the so-called "erotic" lithographs that first went on sale and display January,

A is for Parrot which we can plainly see.

B is for glasses which we can plainly see.

C is for plastic which we can plainly see

D is for Doris

E is for binoculars 9'll get it in five

F is for Ethel who lives next door

G is for Orange which we love to eat when we can get them because they come from abroad.

H is for England and (Heather)

I is for monkey we see in the tree

J is for parrot which we can plainly see

K is for shoetop we wear to the ball

L is for land because brown

M is for Venezuela where the oranges come from

N is for Brazil near Venezuela (very near)

O is for football which we kick about a bit

T is for Tommy who won the war

Q is a garden which we can plainly see.

R is for intestines which hurt when we dance

S is for pancake or whole wheat bread.

U is for Ethel who lives on the hill

P is arab and her sister will.

V is for me

W is for lighter which never lights

X is easter — have one yourself

Y is a crooked letter and you can't straighten it.

Z is for Apple which we can plainly see.

This is my story both humble and true
take it to pieces and mend it with glue.

John Lennon 1969. Feb.

1970 at the London Arts Gallery).

Technically it stands out from all 21 of his poems because its original form is actually as a lithograph. While John, because of his impetuous nature, used only litho paper for the suite itself (with the exception of the frontispiece), he felt compelled to hand engrave this poem upon a zinc plate (the more traditional lithographic procedure). Even so, there are — to my eyes, anyway — some visual ambiguities in his "writing" (I have bracketed the words I cannot completely verify):

> "A is for Parrot which we can plainly See
> B is for glasses which we can plainly See
> C is for plastic which we can plainly See
> D is for Doris
> E is for binoculars I'll [get] it in [five]
> E is for Ethel who lives next door
> G is for Orange which we love to eat when we
>   get them because they come from abroad
> H is for England and (Heather)
> I is for monkey we see in the tree
> J is for parrot which we can plainly See
> K is for [shoe top] we wear to the ball
> L is for lana because [bum]
> M is for Venezuela where the oranges came from
> N is for Brazil near Venezuela (very near)
> O is for football which we luck about & [kif]
> T is for Tommy who won the war
> Q is a garden which we can plainly See
> K is for intestines which hurt when we dance
> S is for pancake or wholewheat bread
> U is for Ethel who lives on the hill
> P is [arals] and her sister will
> V is for me
> W is for lighter which never lights
> X is easter — have one yourself
> Y is a crooked letter and you can't straighten it.
> Z is for Apple which we can plainly See
>
> This is my story both humble and true
> take it to pieces and mend it with glue
>
> John Lennon 1969 Feb."

As you undoubtedly experienced for yourself, the style of the poem is rather surreal. Initially, the poem appears to be an alphabetical

171

acrostic: "A is for," "B   is for," etc. That is, until you notice two "E's" and no "F"! Then the expected order breaks down even further: after "O" comes "T," after "Q" is "K," and after "S" is "U," etc.

To be sure, some of the lines are ludicrous in and of themselves, irrespective of the calculated chaos in the poem: "K is for intestines which hurt when we dance;" "Y is a crooked letter and you can't straighten it." Ultimately, the poem works effectively on its own surrealistic level: it helps free the mind of preconceptions regarding form and content; it urges us to let go of habitual ways of seeing; it introduces a sense of humor to our otherwise "serious" gallery gazing. In short, the poem implicitly asks us to accept, without judgment, what is right in front of our eyes (an apt introduction to *Bag One*, whose honesty and beauty were nevertheless misconstrued as "obscenity" by uptight people the world over. Case in point: the London gallery holding the exhibit was closed down on obsceni- ty charges January 16, 1970. And in the United States, *Bag One* was banned in Boston in 1981!).

"Four in Hand" is a short scene in *Oh! Calcutta!*, a theatrical work devised by Kenneth Tynan and conceived and directed by Jacques Levy, which opened June 17, 1969 at the Eden Theatre in New York City. This work has fifteen contributors, including Samuel Beckett, Jules Feiffer, and John Lennon. It is interesting to note that on the *original* Theatre Program, Lennon is given *fourth* billing; one would suspect that a fairly substantial contribution was made to this work. However, this is not the case; it was John's name and fame only which accounted for such auspicious placement on *Calcutta*'s playbill.

To set the record straight, John did not write even one single scene for *Oh! Calcutta!* What he did do was contribute a two or three line "premise" for a scene (which somebody else developed into the scene itself: "Four in Hand"). We are fortunate that Jann Wenner asked Lennon about *Oh! Calcutta!* in his *Rolling Stone* interviews:

> "Wenner — 'You also did a scene for the Tynan play. How did that come about?'
>
> Lennon — 'I met Tynan a few times around and about and he just said — "I'm getting all these different people to write something erotic, will you do it?" And I told him that if I come up with something I'd do it and if I don't, I don't. So I came up with . . . two or three lines which was the masturbation scene. It was a great

childhood thing, everybody's been masturbating and trying to think of something sexy and somebody'd shout Winston Churchill in the middle of it and break down. So I just wrote that down on a paper and told him to put whichever names in that suited the hero and they did it. I've never seen it."

Below is this scene in its *final* form (chances are that Tynan himself wrote the piece):

Four in Hand

Four chairs, backs to audience. Facing them, a large projection screen divided into four sections, one for each chair. Three men impatiently waiting. A doorbell rings.

1: There he is now. I told you he'd make it. (He opens door.)

GEORGE enters: he wears a fedora.

If you're going to join the group, George, you have to remember we always start on time.

GEORGE: Sorry I'm late, fellas.

2: We don't like people breakin' the rules, George.

GEORGE: I already said I'm sorry.

3: Look — We gonna talk, or we gonna jerk off?

1: O.K., let's get started. This is your seat, George. Now this (pointing to screen) is a new kind of machine — a telepathic thought transmitter. Whatever you think about flashes on the screen. Now the rules of the game are this: all of us think of things to jerk off to — until somebody comes — and the first guy who comes has to stop everybody else from coming. Got it?

GEORGE: Got it.

1: All right. Let's give it a try. Whatever comes to mind, George.

1. goes to his seat. GEORGE sits between 2 and 3. Rhythmic music starts. Images start to flash rhythmically on the screens. The men's arms start to move rhythmically in front of them. The screens facing 1, 2, and 3 show Hollywood and Playboy-type pinups. GEORGE's screen remains blank. The rhythm builds up while screens 1, 2, and 3 are all pulsating with glamorous women. Suddenly, we hear the strains of the "William Tell Overture," and during a crash of cymbols a picture of the Lone Ranger flashes on GEORGE's screen. All screens go blank and all four men stop masturbating.

3: What the fuck was that?

1: What are ya tryin' to do, George?

GEORGE: What's wrong?

2 (rises, adjusting his pants): I told you not to invite outsiders.

GEORGE: I'm sorry, fellas, it's the first thing that came into my mind.

2: We haven't had a vacancy in six months, George! Harvey only left because he got a divorce.

3: How'd you like a silver bullet up your ass?

1 (walking to GEORGE): You sure you're all right, George?

GEORGE: I'm fine, thanks.

1: All right, let's try it again.

They all sit down again.
    And cut the horseshit, George.

The music starts again and the images start to flash. They are slightly more nude than before — close shots of breasts and bottoms. By trial and error, the four screens begin to form a composite picture. GEORGE is dutifully collaborating. Finally, at the height of the rhythm, screen facing 1 shows a nude model's head, screen facing 2 shows her breasts, screen facing 3 her legs. Pause. The recumbent image of the model is almost complete. Suddenly, the strains of the "William Tell Overture" again and another image of the Lone Ranger on GEORGE's screen.

GEORGE (exultantly): Aha! A-a-a-ah!
He rises. His screen continues to flash the Lone Ranger. With one jabbing sweep of his arm he flashes Ranger pictures on the other screens as the music builds. As each image flashes, 1, 2, and 3 lose their concentration completely and give up the contest.

GEORGE (turns as he goes to exit): See you next week, fellas.

1: Get the fuck outta here!!!

Sound of four "whistling" gunshots as each remaining screen blacks out.

END

One final footnote regarding Lennon and *Oh! Calcutta!* All of the "contributors" were asked to provide a biographical sketch to be printed in the playbill. John submitted the following:

"Born October 9, 1940. Lived. Met Yoko 1966!"

Few people realize that Yoko Ono's book *Grapefruit* actually dates to the American explosion of Beatlemania in 1964. At that time, Yoko had published an edition, limited to 500 copies, in Japanese and English, of her unique volume of poetry. Oddly enough, most of what has been written about *Grapefruit* was derived from interviews with John Lennon long after the book first appeared.

John often spoke of *Grapefruit* because it had a significant impace on his creative and social life. For instance, while still married to Cynthia, Yoko's book was providing John with bedside mysteries, goading him, delighting him and confusing him. Later, *Grapefruit* even provided the lyrical basis of *Imagine* (though Lennon admitted his chauvinism prevented him from giving Yoko co-author credit).

So, it is fitting that in 1970 John wrote his one and only "Introduction" to another author's book — *Grapefruit*. The introduction is minimalist like Yoko's text, and stands only as a personal anecdote, rather than any example of John's writing ability:

"Hi! My Name is John Lennon
I'd like you to meet Yoko Ono."

The book jacket also included a one line Lennon "review" (in response to Yoko's request that all readers of *Grapefruit* should burn it upon completion): "This is the greatest book I've ever burned — John."

Well folks, here it is, if not *the rarest of all John Lennon publications*, certainly the most mysterious. In 1971, Mini-Books, Inc. printed *ten* copies of a work called *My Mummy's Dead* by John Lennon. To this day I have never read any information regarding *My Mummy's Dead* (I thank Tom Schultheiss at Pierian Press for the library citation that informed me of its existence).

As most students from U.S.C. know, the best university research library in town is at U.C.L.A.! So off I went to search for this obscure volume in the "enemy" camp. I found *My Mummy's Dead*, copy number seven, in the Special Collections downstairs (PS509/B31/1971/L548m.).

My suspicions were confirmed: *My Mummy's Dead* is a privately printed, deluxe edition of the lyrics to, you guessed it, *My Mummy's Dead* (**John Lennon** — **Plastic Ono Band**, 1970). Now, the publisher wasn't kidding, this is literally a "Mini-Book." It is 3 by 5 inches and consists of just eight single sided leaves. The lyrics are printed in black ink upon a grey cardboard type paper. Each line is centered and printed all in capital letters.

There is no way to know if this curious little project had Lennon's approval or if a fan just printed up his favorite Lennon lyric on his own initiative. I include this documentation to preempt any confusion one would encounter if this citation popped up in a bibliography or was "mentioned" somewhere without clarification.

Those of you who have researched John in the library no doubt have also spotted a rare 1976 citation to a book entitled *A Canoe for Uncle Kila (No Kila Ka Wa'a Kaulua)*, by Stanley Kapepa, with "Illustrations by John Lennon." As this book is typically listed with, or cross referenced to, all of John's other published work, one naturally assumes it to be John's one and only project as bona fide "illustrator."

What an exiting find! A Hawaiian children's book, 48 pages long, filled with John's quirky and humorous illustrations! It makes perfect sense, too, that John would choose a children's book to illustrate, since it would aptly showcase his own "primitive" drawing

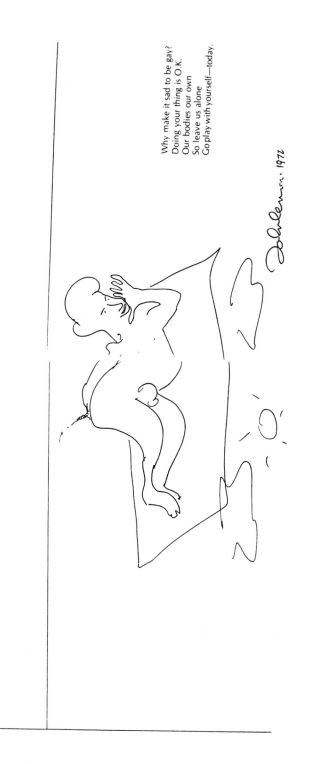

Why make it sad to be gay?
Doing your thing is O.K.
Our bodies our own
So leave us alone
Go play with yourself—today.

John Lennon. 1972

177

style. Furthermore, it seems possible the project could have been at the behest of a friend of Yoko's, as Hawaii has a large Japanese population (though, of course, Yoko's friend could be other than Japanese/Hawaiian).

Since the book was not available in any libraries in my area, and since John's "secret treasure" was also out of print, I decided to call the publishers direct in Honolulu. To my surprise and, despite the above "evidence" to the contrary, the illustrator of *A Canoe for Uncle Kila* was "a local boy" and *not* "The" John Lennon. So, sadly we must move on.

I have previously documented John's second longest and finest poem was never collected with his other works before *The Literary Lennon*. Well, interestingly enough, the shortest poem John ever published has, until this volume, also remained uncollected. There are several features about this piece that make it unique. First, it is the only poem and illustration appearing in an anthology. In this case, Lennon's work rests alongside special contributions offered by Gore Vidal, Alan Watts, Huey Newton, Allen Ginsberg and William Burroughs, among others. The issue is Gay (Men's) Liberation and the book is simply entitled *The Gay Liberation Book*, 1973.

Second, as stated above, this is the shortest poem John ever published: an untitled, five-line limerick. Third, it is the *only* Lennon limerick in print:

> "Why make it sad to be gay?
> Doing your thing is O.K.
> Our bodies our own
> So leave us alone
> Go play with yourself — today."

This lighthearted limerick is accompanied by a two-page illustration. Depicted is a nude male, sprawled and smiling upon a magic carpet (that flies over a bright sun and drifting clouds). The drawing is signed and dated 1972.

On Sunday, September 30, 1973 a swansong of John Lennon's made its auspicious appearance. It was the *only* book review Lennon ever penned and it appeared in no less a newspaper than the *New York Times*. This 700-word review is a heartfelt tribute to Spike Milligan, Peter Sellers and Harry Secombe, collectively known as the Goons. There is very little to say about the review, as it is quite self-explanatory and reveals John's honest admiration for a major influence in his life. Due to its rarity, the review is printed below in its entirety.

178

You had to be there, and he was

THE GOON SHOW SCRIPTS

by Spike Milligan
Illustrated. 189 pp. New York:
St. Martin's Press. $5.95.

On May 28, 1951, three actors named Spike Milligan, Peter Sellers and Harry Secombe, employing a variety of sometimes maniacal voices, launched The Goon Show in the hitherto staid precincts of B.B.C. radio. For Americans who never heard it (it has been broadcast on WBAI in New York) The Goon Show is difficult to describe. Call it pure radio and pure comedy with a good dollop of the Marx brothers veering off into the empyrean of pure surrealism. The program did have scripts, of course, written mostly by Spike Milligan, and there was a plot of sorts which was somewhere between a Chinese opera and World War II in comprehensibility. The "stories" bore such pregnant titles as "The Dreaded Batter Pudding Hurler (of Bexhill-on-Sea)," "The Phantom Head-Shaver (of Brighton)" and "Foiled by President Fred." Milligan, Sellers and Secombe impersonated a variety of characters including Ned Seagoon, Maj. Denis Bloodnok, the nefarious Moriarty, Gryptype-Thynne and Blue Bottle. Goonery was not so much a show, more a way of life, and if you have to ask what it was, we'll be here all day explaining the joke. The Goon Show expired, to eternal regrets in Britain, on Jan. 28, 1960.

By JOHN LENNON

I was 12 when the Goon Shows first hit. Sixteen when they finished with me. Their humor was the only proof that the WORLD was insane. Spike Milligan's (may he always) book of scripts is a cherished memory, for me, what it means to Americans I can't imagine (apart from a rumored few fanatics). As they say in Tibet, "You had to be there." The goons influenced The Beatles (along with Lewis Carroll/Elvis Presley). Before becoming The Beatles' producer, George Martin, who had never recorded rock-n-roll, had previously recorded with Milligan and Sellers, which made him all the more acceptable — our studio sessions were full of the cries of Neddie Seagoon, etc., etc., as were most places in Britain. There are records of some of the original radio shows, some of which I have, but when I play them to Yoko, I find myself explaining "that in those days there was no monty pythons 'flyin' circus,' " no "laugh-in," in fact, the same rigmarole I go through with my "fifties

179

records," "before rock it was just Perry Como," etc. What I'm trying to say is, one has to have been there! The Goon Show was long before and more revolutionary than "look back in anger" (it appealed to "eggheads" and "the people"). Hipper than the Hippest and madder than "Mad," a conspiracy against reality. A "coup d'etat" of the mind! The evidence, for and against, is in this book. A copy of which should be sent to Mr. Nixon and Mr. Ervin.

One of my earlier efforts at writing was a "newspaper" called the Daily Howl. I would write it at night, then take it to school and read it aloud to my friends; looking at it now it seems strangely similar to The Goon Show! Even the title had "highly esteemed" before it! Ah well, I find it very hard to keep my mind on the BOOK itself, the tapes still ring so clearly in my head. I could tell you to buy the book anyway because Spike Milligan's a genius and Peter Sellers made all the money! (Harry Secombe got SHOW BIZ.) I love all three of them dearly, but Spike was extra. His appearances on TV as "himself" were something to behold. He always "Freaked out" the cameramen/directors by refusing to FIT THE PATTERN. He would run off camera and DARE them to follow him. I think they did, once or twice, but it kept him off more shows than it helped get him on. There was always the attitude that, he was "wonderful but, you know . . . . (indicating head). I think it's 'cause he's Irish. (The same attitude prevails toward all non-English British.)

I'm supposed to write 800 words, but I can't count. Anyway, Spike wouldn't approve. I could go on all day about the Goons and their influence on a generation (at least one), but it doesn't seem to be about THE BOOK! I keep thinking how much easier it would be to review it for a British paper. What the hell! I've never REVIEWED anything in my life before. Now I know why critics are "nasty." It would be easier if I didn't like the book, but I do, and I'd love you to love the Goons as I do. So take a chance.

p.s.: Dick Lester (of Hard Days Beatles fame) directed the TV version of the Goon Show, "a Show called Fred"; it was good, but radio was freer — i.e., you couldn't float Dartmoor prison across the English Channel on TV (maybe the B.B.C. should have spent more money). Also there is a rare and beautiful film (without Harry Secombe) called "The running, Jumping and Standing Still Film." Ask your local "art house" to run it — it's a masterpiece, and captures the Goon "spirit" very well.

John Lennon, the now and former Beatle, studied capitalization in the Liverpool school system, and is the author of "In His Own Write," "Spaniard in the Works" and other works.

In 1975, John Lennon participated in an "Exclusive Symposium on Utopia," which was published in *The People's Almanac* (by David Wallechinsky and Irving Wallace). For this Symposium, nine diverse individuals "well known in their respective fields" were polled as to their "personal version of utopia." Specifically, this panel, which included Buckminster Fuller, Jr. (designer, inventor, philosopher, etc., et amazing), Monty Hall ("Let's Make a Deal"), Spock (Dr. Benjamin, not our favorite Vulcan), and Eartha Kitt (singer and entertainer) all answered the same nine questions.

Now, in the *Almanac*, John's answers were sandwiched between Eartha Kitt's and Desmond Morris's (he authored *The Naked Ape*). Everyone's response, *except* for John's, is quite serious and specific (particularly Buckminster Fuller, Jr.'s). Below is a compiled version of *all* of Lennon's responses to the nine questions:

Q. What would the physical environment of your utopia be like?
A. Typical.
Q. What family structures would exist?
A. Any.
Q. How would the government be organized?
A. Toss a coin.
Q. How would work and goods be divided?
A. Color of eyes.
Q. How would education take place?
A. Slowly.
Q. What crimes would there be, and how would they be punished?
A. Plenty. Somehow.
Q. What would be YOUR role in this society?
A. Heavenly.
Q. Why isn't life like this now?
A. Isn't it?
Q. Any other comments?
A. No.

It appears that seven years after *Revolution*, John still had "no plan" for instituting utopia — although, of course, his musings in *Imagine* (October 1971) provide more in the way of details than do the whimsical responses above.

The penultimate citation of John Lennon's writings I have been unable, as yet, to fully track down. Nicholas Schaffner in his fine *The Beatles Forever*, 1977, states that around 1975 "John began to enjoy lending his off-beat literary talents to an unlikely assortment of publications." Now, we've already documented *all* the publications Schaffner refers to but one: "A West Coast rag called *Sundance*, which featured a weekly column by the Lennons."

Unfortunately, there appears to be some inaccuracy with Schaffner's citation. The only *Sundance* on the West Coast during this period made its debut in 1972 and became defunct in 1974. It was published by Running Dog Incorporated on Fillmore Street in San Francisco, and was edited by Kenneth Kelly and Greg Pyes. However, this *Sundance* was bi-monthly, so "the Lennons" couldn't have had "a *weekly* column," assuming this is the same publication.

Sundance consisted primarily of book and film reviews (though it's possible John and Yoko had a special "open" format). As I've not been able to personally view the issues in question, I present the above as a "questionable" citation.

With the following piece, we have completed our course of study on *The Literary Lennon*. "A Love Letter From John And Yoko To People Who Ask Us What, When, And Why" is the last example of writing to be covered; and appropriately, as with **Double Fantasy**, it is a collaborative effort with Yoko. It was printed in several major newspapers and appeared in *The New York Times* Sunday, May 27, 1979:

A Love Letter From Yoko And John
To People Who Ask Us What, When And Why

The past ten years we noticed everything we wished came true in its own time, good or bad, one way or the other. We kept telling each other that one of these days we would have to get organized and wish for only good things. Then our baby arrived: We were overjoyed and at the same time felt very responsible. Now our wishes would also affect *him*. We felt it was time for us to stop discussing and do something about our wishing process: The Spring Cleaning of our minds! It was a lot of work. We kept finding things in those old closets in our minds that we hadn't realized were still there, things we wished we hadn't found. As we did our cleaning, we also started to notice many wrong things in our house: there was a shelf which should never have been there in the first place, a painting we grew to dislike, and there were the two dingy rooms, which became light and breezy when we broke the walls between them. We started to love the plants, which one of us originally thought were robbing the air from us! We began to enjoy the drum beat of the city which used to annoy us. We made a lot of mistakes and still do. In the past we spent a lot of energy in trying to get something we thought we wanted, wondered why we didn't get it, only to find out that one or both of us didn't really want it. One day, we received a sudden rain of chocolates from people around the world. "Hey, what's this! We're not eating sugar stuff, are we?" "Who's wishing it?" We both laughed. We discovered that when two of us wished in unison, it happened faster. As the Good Book says — Where two are gathered together — It's true. Two is plenty. A Newclear Seed.

More and more we are starting to wish and pray. The things we have tried to achieve in the past by flashing a V sign, we try now through wishing. We are not doing this because it is simpler. Wishing is more effective than waving flags. It works. It's like magic. Magic is simple. Magic is real. The secret of it is to know that it is simple, and not kill it with an elaborate ritual which is a sign of insecurity. When somebody is angry with us, we draw a halo around his or her head in our minds. Does the person stop being angry then? Well, we don't know! We know, though, that when we draw a halo around a person, suddenly the person starts to look like an angel to us. This helps us to feel warm towards the person, reminds us that everyone has goodness inside, and that all people who come to us are angels in disguise, carrying messages and gifts to us from the Universe. Magic is logical. Try it sometime.

We still have a long way to go. It seems the more we get into cleaning, the faster the wishing and receiving process gets. The house is getting very comfortable now. Sean is beautiful. The plants are growing. The cats are purring. The town is shining, sun, rain or snow. We live in a beautiful universe. We are thankful every day for the plentifulness of our life. This is not a euphemism. We understand that we, the city, the country, the earth are facing very hard times, and there is panic in the air. Still the sun is shining and we are here together, and there is love between us, our city, the country, the earth. If two people like us can do what we are doing with our lives, any miracle is possible! It's true we can do with a few big miracles right now. The thing is to recognize them when they come to you and to be thankful. First they come in a small way, in every day life, then they come in rivers, and in oceans. It's goin' to be alright! The future of the earth is up to all of us.

Many people are sending us vibes every day in letters, telegrams, taps on the gate, or just flowers and nice thoughts. We thank them all and appreciate them for respecting our quiet space, which we need. Thank you for all the love you send us. We feel it every day. We love you, too. We know you are concerned about us. That is nice. That's why you want to know what we are doing. That's why everybody is asking us What, When and Why. We understand. Well, this is what we've been doing. We hope that you have the same quiet space in your mind to make your own wishes come true.

If you think of us next time, remember, our silence is a silence of love and not of indifference. Remember, we are writing in the sky instead of on paper — that's our song. Lift your eyes and look up in the sky. There's our message. Lift your eyes again and look around you, and you will see that you are walking in the sky, which extends to the ground. We are all part of the sky, more so than of the ground. Remember, we love you.

John & Yoko

John Lennon & Yoko Ono
May 27, 1979
New York City

P.S. We noticed that three angels were looking over our shoulders when we wrote this!

Now, in retrospect, we all understand the "Love Letter's" metaphors: the "Spring Cleaning" of their minds, the need for "quiet space," etc. This message stands, and always will remain, a tender credo of their personal and public caring. It's stylistic simplicity fits the simple truth of its content:

We made a lot of mistakes and still do . . . . Magic is real . . . . Two is plenty. A Newclear Seed . . . . We still have a long way to go . . . . Thank you for all the love you send us . . . . Remember, we love you.

Part III
The Future Works

Chapter Seven

Loose Ends
and New Starts

There remain only two key questions to be answered in our study of the Literary Lennon. First, did John leave us any unpublished manuscripts with which to form a "final" volume? Second, do we know of any proposed writing projects that John intended to complete in the future?

The answers to both questions have recently been provided by the publication of *The Playboy Interviews with John Lennon and Yoko Ono*, 1981. This "complete" transcription of David Sheff's massive 20-hour interview includes John's last words regarding his writing career.

While answering Sheff's persistent Beatle reunion queries, John digressed onto the reason he stopped writing books after *A Spaniard In The Works*. He candidly admitted that he simply could *not* handle the pressure of producing another literary "hit." (Remember, *In His Own Write* had been for John a giggle, just pure fun, and his writing flowed effortlessly, spontaneously, but *Spaniard* was pure torture.) Lennon had literally relied on hard liquor, *every* night, to get himself through *Spaniard*, all the fun of writing was gone, and now John *self-consciously* worked to produce a follow-up to the critical and financial success of *In His Own Write*. The emotional strain and anxiety were too much of a price to pay.

Fortunately for us, Sheff pursues John on this question, so that Lennon reveals — for the *first* time — that in 1975 he completed a first draft of a new book . . . . A book penned one decade after *A Spaniard In The Works*!

Apparently, after John "retired" from music, he was seized with the feeling that he must be producing "something" creative, so he wrote, in the style of *In His Own Write*, a new book. But John was never happy with it, feeling it needed more work, that it somehow didn't gel, so he just put it in a box for resurrection at some future date.

Now, most probably, John is exaggerating when he states that he wrote "two hundred pages." (After all, *In His Own Write* is 81 pages and *A Spaniard In The Works* is 91 pages.) Of course, it is apparent that John's manuscript was a work in progress, and therefore likely contained many pages that would have been cut. At any rate, John's *Scrapbook of Madness* (my personal title derived from his closing words during the *Rolling Stone* interviews) could be published in some form in the future. Perhaps the best of these "new" tales, judiciously edited and with commentary, could be combined with any remnants of *The Daily Howl* or other juvenalia that remain. I hope so.

As to the question of proposed works that had tantalized Lennon's fertile imagination? Well, thanks again to *The Playboy Interviews*, we know of two such projects: the first was a children's book, and one imagines an extended story a la *Lucy In The Sky With Diamonds* (for John maintained to David Sheff that the images in *Lucy* were *not* drug inspired, but were derived "from *Alice in Wonderland*"). Such a children's book would have been a natural progression for John, as he had touched on this form in his prose and poetry (particularly in "The Wumberlog (or The Magic Dog)" in *Spaniard*).

The greatest departure for the literary Lennon, however, would have been a docu-drama of the five women that constituted John's "family." As described to Sheff, all of these women were sisters and included John's mother Julia and his Aunt Mimi, and Lennon had envisioned a series along the lines of *The Forsyte Saga*. Sadly, these ideas never had a chance to become fully grown.

The remainder of this final chapter of *The Literary Lennon* brings together various loose ends: Documentation and a critique of *The Lennon Play: In His Own Write* (1968); an annotated review of radio, record, newspaper and television material relevant to the study of "author" John Lennon; a list of the pseudonyms that John used on the liner notes of his solo albums; a statistical fact sheet summarizing John's literary output; and, finally, suggestions of pertinent areas of research for future literary studies.

It was some fifteen years ago that the revised and expanded version of *The Lennon Play: In His Own Write* was performed at the National Theatre in London. To my knowledge this script is still the *only* adaptation of John Lennon's writings for the legitimate stage. Its adaptors, Adrienne Kennedy, an American dramatist, and Victor Spinetti, an actor, edited and spliced together approximately 28 items from Lennon's major canon. (Tom Schultheiss in *A Day In The Life* (1981) states that Victor Spinetti produced and directed the show, which implies that Kennedy alone "adapted" the material. However, the published script makes no such designation, and though the foreword is penned by Spinetti, it uses "we" throughout — suggesting a total collaboration to follow. I will therefore attribute the adaptation to "Kennedy-Spinetti.") The result was a one-act play, the script of which was loosely based on five poems and 12 prose pieces from *In His Own Write*, as well as five poems and six prose pieces from *A Spaniard In The Works*. In order to make this compilation plausible onstage, the adaptors tell us in their foreword "We invented a family who were confirmed T.V. addicts, rarely speaking to ME, the central character, so he created his own fantasy world and spoke to his own familiars."

As one who has studied adaptation on the doctoral level at U.S.C. and who himself has adapted the works of an author into an "original" two-act play, I feel I know first-hand the difficulties involved in such a project. My *A Pretty Brick Story For Childsize Heroes* (1974) was adapted from *all* the major, minor, and uncollected prose and poetry of — you guessed it — James Joyce. At any rate, all I wish to present here is a cursory critique of *The Lennon Play: In His Own Write*.

I think the weaknesses of this play begin with its title, for it misleads the audience into believing that the play is a staging of only one thing — John's inaugural work, *In His Own Write*. The play's original title was more effective: *Act 1, Scene 3*. This first appellation was derived from the title of one of John's own play scenes (pp. 40–42); it's also more appropriate because the play is, in fact, a one act.

For me personally, the most lamentable aspect of Kennedy and Spinetti's adaptation is the unbounded license they took — of *re*-writing Lennon's original work! The most glaring example is "The SinguLarge Experience of Miss Anne Duffield"; John's story becomes, in the Spinetti/Kennedy version, a sequence of events in which "Jock The Cripple" is really Inspectre Basil! And where Mary Atkins is (arbitrarily) kept alive!! And where "Womlbs," *as* Mary Atkins, captures Jock!!! Only to have Jock-Inspectre commit suicide onstage!!!! Unfortunately, there is yet more damage to report, for there are, throughout the play, *many* awkward and pointless attempts to ape Lennon's style. Needless to say, I find this situation to be a serious infringement on the integrity of John Lennon's work — simply because John's writing is repeatedly misrepresented before the audience (who assume that what they hear onstage is what John wrote). Ironically, even such experts as Philip Norman (*Shout!*) and Anthony Fawcett (*One Day At A Time*) were fooled; they both cite "Pregnant De Gaulle" as Lennon's, but it isn't! "Prevelant ze Gaute" is! (*In His Own Write*'s "You Might Well Arsk," p.57).

I am not saying that Kennedy and Spinetti had bad intentions, or even that their "additions" weren't fully thought through. What I am saying is that it is *totally unnecessary* for any adaptors to formulate "new" material when adapting Lennon's work for the stage. His writing literally speaks for itself; it therefore only needs judicious editing, not rewriting of *any* kind. To be fair to Kennedy and Spinetti, however, I must admit that they clearly print their own names right underneath Lennon's (and in the same size) on the script's title page. Also in their defense, I'll state here that, alas, it's common practice for adaptors to "creatively compile" the work of an author in the same way Kennedy and Spinetti have done with John Lennon.

The theme of *The Lennon Play*, according to its adaptors, is as follows: "This play is about the growing up of many of us: the things that helped us to be more aware . . . .". I find no fault with this theme per se; unfortunately, the cut-and-paste Kennedy/Spinetti script does not capture such a human "journey." Almost no story or poem is presented intact; rather, a confusing fragment from one item is attached — arbitrarily, it seems — to another fragment. And in this way, no thematic momentum is developed. All in all, I find *The Lennon Play: In His Own Write* to be a first, and not highly successful, attempt at adapting the writings of John Lennon for the stage.

The final item on the agenda is a brief, annotated bibliography and literary summary regarding John Lennon:

Radio

1) January 9, 1965. John guests on BBC 2's "Not Only . . . But Also." Citations state that John "read his poetry" on this show, but no specifics are offered. Since *A Spaniard In The Works* would not be published for another five months (June 24), it seems reasonable that John may have restricted his reading to selections from *In His Own Write*.

2) July 3, 1965. John makes an appearance on BBC's "World of Books." Here we know for certain that Lennon was interviewed specifically on *A Spaniard In The Works* (it having only been out for nine days).

Recording

1) The Apple release **From Then To Us** (1970) contains all the orally published material covered in *The Literary Lennon*: "Gary Crimble," "Old King Wenceslas," "Jock And Yono," and "Once Upon A Pooltable."

2) The Beatle magazine *Strawberry Fields Forever* has provided its readers with special Christmas 10-inch flexidisc recordings of rare Beatle material. We are fortunate that one such recording, The 1978 Christmas Record (Audio Disc No. 32; Eva-Tone 128781 A and B) contains John Lennon reading the following:

A. One poem from *In His Own Write*, "I Sat Belonely" (p. 66). John's delivery here is tentative, and seems to get even more so as he continues (tagging on a nervous "The End" at its conclusion). Yet the record captures an apt simplicity, an unadorned interpretation, which is satisfying to the ear (on this most poignant of *Write*'s poems).

Unlike the selections that follow, this reading has neither background music nor any apparent audience, so it is very easy to concentrate on John's performance.

B. One complete poem from *A Spaniard In The Works*, "The National Health Cow" (pp. 144--145). John's fear of failure as a poet is greatly heightened by two circumstances surrounding this reading. One, it takes place in the context of a crowded press conference. Two, Paul's subverting presence makes John extra self conscious:

John: Are we gonna read one?
Paul: Yeah, go on read that . . .
John: Why don't we *all* read it?
Paul: [Testily] Come on, [stubborn?]
John: Alright; "The National Health Cow," page 62

After John completes the first stanza, he anxiously throws in "Don't like that" (it's unclear if he is referring to the poem, to his performance, or to both). Then, after the next three stanzas, whether by John's nonverbal cue or his own initiative, Paul joins in on the reading of the final stanza.

Because of the background music (possibly inserted by magazine editors), the chaos of the press conference, and Paul's sudden, out-of-sync delivery, there's not much of an interpretation to comment on.

C. One incomplete reading of another poem from *A Spaniard In The Works*, "The Fat Budgie" (pp. 100--101). John's performance on the first two stanzas of this poem is the best of the batch. But Paul's implicit jealousy and disapproval quickly becomes explicit. For he rudely interrupts John as John is just beginning the next stanza:

Paul: Same kind of rubbish . . .
John: [Ostensibly falling in line with Paul's put-down, but not without a subtle tone of irony] Yeah, the same kind of rubbish, that's right Paul.
Paul: Just like the first one . . . .

It's obvious to the listener that Paul had great difficulty accepting that area of John's talent in which he could not participate, and so in petty fashion he tries to humiliate John (thus giving himself a false sense of superiority). This moment, recorded in 1965, hints at the reality of the perpetual power struggle between John and Paul (which reached its height publicly in the film of *Let It Be* . . . five years later).

Newspaper

1) *Seattle Post Intelligencer*, August 22, 1964:

> "John read some excerpts from his book *In His Own Write*, but hammed it up toward the end and read the last few sentences through clenched teeth, then laughed along with everyone else in the room."

This account reveals (once again) John Lennon's insecurity concerning his "writing persona," and how it felt to be in the spotlight with his work. The report also falls neatly in line with the tone and texture one hears in the *Strawberry Fields Forever* recordings.

2) *The News Tribune* (Tacoma, WA) August 22, 1964:

> "John entertained the group [of reporters] by reading — in a heavy accent — a short poem from a book he has written [*In His Own Write*]. It drew enthusiastic applause."

Television

1) March 23, 1964. John Lennon makes an appearance on BBC's "Tonight" program. This broadcast contains an interview with John about *In His Own Write* (which had hit the streets that same day).

2) June 18, 1965. John makes a return visit to BBC's "Tonight." This time, predictably enough, he is discussing and promoting *A Spaniard In The Works* (which would be on sale in less than a week).

3) June 24, 1965. John Lennon guests on ITV's "Today" show. He promotes *A Spaniard In The Works* (which was published on the same day).

4) June 22, 1968. John Lennon shows up on a BBC program called "Release." In this broadcast John takes part in a discussion of the stage adaptation of *In His Own Write* and *A Spaniard In The Works* (AKA *The Lennon Play: In His Own Write*).

Though John Lennon used the pseudonym "Beatcomber" for his *Mersey Beat* column, we know that Lennon was given that nom de plume by Bill Harry. It is not commonly realized that John often chose his own pseudonym when recording. The following eleven examples are derived from the liner notes on John Lennon's solo albums:

1) Dr. Winston and Booker Table and the Maitre d's (*Beef Jerky* – It is obviously a pun on the jazz group "Booker T and the MG's").

2) Rev. Fred Ghurkin (appropriately this clerical disguise was used on *Bless You*).

3) Dr. Winston O. Boogie and Los Paranoias (Dr. Winston O. Boogie was John's "on the air" name when he was interviewed for WNEW-FM New York promoting **Walls And Bridges**. The only printed use of "Dr. Winston O. Boogie," however, was on **Mind Games**. "Los Paranoias" was John's translation of the traditional Latin number, *Las Paraguayas*! John was known to instantly break into this number while rehearsing during the "White Album" sessions, 1968).

4) Dwarf McDougal (*Nobody Loves You When You're Down And Out*. Chances are that *anyone* named "Dwarf McDougal" is both "down" and "out"!) But the name has another referent. "Dwarf" is the name of Bob Dylan's music company, and "McDougal" is the Greenwich Village street where the early folk scene began in New York).

5) Dr. Dream (*No. 9 Dream*).

6) Rev. Thumbs Gurkin (Fred's brother?! Anyway, "Thumbs" gets his hands into the earth on *Old Dirt Road*).

7) Mel Torment (even Mr. Mellow, Mel Torme, would be in torment if he wrote and sang *Scared*!).

8) Dr. Winston O. Reggae (John says the Beatles' first attempt at a reggae beat is the middle eight of *I Call Your Name*, found on the **Beatles Second Album**. This signature, however, is for *Steel And Glass*).

9) Hon. John St. John Johnson (seeing that *John* Lennon and Elton *John* got together on *Whatever Gets You Through The Night*, this multiple "John" is quite appropriate).

10) Kaptain Kundaline (*What You Got*).

11) Dad (the most poignant of all, as John's son Julian played drums on his father's cut of "Ya Ya").

It is interesting to note that the title most used by Lennon, "Dr." was also the *original* title of "Sgt. Pepper." That's right, Mal Evans confirmed that **Dr. Pepper's Lonely Hearts Club Band** was the official album name until the Beatles discovered that "Dr. Pepper" was a registered U.S. trademark!

Also we can note that John Lennon used these pseudonyms in a similar fashion to the way he had used the classified ads section of *Mersey Beat* — as a way to let loose a private joke or two (and to "slip" one in while no one was looking).

Literary Summary

The next "loose end" is a statistical fact sheet that quickly summarizes John Lennon's literary output:

I.   *In His Own Write* (March 23, 1964)

   A.   15 stories
   B.   5 special forms
   C.   3 play scenes
   D.   8 poems
   E.   6 portraits (4 self-portraits, 2 Beatle portraits)
   F.   19 illustrations
   G.   1 cartoon (self-contained)

   Thus, 57 total items comprise *In His Own Write*:

      23 prose pieces
      8 poems
      26 drawings

II.   *A Spaniard In The Works* (June 24, 1965)

   A.   8 stories
   B.   4 special forms
   C.   6 poems

D. 5 portraits (3 self-portraits, 2 Beatle portraits)
E. 25 illustrations
F. 8 cartoons (self-contained)

Thus, 56 total items comprise *A Spaniard In The Works*:

    12 prose pieces
     6 poems
    38 drawings

113 Total for both major works:

    23 stories
    14 poems
     9 special forms
     3 play scenes
    64 drawings
      OR:
    35 prose pieces
    14 poems
    64 drawings

III. *Uncollected Items*

A. 3 stories
B. 6 special forms
C. 1 play scene (adapted from an original idea of John Lennon's)
D. 8 poems
E. 9 illustrations

Thus, 27 total items:

    10 prose pieces
     8 poems
     9 drawings (8 of which illustrate *Harmony*)

IV. *All Writing Combined*

A. 26 stories
B. 15 special forms
C. 4 play scenes (one "adapted")
D. 22 poems
E. 73 drawings

Thus, 140 items total:

45 prose pieces
22 poems
73 drawings

It can now be asserted, beyond any doubt, that John Lennon's literary canon is significant. Not only did he produce a considerable amount of work — in a variety of styles and genres — but he maintained a very high caliber and consistency in his writing. Hence, the idea that composer-singer John Lennon "also wrote" (implying that his writing was a second-rate hobby) is totally incorrect. Indeed, John's literary output would have been noteworthy even if that had been his sole form of creative expression.

Furthermore, we now realize that John Lennon's literary legacy provides the reader with the most accurate and incisive chronicle of Beatlemania ever written. It completely punctures the mask of those "luvable Liverpool lads" and reveals the face of isolation, rage, and confusion. We also have discovered that John Lennon, more than any other post-Joycean author, has continued Joyce's complex verbal inventiveness (an achievement for *any* writer!).

Given this kind of importance, what new areas of research does John Lennon, the writer, deserve to have undertaken?

1) We need *all* heretofore uncollected writing to be reviewed and studied:

A. Letters.
B. Prose and poetry still in manuscript.
C. Miscellaneous published works in the order of "The Short Essay on Macrobiotics."
D. Scripts to all orally published work.
E. Screenplays (from John's cinematic collaboration with Yoko).

2) We need *transcripts* made of *all* Lennon interviews regarding his writing (on radio, television, or in print media).

3) We need fresh *adaptations* — ones that do justice to John's original writing (including his uncollected work):

A. Adaptations for legitimate stage
B. Adaptations for feature films
C. Adaptations for television

So, what are you waiting for? Get to it!

Index to Titles